Jumping Ships

David
Baboulene

summersdale

JUMPING SHIPS

Published in 2009 by
Dreamengine Media Ltd.
Email:publishing@dreamengine.co.uk
www.dreamengine.co.uk

In association with:
Summersdale Publishers Ltd
46 West Street
Chichester
West Sussex
PO19 1RP
www.summersdale.com

Cover illustration by Jenny Daley
Stamps by Jimmy Cauty

Printed and bound in Great Britain

ISBN: 978-1-84024-591-2

Jumping Ships

The Global Misadventures of a Cargo Ship Apprentice

David Baboulene

No man would go to sea if skilled enough to get himself into prison, for a jail has more room, better food, more honest company and one is somewhat less likely to drown.

(Adapted from) Dr Samuel Johnson 1708–1784

To my dad, Bernard Baboulene

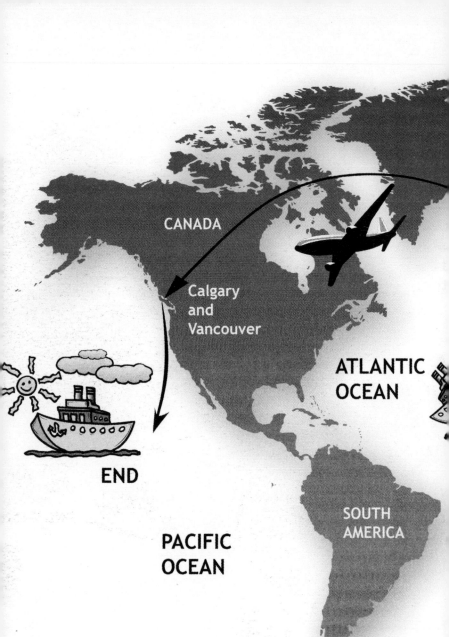

CANADA

Calgary
and
Vancouver

ATLANTIC
OCEAN

END

SOUTH
AMERICA

PACIFIC
OCEAN

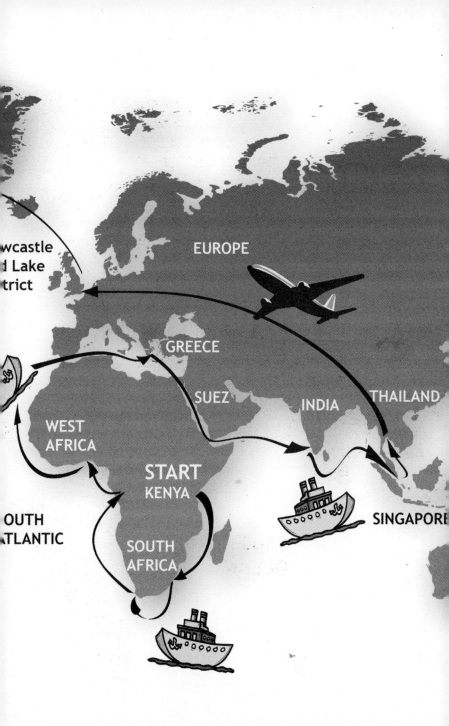

Contents

Author's Mitigation

As you climbed the gangway and headed with feverish anticipation towards page one of *Ocean Boulevard,* you no doubt noticed that a good deal of effort was made to convince you of the sheer veracity of that now legendary tome. As I welcome you aboard for our second trip together, I find myself obliged to make a similar point all over again. However, these mitigations are notoriously dull, so I thought it might be more entertaining to use the space to annoy somebody instead.

It's a funny thing, writing a non-fiction book. What starts off as a personal journey suddenly becomes public property, and all sorts of people start popping out of the woodwork to tell you what they think. Don't get me wrong – I'm not complaining. Far from it. For me, finding out that I have made a complete stranger laugh his head off in some far off corner of the world is easily the most rewarding aspect of writing the thing in the first place. And yet it is this proof that people are actually reading it that sets the legal chaps all a-jitter. They come round and wring their hands and wind one leg round the other and beg me to make a statement denying everything in advance.

Although this book represents genuine journeys and events that took place with real people, I'm amazed to find that some of these same people may not wish to be associated with the stories between these covers. Some have wives and children now. A few have friends who know nothing of the sailor hidden carefully at the back of the family closet, and think my ex-colleagues to be fine, upstanding, blameless souls who wouldn't know one end of a Bangkok hooker from the other. I'm assured one or two of them even have jobs. I know it seems incredible, but this is what I am told. For that reason alone, I am bound to distance myself from the absolute truth, even if I have to lie to do it. So off we go.

In every story within this book, you can safely assume the following:

It wasn't me. It certainly wasn't you, your loved ones or anyone else you know, think you know, may one day know or have ever known. It wasn't even the rank I've implied, and anyway, it wasn't actually on that ship. It was a different ship (if there ever was a ship). It didn't happen when I said it did. It didn't happen where the book implies it did and, in any event, whatever 'it' was (or wasn't), what really happened was entirely different from that which it might appear to be now (unless it wasn't, in which case it was incontrovertibly the opposite way round).

There. That should do it.

However, if you are just along for the ride, between you and me, you can see for yourself that this mitigation is part of this book, and is therefore subject to itself, and it follows, therefore,

M'lud, that this isn't the truth either, even though it clearly is. (I hope you're keeping up.)

Most importantly, I hope you can find apt reward in this mitigation, sharing with me the joyful knowledge that it has given a lawyer somewhere a thumping great headache.

Well, I like to do my bit.

David Baboulene
Sifnos Island, Greece

www.baboulene.com

Global Princess – Personnel Chart

Captain Benchmerson, aka 'the old man'

Navigators:
Chief Officer (first mate): Harry Tate
Second Officer (second mate): Payphone
Third Officer (third mate): The Famous Dick Wrigley

Radio Officer: Sparky

Engineers:
Chief Engineer (the chief): Chiefy
Second Engineer (the second): Jinx
Third Engineer (the third): MoneyBox
Fourth Engineer (the fourth): Benny the Dog
Fifth Engineer (fiver): SmallParcel
Sixth Engineer (sixth): Corkage

Electrician: MegaWatt
Second Electrician: KiloWatt

Navigating Cadets (Apprentices):
Giewy
NotNorman
Windy (that's me)

Engineering Cadet: Ffugg

Chapter 1

The Departure Lounge
at Life's Crossroads

Windy gets the letter. A meeting of minds. New Faces and Opportunity Knocks. Windy lays down the law. A Ffugg rewrites the law. Joining up – an early escape!

'**M**ombasa.'
I received a letter from the London office of Global Line – the shipping company I worked for as a navigating apprentice – telling me I was to join the merchant vessel *Global Princess* in Mombasa. That was the first time I'd ever even seen the word 'Mombasa.' It jumped off the paper and sang to me with the exotic promise of faraway lands.

'Mombasa.'

In the previous year I had travelled the world on a cargo ship called the *Global Wanderer*. As the first tripper I was ripped apart a bit but – wow – what a journey: Gulf of Mexico, Barbados, Jamaica, Panama, Australia, Pacific Islands, the Azores. It was an absolute blast. You read all about it, of course, in the *opus momentus* known as *Ocean Boulevard* (and if not, why not, all good bookshops etc., etc.).

I enjoyed a few precious weeks at home catching up with family and friends, and then The Letter arrived from the London office. Apart from conveying the word 'Mombasa' to me, the letter explained that my new ship was scheduled to work cargo through East, South and West Africa, beetle across the Mediterranean and out through the Suez Canal, then over to India and the Far East. Can you imagine, as a seventeen-year-old, getting a letter like that? It fizzed with travel and adventure. Outside my South London window, I saw grey skies and drizzle. But in my hands, floating like holograms above the letter, I saw African landscapes, Indian sunsets and Thai temples. I could feel the sun, I could see the people and the colours, I could smell the Eastern Promise. I still needed to find out where in the world Mombasa actually was, but in that delicious moment I loved not knowing. If I knew where it was, some of the mystique would be dispelled. I revelled in the excitement of the unknown as I mouthed the word:

'Mombasa.'

What I did know was that I was about to embark on another fantastic adventure all around the world. It made my tummy go all funny.

So it was that on the morning of 17 July 1978, I could be found in the hallowed corridors of the London office of Global Line Ltd, in Bury Street, in the City of London. I found it intimidating to attend the London office. It was sternly Victorian and overawing. The oak-panelled walls were hung with ancient oil portraits of ships' captains going back 150 years. Global Line had its place in British maritime history, and these captains looked down on me with severe eyes as if to make sure I didn't forget it. I felt a strange compulsion to hand in homework. Beneath the portraits were glass cases containing detailed models of the ships these captains had commanded – from the four-masted barques of the nineteenth century right up to the gleaming new ships rolling out of Tyneside that month. The ships sat strangely motionless on papier-mâché seas, with small captions giving name, tonnage and years of service. If I stared at any one of these old ships for long enough, I could see the southern oceans buffeting the tumble home. I could taste the salty spume. I could hear the shouts and the wind in the rigging as the crews worked to their limits to sail the ship and live to fight another day. It seemed somehow wrong to see those ships so static and silent, landlocked in a stuffy London corridor. I wanted to break the glass and set them pouring to freedom. With the portraits of dead captains looming above, the place felt like a morgue. I never did feel comfortable at the London office.

I creaked open a wooden door that was four times taller than me and entered a reception room the size of a castle's banqueting hall. It was like a library, with musty old books about shipping law running from oak floor to corniced ceiling. All it needed was Lurch to open the door for me to complete the creepy picture. My colleagues sat waiting in doom-laden silence. Although I recognised some of the faces from my previous trip, the mood was sombre and nobody spoke. They looked like the accused in ill-fitting suits in a courtroom antechamber. It seemed strange to me that the beginning of a travel adventure should be shrouded in misery, but for experienced seamen, their leave was all too short, and the occasion of joining a twenty-year-old ship was not one for celebration. For them, today was day one of a six-month stint on duty, and not a day they looked forward to. I had to hide my own excitement behind a veil of feigned misery, when really I wanted to run around the room and kiss them all, shouting, 'Mombasa, Mombasa!' and then do the splits. Yes, really. That's how excited I was.

But good sense prevailed, and once the paperwork was done, we were led out into the drizzle and loaded onto a coach bound for Gatwick Airport. I sat on my own and watched London pass by as we made our way through the City, across Tower Bridge, down towards the Old Kent Road and across to the Elephant and Castle. London was tired and grey, as if it didn't want to get up this morning. The people on the pavements looked weighed down with it all. It was one of those heavy days that needed a storm to clear all the headaches. The drivers on their way to the City sat tight-lipped in stationary traffic. I saw a man arguing with a traffic warden. A mother scolded her child. Teenage schoolboys hung around on a street corner, smoking cigarettes and trying to look hard. That could have been me. But I was getting out. I was free. I was going to 'Mombasa'.

The lads began to relax a little once we were settled in the departure lounge at the airport. From left to right, we had my good friend NotNorman (my fellow first tripper on the previous voyage); MegaWatt and KiloWatt, the electricians; The Famous Dick Wrigley coming in at third officer; Sparky, who with his oversized head and penchant for heavy drinking was perfectly qualified to be radio officer; Chiefy, the chief engineer, with his huge, hairless frame and Sybil Fawlty voice; good old Jinx, the provider, at second engineer; Benny the Dog, the busting great Mancunian, at fourth engineer; and SmallParcel, in his vague and transparent sort of way, hazing around at fifth. We also had some new faces: Payphone, a skinny Londoner with quick eyes, a suit that was too small for him, a roll-up in the corner of his norf-n-sarf, and a fidgety manner, was the new second officer. He had earned his nickname from his determination to phone home against all the odds that the third world might throw at him. The new third engineer went by the name of Corkage, for his habit of carrying an unspecified quantity of alcohol hidden about his person at all times (a handy man to know in an emergency). The new sixth engineer was a fat, Midlands lad called MoneyBox. He got his nickname not from manoeuvres in the financial markets, but from his habit of wearing his jeans too low, like a construction worker, so there was, ever-present, just above his lack of belt at the back, something akin to a penny slot. My nickname was Windy. I don't want to talk about why.

I wasn't pleased to discover that we were to have the same chief officer as the previous trip. He was commonly known as Harry Tate, and he was the man in charge of us navigating apprentices. By nature and instinct he was an overbearing bully who had no purpose in his life but to make mine a misery.

We also had the same 'old man', as Captain Benchmerson was known. This was also bad news for me. I had got myself tangled up in a fair deal of shenanigans on my first trip and the old man had somehow got it into his head that the thing I loved most was to be at the centre of all the mischief. Although it was true that I often found myself in residence at Guilty Central, it was usually as a victim, not as a ringleader. I would rather have started afresh with a new captain and a clean slate.

Of all the new faces, the one in which I was most interested belonged to a lad called Ffugg. He was our one and only first-tripper for this tour. I was now officially a hairy-arsed, second-trip apprentice. I looked furtively across at Ffugg as he stared around the departure lounge, taking it all in with eyes like saucers. All that gullibility. All that naivety. Oh, man. He was the new cannon fodder, and I was one of the lads. Ffugg was an engineering apprentice so I would not be working with him directly, but he was still the first tripper, and that meant he was the new target for all the practical jokes (instead of me). He was a big lad – huge, in fact – but he was wide-eyed and innocent. He had curly blond hair like a baby girl, with chubby, smooth white cheeks. He had a small mouth and pert little nose (also like a baby girl). He only had to stick his thumb in his mouth and the effect would be uncanny. Even his arse was like a baby girl's – big and broad, as if his nappy needed attention. He was a walking victim, ready to be torn to shreds week after week, just as I had been during my first trip. As I looked at him, I realised I was drooling and flexing my fingers. This trip was going to be even more fun than the last one, and I had my part to play in his education. I would not be doing my duty if I didn't make his first trip as rich and fun-filled as my colleagues had made mine, and as there's no time like the present so I edged across to Ffugg and got straight down to business.

'Sooo, first tripper, are you?' I enquired innocently.

He looked back at me with Disney-blue eyes that begged for help.

'Oh dear,' I sucked my teeth. 'Oh dear, oh dear, oh dear. You really don't want to be one of those, you know.' I shook my head as if deeply concerned on his behalf. This was just what the lads had done to me on my first day, and I wanted to ensure equality. I put my hand on his shoulder and spoke in a low, conspiratorial tone. 'You should leg it whilst you still have the chance.'

Ffugg looked at me with trepidation. I flicked my eyebrows sagely towards the exit doors. His eyes became wider and he bit his bottom lip. He already looked pretty edgy. I remembered how I felt when this was done to me. He would have heard horrifying stories during the induction course at college. He would have been warned by the cadet-training officer of the perils that lay in wait. He was away from mummy for the first time since his birth; homesick, full of doubts and troubled by uncertainty. I leaned forward and spoke in a loud, urgent whisper.

'Leave now,' I urged. 'Leave now, whilst there's still time to change your mind.'

I nodded at him with pity in my eyes. It was getting through. I couldn't believe the power I had! He was actually shaking! If anything, he was even more anxious than I had been under the same pressure. I saw him swallow hard. His lips were twitching. I even began to think he might crack, when suddenly, he did.

He threw my arm off his shoulder and leapt to his feet.

'Are you fffreatening me?' he shouted in a wide-boy, Essex accent. He then began bouncing up and down on his toes in front of me like a heavyweight boxer. 'Come on ven! Let's do this fffing! Noooww!'

All the other lads stopped what they were doing and looked at me and Ffugg. I didn't know it at the time but his nickname was derived from his own pronunciation of the word, 'thug'. I looked back at the lads hoping for support. Surely we were all in this together, shoulder-to-shoulder, ragging the first-tripper? Weren't we?

Lads?

Ffugg curled his top lip under to bear his teeth at me. He beckoned me with his fingers to get up and fight him.

'Come on, ven! You fffaaaancy yerself, do ya? Eh? Eh? Eh?!'

I remained resolutely attached to my seat, as a giant baby lollopped up and down in front of me, inviting me to fight it. It was almost too surreal to be scary. I refused to stand up, but he was already well into the fight all by himself. He bobbed and weaved, shadow boxing round my chair, throwing practice punches at my head like a demented hairdresser for whom the day had gone all wrong. People waiting for their flights, and grateful for any distraction, dropped their luggage, grabbed each other and ran over to get a ringside seat for the violence to come. I even saw one bloke hoist his three-year-old son onto his shoulders to give him a better view.

I had taunted a violent mental case and prospects for a happy outcome did not look good. I was hoping his display might spark some other random nutter to life – there are usually plenty about, lying dormant in public places until a fellow patient shows up with whom they can exchange opinions until the police arrive – but no such luck today.

Suddenly Ffugg jumped back into the space in front of me, landing in a karate stance and shouting, 'Aaaah HAAA!' chopping and posing like a Teletubby in a martial arts class. He stared me directly in the eye, stood on one leg miaowing like a cat which has had his saucer of milk taken away and circled his hands in front of my face in mystical, oriental ways. I had no idea what to do, but getting out of my chair was definitely not on the agenda. This seemed to frustrate him and suddenly he was up and off again, in true thug mode, jumping up and down around the airport, headbutting to the left and right between demands to know if I fancied myself. I sat in front of him looking small, the surrounding crowd baying for me to take him on. This was unbearable. I couldn't back down to a first-tripper – that would be social suicide. But then fighting him might be *actual* suicide. I watched his great, puppy-fat pecs lollop up and down in time with his bounce. Every now and then he dropped down onto flattened feet and reeled off a dozen or so short jabs in front of his own face. Then he shot back up onto his toes, raised himself to his full height, arms by his side, and ghosted sideways in front of me like Mohammed Ali.

'Come ooon ven champ! Do ya want some? Do ya? Do ya?'

Help!

Once Ffugg had drifted sideways far enough, he dodged this way and that, did a little high-speed *Riverdance* thing, then did that stupid jogging on the spot and kicking his feet out to the sides that runners do when they get stuck at the lights. He then straightened back up to his full height and tracked back the other way, nodding dismissively as if he had the full measure of me. I had no idea what to do, except hope he might run out of puff and need to sit down again soon. Onlookers were trying to coax me to my feet, shouting at me to fight. One guy was even pushing me to get me up, but I clung firmly to my chair with both hands.

Help!

I felt the heat rising in my face. The lads were going to put a lot of stock on the outcome of this episode. This was day one and it could make or break my trip.

Then came a moment of inspiration the like of which I have never delivered to the world before or since. I don't know where it came from, and I certainly don't remember consciously thinking it up, but there it was. For centuries, we Baboulenes have been known for a hot line in instinctive brilliance and it was at this very moment that I connected with my genetic bloodline. Forces beyond my comprehension – perhaps a link to my forefathers and their fathers before them – synthesised into an act of devastating genius: I leant forwards and deftly swiped with my left hand at ground level, connecting perfectly with Ffugg's right foot. At that moment, he was ghosting sideways, and his feet were kind of crossing back and forth over each other as he went. I'm sure it looks wonderful when a ballet dancer or legendary boxer does it, but it only takes a minor interference with the progress of one foot on its journey across and around the other one to upset the entire machinery. My beautifully timed clip of his foot provided just the interference required. As Ffugg's lower legs wound six times around one another and he catapulted skywards, I remember thinking what an extraordinarily positive effect a simple act of this nature might have on a dull performance of, say, *The Nutcracker Suite*. 'Now, that's more like it!' they would say, leaning forwards in their seats and calling for more. As Ffugg's face switched from focused boxer to surprised baby, he began to keel over sideways like a falling tree, I had pictures in my mind of audiences queueing round the block at Sadler's Wells to see ballet dancers going over like this all over the stage. It was magnificent.

Perfect. A good day's work. Well not quite perfect. As Fugg made his heavy touchdown in the departure lounge and the ground shook beneath us, harsh tones roared out behind me.

'Baboulene! What in the blue blazes do you think you're doing?!'

The captain and the mate had returned from the check-in and were just in time to see my impressive combination of timing and brilliance. Before I knew what was going on, I was getting the blame.

'Good God, Mr Baboulene! I had hoped you would welcome our new recruit, not start abusing him in airports. I am not going to allow you to turn this ship into a bear garden like you did the last one. I want you in my day room the moment we are on board, understand? This behaviour has to be nipped in the bud.'

Ffugg sat on the floor with a vacant, happy stare, looking for all the world like a giant baby in the process of filling his nappy with deep satisfaction. I couldn't believe this. We hadn't even got on board yet, and already I was in the captain's bad books again. I had been so determined to keep on the right side of him, and here I was hitting rock bottom from day one. I looked at Giewy. You may remember him as the knock-kneed, sunken-chested, spanner-brained, hook-nosed berk with the face like a Photoshop accident, who had made my first trip such a misery. This trip, Giewy was the new senior apprentice, and therefore directly in charge of me and NotNorman. He smarmed at me through buck teeth. I now saw that he had a soulmate in Ffugg, and that I had two idiots to deal with this time around. I felt numb. Giewy had been enough trouble without adding a Ffugg. I could see I was going to have to assert myself if I was to keep control of my inferiors on this trip.

Chapter 2

Mooning the Bongo

Nature's wonders fail to grip. The big game hunters' search for a Big Chicken. 70s Nite at the fever tree. The name's Bond... Jumbo Bond. Windy – lone survivor.

We arrived in Mombasa to two pieces of unexpected news. Firstly, the ship hadn't arrived yet. In fact, it was drifting hopelessly in the middle of the Indian Ocean with engine failure, and was still days away from Mombasa. We would be put up in a hotel to wait for it. Secondly, I found out that Mombasa is in Kenya, Kenya is in East Africa and the whole region is extraordinary from the very moment you touch down. The adventure was beginning, and it was doing so in fine style.

We had time to fill. And what do a dozen feisty young men do when they find themselves at a loose end in some far-flung corner of the world? They summon the Jinx. Simple as that.

It was said of Jinx that if NASA wanted to find life on Mars, they simply needed to send Jinx up there. With his sheepskin coat, spivvy moustache and his purring Leslie Phillips tones, life would emerge from every nook and cranny of Mars, probably in the form of pole dancers, wanting to make up for lost time having been deprived of male company as they devoted themselves to their studies. Jinx was just kinda gifted like that – he had The Knack for finding fun and mischief. And here in Mombasa, it seemed he would come through in typical fashion.

Word went round the table after breakfast on our first day that he had a 'special contact' here in Mombasa (he always had a 'special contact'), apparently going by the name of 'Precious'. Between them they had cobbled together some sort of safari. We were to drive for five days up to Mount Kenya, stop at a couple of lodges, ride the steam trains and enjoy the wild and unparalleled glory of Tsavo National Park. Was this really my job? Was this work? I couldn't believe my luck.

Sure enough, we all convened in the hot Kenyan sunshine outside our hotel and Jinx introduced us to Precious. He was a tall, thin, black gentleman built rather along the lines of one of those rotary washing lines, but with the longest arms I'd ever seen, and feet and hands so large they were like some sort of clown's props. This was the man who was to guide us through the wonders of East Africa. He had a gun (which wasn't his) and a safari truck (which wasn't his), but if his height was anything to go by he was on personal whispering terms with the giraffe population, so everything would be fine, wouldn't it?

There was great excitement as we leapt aboard the truck: Ffugg, Payphone, NotNorman, Giewy, Jinx, The Famous Dick Wrigley, MegaWatt, KiloWatt and me. Precious folded himself up like a collapsible chair into the driver's seat and adopted his very own driving position: one knee on either side of his ears, arms running down outside his legs and under his knees to hold the wheel in-between his calves, and with the back of his neck flat against the cab roof. He looked very uncomfortable; all curled over like a grown-up on a child's tricycle. I looked at him doubtfully. If that guy ever got cramp, it could turn the truck over. Once or twice on the journey he attempted to drive and simultaneously unwrap sweets and place them in his mouth. He was fortunate to be amongst sailors who knew how to untie him.

The first day of the safari passed pleasurably with no unseemly events to report. Spirits were high (the case of beer had not yet run out), and the sight of a wild horizon, the bound of a Thomson's gazelle and the classic silhouette of a fever tree at sunset, had not yet lost their novelty. The first night was spent at a spectacular lodge where we oooh'd and aaah'd over the fine food, spotted big game from a balcony terrace overlooking a watering hole and enjoyed a great night's sleep in the cradle of humanity. It was nothing short of magic.

But on day two, as we bounced off in the truck for another day's wild riding, the cracks began to show through. It is, alas, the nature of man – particularly, the nature of sailors – to find nature's bounty a little short on what one might call 'essential facilities': the kinds of things that speak to a man's fundamental instincts and make him feel that life is worth living; bars and clubs, for example, are not readily available, and that special type of local friend with whom a young sailor, in the prime of his life, can have a fight.

The lads were getting bored.

'Oi, Precious!' shouted MegaWatt, tapping the Long One on the shoulder. 'Where's The Business, then?'

'Yeaaah!' agreed KiloWatt in a slovenly drawl, stoutly supporting his boss. 'Wot he says. Yeaaaah!'

Precious looked puzzled. 'Business? What do you mean, business?'

MegaWatt explained with exaggerated patience. 'Precious, this is *Africa*. We want to see some Business.'

'Yeeeeaah. Wot he says! Yeaaah!'

Precious made a face. He already knew this was Africa. MegaWatt took a deep breath and spelled it out for him. 'We wanna see, like, a giant spider drop out of a tree onto a pig!'

'Yeeeeeah!'

'Eh?'

'And we wanna see some lions killing villagers.'

'Ooooo, yeeeah! Killing villagers. Yeeeah!'

'What?'

The others were getting the hang of it now, and the call for blood grew stronger.

'Yeah! We wanna see tigers and… and…'

'…and… and bears, and… and…'

'Yeaaaah.'

'… and… and sharks!'

'Yeaaah! And… and... and we wanna see a snake eat a whole cow. Yeaaah!'

'Yeah, and we wanna see a cheetah leg it after one of them Bambi jobbies!'

'Yeaaah!'

'Like on the telly!'

'Yeeeahhh! Killing villagers!'

'Yeeeah. Wot he says. Yeeeah!'

There appeared to be a general thirst for blood that no amount of grazing wildebeest could satisfy unless they were being torn apart by something akin to a Tyrannosaurus rex.

Precious stopped the truck and turned around to address us in deep, golden-black tones from beneath his right knee. 'You mustn't expect big cats. It's very unusual that we even see any big cats, and they rarely hunt in the daytime. We will be extremely lucky if we see any at all.'

Well, the lads were deflated. There are only so many merciless plains of Kenya that a chap can take without a kill before he begins looking for alternative forms of entertainment. There didn't appear to be any changes coming over the horizon, so a plan of action was required.

'Jinx,' said The Famous Dick Wrigley, placing a hand on the great man's shoulder with a certain solemnity in his voice. 'It is now perhaps more important than at any other time in your illustrious career that you come up with something brilliant.'

Now here was a challenge even for the notorious Jinx. He had proven himself on so many previous occasions, but surely this was a bridge too far for even the Pied Piper himself.

We looked on with apprehension as the Jinxed brain churned and his moustache twitched like a divining rod above his ever-smirking lips. There were definite signs of activity. I, personally, was not confident that Jinx could create a party under these circumstances. I had a brain, just like he did, and could see no potential around us. There was no raw material here. Nothing to work with. I looked into the trees for the beautiful girls he might conjure out of nowhere. There were none. The lads would simply have to wait until Mombasa's Kilindini Road rolled over the horizon again; a place where they could satisfy themselves easily with a wide selection of diseases.

A smile began to rise at the edge of Jinx's lips. His eyes flitted furtively from one open-mouthed onlooker to the next. Precious looked back in wonder as the sense that something was about to be delivered overtook us all. Suddenly, Jinx clapped.

'OK!' he said. 'If there are no sizeable pussycats around, we'll have to see if we can't hunt down a different species.' He opened his arms wide to emphasise his point. 'We are going to bag ourselves...' he milked the moment as we all waited with bated breath, '... a Biiiiig Chicken!'

We all cheered. We didn't understand why, but Jinx's build-up meant that cheering just felt like the right thing to do. I saw through him at last! He just buzzed people up and then delivered nothing! Africa had exposed him. I was about to ask why it was that anyone had ever rated Jinx so highly, when he continued.

'And Windy. You are the first tripper, so you get to go first. Let's go hunting the Biiiiig Chicken!'

I shut my eyes and counted to ten before delivering my withering retort.

'I am not a first tripper. As you well know, Jinx, I am on my second trip, and I refuse to be treated in any way unbefitting of my status.' Sometimes a chap has to stand up for himself. I wasn't going to be the butt of everyone's jokes for the next six months as well as the last. 'Ffugg,' I said, using both hands to indicate the six-foot embryo sitting next to me, 'is the first tripper.'

'Chic-ken! Chic-ken! Chic-ken!' the lads chorused towards me. Even Ffugg joined in with them. He placed me in a chummy sort of half-nelson and noggied me on the head with his knuckles, and The Famous Dick Wrigley attempted to strut about doing a chicken impersonation (a tough trick in a safari truck, but his commitment to the programme was there to be admired).

Jinx leaned forwards and looked me in the eye. He appeared surprisingly angry.

'Listen to me. When we are all in our old age and we have grandchildren on our knees, and we are telling them of the time we went on safari, we want to be able to show them some special photographs. Now, if I can't show them a picture of myself with one foot victoriously atop a fallen lion, then I want to show them the next best thing: a picture of me victorious atop a Big Chicken. One of us in this truck will go down in history as that poultry figure, and will be derided by generations to come. Is it you, Baboulene? Are you the Big Chicken, and proving yourself to be so before we have even started our search?'

Now, I didn't particularly want to patronise his childish game (or at least, I didn't want to go first) but as he spoke, the Baboulene brain was working. The vacant Ffugg may not have realised it yet, but I could understand the coded message Jinx was imparting to me. He was letting me know that there wasn't a real Big Chicken at all. Quite possibly there wasn't even such an animal in Kenya. This was going to be a test of bravery. I looked from the enigmatic expression on Jinx's face to the gormless one on Ffugg's, and I instantly knew what he was getting at. Jinx and I were communicating on a higher plane of consciousness – and it was Ffugg who was going to suffer.

'OK!' I cried, slapping my thigh in the manner of Hercules approaching the first of his tasks. 'Tell me what I have to do.'

'Good man!' said Jinx, the anger evaporating as rapidly as it had arrived. 'Did you ever play dares when you were a kid? Daring someone to knock a policeman's helmet off, that kind of stuff?'

'Ooooh, yes,' I said. 'Only last week we put a hose pipe through next door's letterbox. Ha, ha! And whilst they were trying to stop the water, we went round the side, rang the bell and ran away. Yes, and then we got a roll of cling film, right, and we stretched it across the toilet, you see, and when my mum came home she didn't realise, and…'

'Yes, yes. OK. I forgot – you're still a kid, aren't you. Well, we're going to play dares now. Africa style.'

A chill ran down my spine as the words emerged from his mouth. These supposed grown-ups wanted to play childish games, but not risking an irate neighbour, the wrath of a village bobby or even a little parental splash-back. These guys wanted to go and take childish risks… on the savage, uncompromising plains of Africa.

Now, I'm sure you realise that it is not actually very difficult to take childish risks on the savage, uncompromising plains of Africa. Indeed, it's very easy to find dangerous things to do. Having said that, it turns out that there is fundamentally only one obviously dangerous thing to do, and that is to leave the safety of the safari truck and the reassuring presence of Precious and his gun. The variety in the dares will only ever come in the manner in which you risk being pounced upon and eaten.

'OK,' drawled Jinx. 'Your first-round test, young Windy, is to re-enact for us a scene from a James Bond movie. Your co-star will be Jumbo over there.'

I followed his pointing finger. There in the bushes, lazily tearing shoots from a camel-hair tree, was a large bull elephant.

'What? You want me to…?'

'Get on with it, then! Nothing more to discuss!'

And they bundled me out of the truck. As I headed away from the truck the earth felt strange under my feet. Was this real? I was walking on Masai earth. Wild earth. The reality of what this meant made me feel instantly insecure. This was dangerous terrain. I had read only the day before about the Tsavo lions, the notorious man eaters in this area. People who didn't stay in their trucks got killed, it was as simple as that. But that didn't seem to matter to my sniggering shipmates whilst it was me out roaming the plains. They had yet to feel the reality of leaving the truck. The sense of vulnerability was instant and alarming.

The elephants are tame in Tsavo National Park. Well, no, that's not the right word. They are not exactly tame, but they are not scared of us – why should they be? You can wander amongst them quite safely, provided someone is there who can recognise when it is best to leap back in the truck and hide under the seat.

I tiptoed gently up to the large bull. He stopped his ruminations and looked down on me with a profound and reproachful eye. His head was huge and wrinkled. Had he been wearing a judge's wig, I would have begun a full confession immediately. I looked back to the truck, some 30 metres away, and was greeted with hand-signals from the lads telling me to get on with it.

I looked the elephant in the eye, took a deep breath and adopted a thespian's pose.

'Sshoo, Mr Bond,' I said in a Sean Connery drawl. 'We meet again.' I changed my pose to place my gun-finger across my chest. 'But this time, you... are an elephant.'

We stared at each other for a few moments as my point hit home. The elephant raised his eyebrows. No doubt about it, he was surprised to be mistaken for James Bond. He was about to make the point that, given that I had called him Mr Bond, it should surely be he who was allowed the Sean Connery accent and that I had therefore just turned myself into Miss Moneypenny, when his co-star suddenly cut the scene short, turned and galloped back to the safety of the safari truck. I was sweating heavily by the time I got back to my seat. I counted my limbs and it became evident that I had not been eaten. I had done it! I wasn't the Big Chicken, and I could hardly contain myself.

'Wow, man, what a buzz! You guys have just got to get out there! This is a great game! Whose turn next?'

One by one, for the first round of dares, we each forayed around 20 or 30 metres away from the safari truck, hardly a trek into the heart of Africa, and yet it was ridiculously scary. In turn, each of us was obliged to creep off nervously, perform some pointless charade, then scramble back to the truck in a blind panic, being pursued by a thousand imagined beasties. Payphone, for his first-round dare, had to score a goal for England. He had revealed a little more of his personality since we first met at the London office, and it was becoming clear that he was more than just an anxious telephonist. He had been born within the sound of Bow Bells, and was a cockney through and through. He had a pork-pie hat to fend off the sun ('a titfer wot set me back a nugget up Whitechapel,' apparently), a permanent roll-up in the corner of his mouth (known fondly as his 'oily rag') and he spoke with such an extraordinary cockney accent that I could barely understand him even though I had grown up not ten miles south of him. He was excited by his task (it was, to be precise, 'aaandsome'), as it had always been an ambition of his to 'stick one in the old onion bag for Queen and country'. He hopped out of the truck, ran over to a patch of open land, took off his left 'ow-do-ya-do and placed it carefully and centrally in line with two acacias which were to act as goalposts. He stepped a few paces back and, in the classic style of Hurst and Charlton, took a long, dramatic drag on his oily rag as he psyched himself up for the penalty that would put Germany out of the World Cup. He eyed the keeper (a small bush, well out of position to the right-hand end of the goal line), stretched his neck, flexed his elbows and his knees, took his short run-up and, with his right boot, booted his left boot high up into the top of a baobab tree.

'Geddin, you beauteeeee!' he yelled, wheeling away victoriously with fists clenched. He pulled the front of his T-shirt over his head in the manner of an Italian striker, and ran in a circle with his arms out to the sides as if pretending to be an aeroplane. Luckily, when he ran headlong into the baobab, it gave the tree such a jolt that it caused his boot to drop back down to earth again. He picked it up and jogged triumphantly back to the truck looking pleased with himself.

'You missed,' said MegaWatt, dryly. 'Go do it again.'

Giewy's first-round task popped up when we stumbled across an apparent rarity. A large, striped antelope known as a Bongo. We all laughed at the name, but Precious stopped the truck some distance from the beast and told us in an excited whisper that it was very unusual to find Bongos in this part of Kenya. They were very rare, very timid and we should feel honoured to see one. Once we heard this news, Giewy was charged with performing a scientific experiment to test Bongo timidity. The research process required Giewy to adopt the professional standards of a medical scientist – and go moon the Bongo. Or for those of you who don't understand all of these scientific terms: show it his arse. If the beast was as timid as Precious said it was, we would shortly be privileged to observe a rare and unusual beast burst into tears.

Giewy prowled, cat-like, up past the bushes to get near to the creature. He then leapt up, dropped his trousers and, with a sing-song 'Nurr-nurr-ne-nurrrrr-nurrrrr!' waved his bottom at the poor defenceless creature. The animal twitched palpably as if it had never seen anything like it before in its entire life. But it did not react as we predicted. There were no tears. It didn't even run away. It merely sneezed heavily – perhaps some sort of allergy to tit-heads – then returned to its ruminations. So much for timid. I guess if you live with the nightly opportunity to be mauled by lions, it takes more than the contents of even Giewy's trousers to make you jump. Mind you, from what I'd seen, I'd take the lions any day. As Giewy climbed back into the truck, KiloWatt cruelly suggested that he should wave his face at it next time, but was immediately told to calm down: we wanted to have a bit of fun, not eradicate a species.

Ffugg was given a childishly simple exercise. He had to go and pretend to take some money out of a cash machine. He acted it out as if there was one in the trunk of a tree, and his performance was rewarded with laughter from the boys. It wasn't funny, but they laughed. It was pathetic. Were these guys actually protecting him? How come they were so brutal towards me on the previous trip, and so easy on him this time? It just wasn't fair.

By the end of the first round of tests, we had not definitively established a Big Chicken. There had been some shaky moments in which a couple of eggs had been laid, but each of us had successfully completed our task. We would have to turn up the heat for round two.

So off we went again, but this time moving further from the truck to perform our pointless charades. A lot further; off into the heart of Africa the length of a football pitch distant from basic safety. This was properly scary, with additional tension in the atmosphere coming from Precious. Even he was getting anxious about the risks we were taking. He was responsible for our welfare and was not happy to see us larking about in this way. His agitation gave a certain additional bite to the second round, not only because it let us all know that what we were doing was now confirmed as genuinely dangerous, but also because he was now refusing to stop the truck. His theory was that if he kept driving, nobody could get out and risk their lives. This was a complication, but, as the saying goes, the show must go on, so the charades now absorbed this additional component: before you could commence your task, you had to trick Precious into stopping the truck. This was achieved in a safe and controlled fashion, of course. For example, you could place your hands firmly over his eyes (and fight hard to keep them there in the ensuing flail of the human washing line).

The charades themselves didn't get any more grown-up in the second round. NotNorman, for instance, was given instructions to travel up to the top of a hill, place a pretend handbag on the grass and perform a little 1970s disco dance around it. We got hold of Precious' gun, pulled it into the back and began larking about with it. Precious knew us well enough by now to see how lethal letting us loose with a high-powered rifle could be, so he stopped the truck and leaned into the back to fight over it with us. Before you could say 'Ernest Hemingway,' NotNorman was mincing outrageously up the hill with his pretend Dolce & Gabbana swinging casually on the end of his outstretched fingertips.

At the brow of the hill, NotNorman placed his handbag carefully on the ground then – as the strains of his rendition of 'Stayin' Alive' by the Bee Gees wafted across Africa – he began gyrating away, pushing his bottom out from side-to-side like some hideous cross between the Pink Panther and a slow death in *Erasure*.

The animal kingdom stopped its hunting and grazing, and looked at NotNorman silhouetted perfectly against the African sky. It was as if they'd never seen or heard anything like it in their lives.

'Well you can tell by the way I use my walk, I'm a woman's man, no time to talk…' NotNorman's grating falsetto rang out horribly across the Serengeti.

Precious couldn't take any more. He roared the engine and spun the wheels. The truck ripped round and bounced off-road in exactly the way they do on those wildlife documentaries when they chase a rhinoceros to shoot a tranquilliser dart into it. But this wasn't one of those occasions. Precious was barrelling across the plains not in pursuit of Big Game, but to stop an errant sailor from poncing about.

I honestly do not think Precious can have been worried about NotNorman's safety. Personally, as I watched him – now deep in the groove and showing no signs of a return to the truck – I couldn't even begin to think about eating him. Any self-respecting carnivore would surely feel the same way. I think Precious was more concerned firstly, about the damage to the environment caused by hundreds of different species all throwing up at the same time, and secondly to the wider image of Africa. I mean, can you imagine being in another safari party, driving along on the other side of the hill? You are enraptured by the sights: to the left – the impala, the giraffe! To the right – the elephants, the wildebeest! Above us – the monkeys, the weaver birds and, oh! Look there! Dappled in the sunlight, a sailor, disco dancing around a pretend handbag as he murders a

Bee Gees song. You see? It spoils the savage imagery of the place. People will stop taking Africa seriously. Perhaps Precious was worried that the animals might start picking up the behaviour. Then where would we be? Whichever way you looked at it, NotNorman – now acting out the letters 'Y, M, C, A' with a chorus line of impala – was not good for the environment.

Once they had eventually subdued NotNorman and got him back in the truck, it was my turn again. I was not looking forward to it. The sun was going down and I was hoping that the game might be wrapped up for the night and get itself forgotten. No chance. We browed the top of a hill and central to the view that greeted us was a lake.

'There you go, Windy,' said The Famous Dick Wrigley, indicating the lake with a wave of his hand. 'You have to run round that lake. On your way!'

There was general agreement amongst the lads that this was a good task. But this was because most of them couldn't have made it around that lake without a cardiac support team pushing them in wheelchairs. I was young and fit. I could run round a little pond like that in no time – I mean, you could hardly call it a lake – and I'd still have enough puff left to tell everyone how easy it was afterwards. I was well chuffed with getting such an easy task, and set about it right away before they had time to change their minds. I reached forwards, picked up Precious' wallet and lobbed it out of the safari truck. He screeched to a halt, and I was off over the side and swiftly up to an easy cruising speed down towards the pondy-lake thing. It would be nice to stretch my legs and get a little trot. This would be a breeze. Windy's breeze.

What I hadn't bargained for was that this was Africa. It seems I had forgotten.

You see, the thing about Africa is that it is really, really big. Unless you have grown up there, the sheer scale of the place monkeys with your head. For instance, we had been motoring towards Mount Kenya for two days; we could see it, but it didn't seem to be getting any nearer. The sky meets the land on a horizon so distant that the sky seems low. So low it's almost claustrophobic. At night, the canopy of stars we are used to isn't a canopy in Africa. It's a three-dimensional myriad of stars; you can see past the near stars to more distant stars, and more beyond them. Africa is beyond the understanding we gain from growing up elsewhere on the planet. My point is that this pondy sort of lake was much, much bigger than it had first appeared. I hadn't been running three minutes when it hit me, quite hard, that it was a darned sight further to run round than I first imagined. Of course, this also meant it was going to take me proportionally longer than my initial estimates. So long, in fact, that it would get dark in the time it was going to take me, and when it gets dark in Africa, it gets seriously dark and it does it quickly. As my mind filled with what you might call sobering thoughts, it also hit me, quite hard, that this was not a lake, was it? Nor was it a pond. I suddenly knew exactly what it was.

It was a watering hole.

At sunset.

In Africa.

And here I was, trotting round it looking like a giant sandwich on legs. All I needed to complete the mistake I was making was a big, neon sign above me, with a pointy finger aimed at my head, flashing the words 'Eat Me'.

There was a varied mix of wildlife around the watering hole already, chatting of their day and, one could safely assume, a good deal of other wildlife lying in wait for it in the long grass nearby. I realised that perhaps running round a watering hole at sunset wasn't such a clever idea after all. In fact, it was life-threateningly dangerous and – for a Baboulene so renowned as an intellectual force – a notably stupid thing to do.

I felt the spring go out of my stride and a wave of doubt wash over me. I also experienced a major and involuntary adjustment in my priorities. I no longer cared if my shipmates called me names. I could be a Big Chicken if that was what pleased their juvenile minds. I had to rise above their childish games and make a grown-up, responsible decision for everyone's sakes. They would lose their ebullience pretty quickly if I was to get eaten alive, wouldn't they? It wouldn't be so funny then, and it was best for everyone if I simply let them have their fun and resigned myself to the status of Big Chicken. I had to choose between losing a childish game and losing life and limb. It wasn't a difficult decision.

Despite all these thoughts I was still running forwards, albeit without enthusiasm, when suddenly the decision seemed to be made for me. In the middle of the watering hole a large hippopotamus surfaced and set about his evening yawn. It gave me a shake which stopped my legs turning. I stopped and stood frozen to the spot, looking around at some of the other local gang members sent to spoil my day. For some reason, the clincher was a large bird waiting for me about half way round. It was one of those big crane-like jobbies – almost as tall as me – on long, spindly legs. It had hunched shoulders, no neck and a huge, heavy beak like a wind sock full of sand. The Godfather of Africa. It had the angry deportment of a bird who has just been informed that Windy Baboulene has been going about the town calling his mum a chaffinch. He looked all shifty, like he was packing heat.

And that was it. All the evidence suggested that a return to base was the only sensible course of action. It was nearly dark, I was nearly knackered and there were miles to go – particularly with the extra ten minutes it would take to get round the Mafia hit-bird. I knew what had to be done. It would take possibly more bravery to go back and face the boys than it would to continue my run around the watering hole, but I made my decision. I would rise above their childish games and go back.

I stopped. I turned round. I looked back the way I had come and...

... and...

... and...

... there was nothing there.

The truck had disappeared.

They had gone.

I rubbed my eyes and stared, dumbfounded, through the shimmering heat haze. There was nothing in the direction from which I had come except more Africa.

They had gone.

I felt my knees go weak and an enormous adrenalin rush remove my stomach. My blood froze in my veins.

THEY HAD GONE.

I spun round through three-sixty to check I had my bearings right. There was nothing but a heat haze, wildlife, fever trees, acacias and more Africa in every direction. No safari truck. No shelter. No Precious with a gun. No safety.

The world stood still. I had nothing with me; no protection. No weapons. Nothing. I was bereft of the basics for supporting life, and closer to nature, red in tooth and claw, than humans can advisably get. I felt a kind of static, sickening panic and an indescribable hollowness in my stomach as all the blood rushed away to serve my muscles. My muscles! How laughable! My speed, my youth, my agility, my brain! All were worthless in this merciless terrain. I felt as though someone had removed all the flesh from my midriff – all the organs and fat and meat – and was blowing a chill wind through the exposed skeleton that remained. It was the feeling of death's arrival. The kind of priming one's body does when it thinks it's going to die. A horrible feeling I hope never to experience again.

As I stood in the enormous silence and stifling African heat, the details of my local area began to come to life. It wasn't just lions and leopards one had to fear in this part of the world. There were insects that could kill you! Plants that could maim! Spiders, snakes, crocodiles! Who knew what might drop out of a tree?

Even the dogs would tear you limb from limb – none of that 'nice-doggy-fetch-the-stickie-have-a-bonio' stuff around here. Just death. This was nature with the roof off. In the West we live in ivory towers, insulated from the workings of nature. Here I was now, a tiny cog being turned remorselessly in the wheel of life. I would be unlikely to survive a single night on my own.

And night was upon me. It was getting dark. In Africa, the sunsets are spectacular but very short. The sky goes from slanting warm daylight through a laser show of brilliant yellows and oranges, through vivid scarlets and violets, through blood reds and portentous purples until pitch darkness comes down like a cold blanket, and the hunters and hunted change shifts. You can feel the creatures of the night stirring to life. You can sense the foreboding amongst the prey. In the morning some of their number will be gone.

I don't honestly know how long I stood there. A sunset takes around twenty minutes, and I guess I was alone for around half that – but let me tell you now – it felt like a lifetime.

When the lads finally returned, I climbed shakily back into the truck, a significantly older man than the one who had hopped out a few short minutes earlier. They didn't understand what I had been through. They thought it was hilarious, but I was too traumatised to hear their taunts. What I did divine was that they had chipped Precious about a year's money, in his terms, to drive off. Precious, our guide and protector. Precious, the faithful man who had been so concerned for our safety. Yeah, right. As soon as he was offered enough cash, before you could say, 'Daktari', he was into gear and off over the hill, steering with his knees and counting notes with his fingers. To them, it was just a laugh, and I hid my feelings as best I could, but I had suffered a trauma that would last me a lifetime. I would never forget the day I survived alone on the plains of East Africa.

But, you know, there was some good news too. You see, the boys didn't know I hadn't run round the watering hole. They thought I had completed the task, so I was not the Big Chicken. Ha! I was officially brave, despite being more scared than I had ever been in my life before or since. Strange old world, isn't it?

The Big Chicken was later revealed to be none other than Ffugg. Ha, haaaaa! The new boy was exposed for the lily-livered spineless child he truly was when he refused to run a mere forty or fifty paces into the Serengeti. I mean, how weak is that? What a girl! Admittedly, it was pitch black out there, and there were some blood-curdling roars from quite close by, but really. I mean, what sort of animal would want to eat a giant baby? Yeesh. He would have been all right, wouldn't he? Some blokes just don't understand a bit of fun.

No guts, kids nowadays. No guts at all.

Chapter 3

Revving the Chevvy

All aboard! Thoughts on modern methods. A cook's tour. Africa is eclipsed. Motorbikes and sandy bottoms. Life in the ladies'. Dressing up time.

I was very excited to get on board the *Global Princess*, but the feeling was not shared amongst the lads. As we climbed the gangway, everyone was complaining about the ship's age and the endless problems associated with an old girl like this one. There was no denying that, as princesses stack up, she'd certainly let herself go a bit, but I wasn't bothered that she had been tramping the world since the late 1950s. These old ships were all I knew, and I can't say I liked the sound of the new ones particularly.

The new ships had been got at by the psychologists who had taken a long, hard look at sailors as a species and had decided we were all losing our minds because the old ships represented such an alien world. A floating metal platform with portholes, cabins and decks was not a healthy environment in which a man could thrive. They decided that what we needed to improve our mental condition was Formica, fibreglass and reinforced plastic. 'They' had never been to sea, of course, but 'they' knew best. So the new ships featured no wood, canvas or brass, but square replacement windows, art deco-style plastic bedrooms and linoleum floors. They even had polyurethane ropes! The nautical heart was being torn out of the ships, and in its place were moulded fixtures and wood-look veneers covered in whizzy technology that was brilliantly marketed to convince us that it made our lives better. No need for sextants – there was GPS (Global Positioning Systems using satellites). No need for Morse code or even a radio officer on the new ships – there was an 'electronics officer' instead, armed with an anti-static mat and a computer full of smoke and mirrors. The world was changing and – although I didn't appreciate it at the time – I was massively privileged to experience the Old World. Apart from anything else, the new ships turned around much more quickly, sometimes staying in port only a matter of hours before heading off again. Indeed, some of the bigger tankers could barely get alongside at all! My lovely old ships spent around two-thirds of their time in port. You could get up the road, meet some people, get time to feel a part of the place and get involved. When I spoke to cadets at college who worked on the oil tankers, they sung the praises of the ship's gym, the swimming pool and the direct line to the company psychologist, but the closest they got to visiting anywhere was to stare longingly at Rotterdam through binoculars from the oil terminus out at sea. I knew which I preferred.

We were shown around the *Global Princess* by the two departing apprentices. They were an odd couple. One was extremely tall and thin with a tall, thin head, sticky-out ears and a flat-top haircut; the other was short and fat with a short, fat head, sticky-out ears and a flat-top haircut. NotNorman whispered to me that they looked like a 'before' and 'after' advertisement for being dropped from a great height. I couldn't stop laughing the whole time they were showing us round, which was unfortunate because they were keen to conduct a sincere and formal handover.

We started at the fo'c'sle head, hanging over the bows to look down at the sea 50 feet below. The huge anchors were drawn up tight against the ship's side like the closed wings of a bird. I understood so much more now – I felt strangely at home already. I looked across at the hawse pipe. It is worth making note of the hawse pipe in passing because we'll be having some fun and games with it later. It is effectively a blooming great hole – a tunnel – running from the outside of the ship to the deck of the fo'c'sle head. The enormous anchor chains run from the anchor outside the ship up through the hawse pipes – one port, one starboard – and across to the gypsy. The gypsy is a huge wheel, shaped to bind with the anchor cable like the teeth of a cog. The windlass (an electric motor) turns the gypsy and feeds the cable into the anchor lockers. I remembered the huge, clattering sound as the anchor is let go and the cable rushes out over the gypsy and down into the sea. I remembered the smell from the friction as the brake is applied to stop that massive weight. I wanted to hear that sound and smell that smell again. Can I tell you an interesting fact about anchors? (Oh, all right then.) If you let the entire anchor out into the sea, right down to the 'bitter end' (i.e., the final link of the anchor where it shackles to the bulkhead in the anchor locker – yes, that's where the expression comes from), and if the sea is so deep that the anchor does not rest on the sea bed but just dangles like some enormous fishing line, then the motors that retrieve the anchor are not strong enough to pull it back up. Normally the weight of the cable does as much to secure a ship as the anchor itself, but if the whole lot just dangles there in the water, it's too heavy for the windlass to fetch it back up. There. Educational, this book. Enriching.

We dropped down onto the foredeck where the biggest surprise was that I knew where I was! On my first ship, not so many months before, I had tripped over cleats and banged my head on blocks, trapped my feet in scuppers and blundered into capstans. Now I felt like a part of the ship. I looked up at the runner wires between the heads of the derricks as the crew prepared them for loading. I knew what they were for! I knew what the crew was doing! I knew about the bottle screws and chains and shackles. I knew my bowline from my clove hitch, my splice from my binding and my port from my starboard. This was excellent.

Before and After were chatty and happy, as if we were visiting the home they'd just spent six months renovating. They looked weathered and worked, bedded in with the ship. We walked the length of the foredeck and into the accommodation. At this level were the engineers' cabins, the officers' galley and mess, the duty mess and the access to the engine room. We opened the huge iron door into the engine room and stood on the plates at the top of the metal companionway that dropped down, section by section, deep into the bowels of the ship. The engine room was fascinating, but as a working environment I could think of nowhere worse. The temperature was forever in the 40s and the hot air wooshed past us as we stood in the doorway. The noise was too much even now, despite the fact that the main engine wasn't even running. The metal steps also ran upwards, high up to the boiler flat and further up into the funnel. We gave a visit to the bottom plates a miss, and went back out onto the afterdeck.

We wandered along past hatch five to the poop deck – the raised section at the stern of the ship. *Global Princess* was built in 1958. She was so old that she had a rounded stern (as opposed to a transom stern which was squared off at the back) and a single propeller to handle all requirements. Even then, modern ships had bow thrusters and stern thrusters that forced jets of water sideways into the sea to allow the ship to turn on a sixpence without involving the propeller at all. There was no such luxury for us.

Inside the poop was the crew's accommodation. The whole area had a somewhat Eastern feel to it, from the incense they burned to the curry and rice that was permanently on its way. The poop deck had a wonderful and very different character. Some fifty crew – from Calcutta, in this case – did a two-year stint on board in one go. One side effect of this was that their accommodation was extremely homely and they were left entirely to themselves. We rarely went into the crew's accommodation, generally only venturing there to cadge fantastic Asian food from the 'bhandary,' or crew's cook. His relationship with Before and After was promisingly good humoured. This was another great sign. Finding food outside the officers' official mealtimes involved either a risky raid on the officers' galley or a good relationship with the crew's bhandary. To set things off on the right foot with the bhandary, I told him I thought it must be odd to go through life with people dribbling every time they see you. He inclined his head sideways and smiled politely even though he didn't have the foggiest idea what I was on about. I knew what I was on about, though: I was dribbling already. I felt a mad compulsion for a chapati. Perhaps with something lambish and tingly with spices. With maybe a foil of rice. Mmmmm. And a nice pint of beer. That's what this guy's face made me think about.

We then met our steward, Ahmed. He was to look after us. He would do our laundry, bring us tea at break time (or 'smoko' as it was called) and wake us gently when it was time to go on watch. Ahmed had grey hair and folded skin. He was at least 160 years old. It seemed somewhat odd, at my tender age, to have someone of his experience working for me in this capacity, but there you are. The British Empire was built upon domination of the sea, and was still evident out here on the ocean wave.

We said our goodbyes to Before and After who grabbed their bags and headed with delight for the gangway. NotNorman, Giewy and I climbed the companionway at the back of the accommodation, up one level to the boat deck. Two large lifeboats, each 30 feet in length (as big as a decent-sized yacht), sat at head height, ready in their davits to be lowered at a moment's notice. Our cabins were at boat deck level – indeed, when the heat was on, we would sleep out here on the boat deck to try and find a cooling breeze. There are no mosquitoes on a ship – at least, not when you are at sea – and no air conditioning on an old girl like this one, so the boat deck was favoured for getting to sleep when deep-sea in the tropics.

Up another level took us to the senior officer's deck – then to the extensive and lavish suites of the captain and the chief engineer, the radio officer's 'shack,' or radio room, and the guest and pilot's accommodation. We were rarely to be found at this level, unless we were passing through on our way to the bridge or, as somehow seemed more common, awaiting a carpeting from the captain. The neighbourhood had an intimidating air. It goes without saying that I preferred to avoid it.

We climbed another companionway and walked onto the bridge where the departing second mate was just finishing his handover to Payphone. They were poring over charts and talking earnestly of navigation and chartwork, the deeply interesting domain of a second officer. In front of the chartroom was the main bridge, with the helm and auto-pilot, radar, depth sounder, direction finder, VHF radio and telephone, the tachometer and commodore log, the engine room controls (or 'telegraphs'), the chronometer and clocks and lots and lots of other lights, bells, alarms, and whistles that I didn't fully understand. Although I hadn't spent much time in the rarefied air of the bridge on my first trip, this was where I would spend most of my professional life as a qualified navigator in years to come, looking out across the seas and cities of the world. I liked it very much.

We walked out onto the bridge wing and the vista opened up around us. We were high and proud. The only way to get higher was to climb onto the 'monkey island' (effectively, the roof of the bridge and charthouse) or scramble up a mast. The view was spectacular in all directions. It made me feel like a captain just to be up there. I looked out onto the fore and after decks of the ship where preparations were being made to load cargo; out to the shore with all the stevedores and cranes in the foreground, the Mombasa cityscape lying behind and the enormity of Africa beyond that; out to sea, where dozens of sun-kissed boats were chuntering about their day's business on a spangled blue sea.

I heard a shout from below and ran to lean over the polished wooden rail to see what was going on. The departing second mate was running to catch the coach. He was last aboard and the others were ragging him for holding up their departure. I saw the coach pull away with the old crowd peering back out of the windows for one last look at the old ship they were leaving. They knew they would never see her again – she didn't have many sea miles left. I felt another set of butterflies in my tummy. It was all down to us now.

So life kicked off on board. In three Mombasa days, the cargo was unloaded, the new cargo loaded and we set sail down the east coast of Africa. The mate was keen, of course, to have us tackle arduous, character-building tasks (for which, he assured us, we would thank him later), but he was also very keen that we learn some traditional maritime craftsmanship. We spent a lot of time on the afterdeck learning how to splice ropes and wires and create perfect bindings. Occasionally the routine was broken by the appearance of Ffugg, who would insist on a painful and extended wrestle with me every time we met. He would come barrelling down the companionway or leap out from round a corner, and off we would go, rolling about; me, struggling for my life engulfed in folds of puppy fat; him, enjoying the romp immensely. In between my rapid submissions, the four of us leaned on the starboard rail and watched in awe as Africa passed by majestically. And we talked lots and lots of rubbish.

In port I devoted myself to falling in love with Africa. We paid relatively uneventful visits to many beautiful ports along the east coast of Africa, including Mahajanga in Madagascar (a stunning country, which I would love to revisit with more time; the nature alone is unbelievable) and Tanga in Tanzania (a surprising oasis of wealth with large cruisers in the bay). In Maputo in communist Mozambique we broke a strict curfew, only escaping arrest at the hands of grim policemen by swimming across a small river that acted as a moat between the ships and the mainland. We dived in and, mercifully, the policemen chose firstly not to follow, and secondly, not to fire their guns at us across the divide. Our triumphant escape was only tempered by the discovery that the moat was in fact an open sewer. Seeing it in all its daytime glory made me feel physically sick – I'd been entirely immersed in it, head, face and all. The entire swim team caught scabies as a result. However, the process of falling in love with Africa was not to be thrown off course by trivial diseases, and when I arrived in Durban, South Africa, that was it. I was smitten. Durban is one of the few places in the world in which I could happily settle for life. It is a cosmopolitan city with great weather and fun at its heart. It has a fantastic seafront and glorious beaches (with huge waves), a great nightlife and an eclectic, mixed population. And in a bar one glorious evening, it had a girl. A girl called Chevvy.

I met her when we were out one night in the city. Sadly, I have to admit, we were in an English-themed pub. Yes, there is such a thing, although strictly speaking it was a Cockney-themed pub recommended by Payphone who was given a hero's welcome at the door. Payphone and the proprietor were gushingly emotional in their home-away-from-home reunion, and before we knew what was happening they had us gavvered rand the old Joanna for a cockney ding dong, a Dame Edna[1] – all round and a right old jolly up. The pub had a bloke dressed as a Pearly King 'ammering the ivories, and after only three or four yards of ale, the rest of us were up there helping Mother Brown get her knees up whilst Payphone explained to us, in rasping tones, his father's millinery preferences in his capacity as a dustman. It was all brilliant in its way, but not really what I was looking for from a night out in South Africa.

I was wondering how we could put an end to Payphone playing the spoons and winking at us as he went on to describe his father's unfortunate predilection for 'gawd blimey trousers' (I can just see them now, and you do have to feel for the man), and how his humble beginnings needed accommodation provided by social services (apparently as a result of the gawd blimey trousers), when Jinx appeared in the pub doorway with a big smile on his face. I knew that smile and, like Pavlov's dog, a wave of expectation washed over me. Sure enough, Jinx stood and held the door open and – with a gallant bow – ushered in a line of gorgeous young ladies. He had done it again. As girl after girl came smiling in, the singing stopped. The piano stopped. Would you Adam 'n' Eve it, even the spoons stopped.

I don't know how many girls there were, but I only saw one. My knees went. My brain blew a fuse. The only thing that was clear to me was the meaning of life and my purpose therein

---

1   Dame Edna Everage = beverage = beer. Geddit?

(which isn't bad going, really, I suppose). But for all orthodox aspects of life, Chevvy left me incapable of cohesive, logical thought from the moment I laid eyes on her. She had hair so deep and black it was like a secret whispered in space, and lips which were permanently three-quarters of the way to a kiss. They simply demanded to be kissed. And her eyes... her eyes were extraordinary – large, blue and unblinking – with an air of permanent wonder, as if she was horrified by your latest suggestion. Once her eyes had locked on to yours, you were helpless. Her Afrikaans English was wonderfully accented and she spoke in a breathy, pulsing tone which, when combined with her parted lips and outraged eyes, made her seem to be eternally on the brink of orgasm. I know men are renowned for thinking of sex every minute of the day, but with Chevvy in the room, it was impossible not to. Her every feature was alive with sexual tension, and seemed to be crying out for you to help her to relieve the problem. She smiled at me and said something, but the only sound I made in response was the one produced by my jaw hitting the floor. She wore a black leather mini skirt and black leather waistcoat. Beneath the waistcoat was nothing; just tanned, smooth skin and glimpses of a red-lace bra that supported a perfect cleavage. I couldn't hear. I couldn't see. I couldn't think. She was perfect. Absolutely perfect, and I was in love. I stood looking at her, thinking that looking at her was exactly the way I wanted to pass the rest of my life, when I found myself being slapped around the face by Jinx.

'Oi, Windy! Hello? Offer the poor girl a drink, will you? Chop, chop! Don't just stand there like a lemon!'

'Eh? What? Get yer own. Oh! Drink! Right! Yes!'

I snapped into action, tripping over a bar stool and spilling a beer someone had carelessly left on the bar. Oh my God, oh my God, oh my God. She was amazing. She had lips like... like... And legs like... I didn't tell you about her legs! Oh, and she had skin. Skin that was... was... indescribable (obviously).

She was poetry. She was nature's greatest wonder. She was an unparalleled beauty and it would be my life's work to make her mine.

Whatever else she was, Chevvy was also a human being and good fun. It was easier than I expected to get chatting and we had a wonderful time getting to know each other. We ignored everyone else as our group moved from one place to the next throughout the evening. We just chatted for hours. Chevvy was demure, and her expression of endless wonderment had me spellbound and talking too much. I couldn't look at her enough. My eyes would not drink her in fast enough. Her beauty was an endless, incomprehensible wonder. Nothing else mattered. I wanted more, more, more.

The night just flew by. At about three in the morning, Chevvy and I ended up in someone's flat. A penthouse high above Durban somewhere. By then I was in a group of about eight of Chevvy's friends. The flat had low-lighting, cool music and extremely well-organised soft drugs. I don't think I have ever been so well prepared for a first kiss. There and then with Chevvy, in amongst the lights over Durban, we lit up the sky. That kiss was an eternity. It was a moment that lasts forever.

When the owner eventually chucked us out, dawn was breaking. We walked for a while back towards the city centre, where Chevvy had parked her 750 cc four-stroke touring trials bike. Jeez, this girl just got better and better. She hitched up her mini-skirt and threw a tanned thigh over the bike. I sat behind her as she fired it up, and I put my arms around her tiny waist as she cruised through the warm night air. We rode fast through the empty city streets back to her place.

Chevvy's leather clothes might have been something of a clue about her preferred mode of transport, but were not any sort of clue to her profession. I was surprised when we drew up in front of a large, imposing building that looked like a Victorian school. In fact, Chevvy was a student nurse, as were all her friends, and she lived in a nurses' dormitory that was disguised as a fortress complete with gestapo guards, alarms and a gate and, to put it bluntly, I was not allowed inside. She had refused to sleep with me anyway that first night – a factor which only served to make her all the more perfect to me.

The sun was coming up when Chevvy finally disentangled herself from my loving embrace outside the prison camp. I begged her to let me see her again and she agreed. But I wasn't happy. I didn't want to be parted from her, or take a risk that I might not see her again. I had no way to get back to the ship anyhow. In order to reassure me that we would definitely meet again, and to give me a means to sod off and leave her alone, she loaned me her motorbike. We agreed to meet on a beach outside of town the next afternoon. Oh man, what a woman. I got on the bike and rode straight to the beach to wait for her. I didn't want to be late.

I love motorbikes. In good weather, with few clothes on and, ideally, without a helmet, there is no freedom like it. Add this to the fact that Chevvy's bike was big and powerful (I was the proud owner of a measly 50 cc moped back in the UK) and top it all off with a ten-mile stretch of beach on which to ride it, and you have a world of wonder and excitement for a teenager feeling he had perhaps got lucky in life. I spun those wheels, turned circles, pulled wheelies and blatted miles up the coast, pausing only to consider the subject of red lace bras and to fill the tank up again.

That afternoon when Chevvy finally arrived, everything changed. The world stopped turning. She made a motorbike seem tame. She was a vision that eclipsed Africa. Oh man, I was definitely in love.

We got a bunch of food and wine, which, as pillion, I had to try and hold on to as Chevvy drove the beasty-bike about half an hour along the beach. Eventually we arrived at a cove. We parked, spread out the food, went for a swim in gigantic waves, chatted, laughed, ate, drank wine, kissed, petted, bathed and fooled about in the sand. Life was perfect. Then as the sun set on our beautiful day, we rode back along the sand, up onto the road and back to the nurses' home.

The guards on the gate were as intimidating as ever, but I had passion to match and would not allow Chevvy to turn me away. She wasn't forthcoming, though, and it was a close thing. I almost said 'I love you,' for God's sake (that's how tough she was). Finally, after some electric foreplay delivered expertly by me, she gave in.

'OK, OK, you madman,' she said. 'I need the loo and you won't go away, so you might as well come in.' I felt my heart lift. I should write a book on foreplay one day. 'Go round the back of the building,' she said. 'There is a lamp post with spikes on it that you can use to climb the wall. Across the gardens there's a fire escape. Climb up to the first floor and I'll open the emergency exit at the top.'

She smiled mischievously at me, her big eyes shone with the kind of promise that could make a man weep. I knew she was serious. She was left staring in wonder at a me-shaped cloud of dust as I legged it round the back of the dormitory.

Getting in was just as she described. I climbed the lamp post, scaled the wall like a shadow and dropped, cat-like, to the ground inside enemy lines. I melded onto the wall and surveyed the grounds, my instinct for tactical management of danger giving me an edge over the impoverished enemy. I should have joined the SAS, not the Merchant Navy. I was at one with the darkness. Normal people were naïve under circumstances like these, but I was perfectly prepared. A silent, lethal assassin, at his most dangerous when working alone. I really believe that given my time over again I could have been a…

'Cooo-eee! Windy! Up here!'

Chevvy was standing at the top of the fire escape. She had somehow seen me in the shadows and was waving and calling to me with no thought for the movements of enemy agents. I don't know. Girls have no idea how to handle these situations. I prowled across the terrain, climbed the metal steps swiftly and silently, slid sideways through the fire door and was kissing Chevvy before any mention of a Black Magic Box.

Chevvy sneaked me along the corridors, checking for guards and goody-goody squealers the whole way. We slinked into her room and shut the door behind us. She had a small bed-sitter all to herself in what was otherwise a girls-only dormitory. Girls only, that is, except for me. Ha Haaaarrr. I was The One. The luckiest bloke on earth.

Now, details of our night together would not be appropriate here, and you will know by now that I am not a purveyor of salacious material. I feel equally confident – knowing a bit about your excellent taste in books – that you are not the type of person who would want me to be indelicate. However, a certain amount of information is necessary to the plot, so to speak, so I guess I have to let you in on the depressing news. Chevvy was not an easy woman to fire up, so to speak. She seemed to be laden with blue-touch paper throughout the preamble, and yet the fireworks display turned out to nothing more than a few sparklers. I couldn't understand it. With all the promise in the overture, the endless wonderment in her eyes, and my own unparalleled technique, it seemed almost impossible, but I could not move the earth for her however hard I tried. She patted me on the head and said it was fine, but we both knew the truth. And the curious thing was that I knew she felt the same way – that it could and should have been something of a night of bangs and explosions to warrant the full orchestra in the park. We fell asleep in a curious mood for which one word was depressingly apt: anticlimax.

I woke early the next morning. The day and the girl were beautiful. The sun was slatting in across Chevvy's glossy hair, golden skin and pouting lips as she slept. I took one look at her in her slumber and felt a sudden urge to have another go with the incendiary areas of this amazing-looking girl. I woke her in the traditional fashion. She awoke like a pussycat, stretching and luxuriating in half-slumber as I kissed her neck, and things were looking promising. But I did need to use the toilet.

'You can't,' she said, pulling me back into her arms. 'There's no gents.'

I pulled away again. 'What do you mean, I can't? I have to!'

'No, really. You can't,' she was waking up now. 'If you get spotted in here, they'll throw me out as well as you. You'll have to hang on.'

This, to be frank, wasn't an option. 'Where's the ladies' toilet? Can't I use the ladies'?'

Chevvy thought for a moment, then smiled an ominous smile. 'You can, but you really mustn't get spotted. You'll have to wear some of my clothes and walk like a girl.'

Despite my protests, she seemed to be strangely happy with this arrangement. I would go as far as to say that her eyes lit up at the prospect and, I'm sorry to say, we had our first argument. A man likes to keep a sense of proportion during the early stages of a new relationship, and I felt that dressing up in women's clothes was not good for my image, particularly when the clothes were of the type Chevvy preferred. She ignored my protests and held pink-plastic and tight-leather clothes up against me as I explained that I wasn't going to wear them. But in the end, she held the trump card. I had no choice, and began trying on girls' dresses.

It was difficult to find clothes that not only came close doing up at the front, but which did not offend Chevvy's sense of style. I was only going to the loo and back, but she insisted that I couldn't go out looking like that… or that… oh no… or that… We argued our way through a bladder-bursting half-hour choosing an outfit which looked just so. In the end, we arrived at an interesting nightie and hooded dressing gown combo which showed a tad too much hairy leg, given the circumstances, but the eye was cleverly distracted from this with a pair of silver sling-backs with three-inch heels.

I pulled the hood up and was ready to go. She opened the door to check that the coast was clear, and a strange thing happened. Her eyes were bigger and more filled with wonder than ever before. That elusive fire appeared to be burning bright. She grabbed my hair inside the hood, kissed me hard and wrapped a shapely leg around me.

'God, I love it when you dress up,' she growled, rummaging inside my nightie. 'Now this is more like it...'

But I still needed the loo. I prized myself away, she opened the door, looking on me as a cat looks on a cornered mouse, then reluctantly let me on my way.

'End of this corridor, turn right, loos are on the left,' she said, watching me scamper off, my bow-legs hardly well disguised by my high heels, which lay flat out to the sides as I limped along on the soles of my feet.

As I made my way to the toilets, I kept close to the wall and kept a watchful eye out for security guards. Getting caught by those large, South African thugs in uniform would be bad enough at the best of times, but dressed like this... And there were other factors too. Not only would Chevvy be in deep trouble, but her apparent hunger for unbridled morning intercourse with me wearing her clothes might evaporate. It was vital that I got in, did the job and got out again without being detected. SAS, that's me.

I peeked gingerly round the corner. I could see the toilets. Excellent. And no one in the corridor. I made it to the door and listened for activity within. This could be the tricky bit. Bumping into two or three nurses as they left the ladies' might not go down well. I could hear nothing. I looked left and right, adjusted my hood over my face and in I went.

There was a short corridor and a second door before the main area of the girls' toilets. It was all very clean and smelled disgusting. How refined ladies can accept washrooms that stink to inflammable levels of Toilet Duck or whatever it is, I don't know. There was hardly enough oxygen to support life; the mixture was more suited to supporting an internal combustion engine. And the pong rather distracted me in that vital second before I entered the main area, so the sight that met my eyes as I opened the door to the inner sanctum did so with some surprise. Standing at the washbasins was a line of men all tending to their ablutions. They were all dressed in girls' dressing gowns and pink slippers, but with shavers buzzing, stubble being removed and, as if to welcome me and simultaneously mask the pong of ladies' toilet, one of them lifted a leg and delivered a strident fart. There were certainly no ladies present. It was more like the men's bogs at a campsite.

'Mornin'!' said the bloke nearest me, stretching his face to shave his jowl. 'You all right?'

Others turned to acknowledge me as they went about their business, including a guy in a cubicle taking a leak, with his back to me, in a light-blue, baby-doll lingerie nightdress which barely covered his arse. And I thought showing my calves was risqué.

'Yo!'

'Mornin'!'

'Hey, dude!'

Despite their own appearances, I couldn't help but notice them checking out my red gown and heels. I had much better style than any of them, and I think they felt upstaged. Some of them appeared to have put no thought whatsoever into their outfits. Another 'good morning!' sounded a tad strained as it came over the top of a closed cubicle door, but I felt it was only polite to respond.

'Morning.'

'Who are you with, then?' asked the Wilkinson Sword and Flowery Shower Cap nearest me.

'Eh? Oh, her name's Chevvy, although I'm not sure what it's short for. It was something like…'

'No, no, no,' said the Rechargeable Twin-Head and Pink Boob Tube at the next bowl. 'What number?'

'Eh? Oh! Errr… room number, you mean? Em, thirty-six, I think.'

'Hey, heeey! Good one, neighbour!' said a Colgate and Estee Lauder Sponge-Bag passing me on his way to the exit. 'I'm forty-two. Straight opposite you. If you need a cup of sugar or something…'

'Twenty-eight,' said the Wilkinson Sword.

'Nine,' said the Rechargeable Twin-Head and Pink Boob Tube, winking at me knowingly as if I should be impressed.

'Fifteen,' said an exfoliating Dove Soap and Sure For Men at the far end. (Who let him in?)

'Hngggg! Forty-aaah! Jeezus! Forty-eight!' strained the cubicle.

'Four!' shouted the Blue Baby-Doll, golf-like, as he turned from the toilet to reveal – NotNorman!

'Hey! Notski!' I shouted, pleased to see a familiar face in all the madness (even if he was rather badly setting off the nightdress). I stepped towards him, but then remembering how little clothing he had on, I decided that my joy at seeing him should perhaps fall short of a hug.

'Hey, Windy! We never knew you got back here! MoneyBox is here too somewhere. And The Famous Dick Wrigley.'

As I stood, eyes closed from the ecstasy afforded by a long-awaited release of pressure, NotNorman described the way the last day or two had panned out for the rest of the lads. The long and the short of it was that there was enough nautical talent in the vicinity to sail the nurses' home to Cuba. I told Notters about my adventures with Chevvy, and we went our separate ways, stumbling back down the corridors in our feminine attire.

Now, I do not wish to make any statements here which could prejudice judgement or lead to awkward questions at some future date. We were all young once, and these things happen, but I have to admit that there was something – I don't know – *intriguing* about wearing Chevvy's clothes. I mean, I don't want to make a habit of it or anything, you understand, but it was a new experience in life's rich tapestry and it felt… soft. It was different from the sullen day-to-day boredom of men's jeans and T-shirts. There is a sensual side to women's clothes which we chaps are denied in our own wardrobes. Not only that, but, well... what am I trying to say here...? I caught my reflection a couple of times and well, I actually have quite a good figure. For a girl. And Chevvy seemed to think so too. As soon as I was through the door she pounced, and we never looked back. She was extraordinarily excited by her own dress sense, and I have to say that the physical side of our relationship exploded into life once I was, if I may speak openly, wearing women's clothes.

As we lay in the afterglow of our umpteenth struggle together, she was one satisfied woman. Well, I thought she was, anyway.

'That was incredible,' I said, smoothing the ravages out of my cotton frock (I mean one hundred per cent cotton – no synthetic mix). 'Really incredible. I – I've never known anything like it. Listen, Chevvy, you know these velveteen gloves of yours? The ones that go with that black ball gown I was wearing? I was wondering if it would be OK for me to borrow them, just for a day or two? I'd like to…'

'It wasn't bad,' she said, lying back on the pillow and staring at the ceiling. There was a pause as a distant longing drew down over her face. She looked like the Greek goddess whatsername, dreaming wistfully of unknowable thingummies. You know the one. She seemed determined to broach a sensitive subject. Suddenly she looked me hard in the eyes. 'It was all right, Windy. But do you know what really gets me going?'

I looked at her in disbelief. 'What? You mean, there's more? You can go better than that?'

She leant up on her elbow and smiled at me with a scary glow behind her eyes. 'Oh, yes,' she purred like a tiger that also had half a chance of achieving unknowable thingummies. 'You wanna know the secret?'

I had to know, of course, but I felt almost scared at the prospect of where we could go from here. Embarrassed, I fiddled distractedly with the straps on the red plastic hot-pants I was wearing under the frock. Not quite my size – much too tight to really do me justice. Such a shame. I only had ten minutes at a time in these before I lost all the blood to the lower-half of my body. Inconvenient, under the circumstances.

'If you really want to get me going, we need a full and manly performance. Could you do that for me?'

I thought I had already achieved new heights in the realm of manly performances, despite being enfrocked, but she was apparently not as impressed with me as I was with myself.

'Here's what you gotta do,' she continued. 'I need you to burgle me.'

I looked at her with eyes that probably looked as big as hers. I thought I knew most of the terminology for the different types of fun and games people got up to behind closed doors, but this was a new one for me. Burgle her? What would I have to do to *burgle* her? I got a picture of what it sounded like it might mean and – no. It couldn't be that.

'It's simple. I want you to dress up as a burglar – and burgle me!' she said, her eyes afire. 'Black balaclava, black leather gloves – the works. I want you to creep in and discover me, all naked and vulnerable in the bath, and I'm like: 'oh, no! It's a burglar and he's going to be rough with me and – and tie me up and have his way with me, and I want you to drag me out of the bath – really roughly – and, and, I'm kicking and struggling but I can't get away, and you're too strong for me, and I can't see your face, and – and – and you hold me down with your big muscular arms, and you tie my hands together and I'm helpless, and you throw me down, and struggle as I might there's no stopping you from having your way, and you bite my neck and force yourself on me and…' Chevvy swallowed. She was panting hard. I think she had forgotten I was there.

I sat in my red hot-pants and fiddled with the black chiffon evening dress I had borrowed (I loved the way it accentuated my hips) and stared at her in disbelief. Chevvy was one fit young girl. If it came down to a straightforward wrestling match between me and Chevvy, I wasn't sure I could win. And I wasn't sure what my entire role would be. I'd never burgled anyone before. 'I… I guess I could, you know, nick the video player…' I hazarded. 'I mean, if that's OK. But I'm going to have to get a bag.'

She closed her eyes and counted to ten. 'Once you've dragged me roughly out of the bath we'll just go with the flow from there, OK? But you must be really rough with me, particularly until you've got me well tied up. And certainly don't pay any attention to my cries for help, or telling you to stop or anything. Don't take any nonsense. Just take me for everything you want, OK?'

'Ah. Right. Everything I want, right?'

'Everything and anything you're strong enough to take. And once I'm tied up, I won't be able to stop you.'

My mind became crammed with good ideas. I wanted an SAS role, and now it appeared I had one. As she escorted me out via the fire escape, I turned back to her.

'So, 9.30 this evening. You'll be in the bath, right?'

'That's right,' she purred. 'Naked. Naked… and helpless.'

'Oh, right. And you don't need these clothes back tonight?' I held up the four hangers and their contents.

'No,' she snapped, waving them away. 'Not ever. Keep 'em. Tonight you must have a black balaclava and leather gloves. And some rope. Don't forget the rope. Some idiot will have left this fire escape ajar and we girls won't be safe. You'll be able to break in, and… and… subdue me and tie me up, and then you'll be able to… to…' She caught her breath and that wistful, glazed look in her eyes told me that my Goddess of the unkownable was already getting a head start with the foreplay…

Oh my God. What a night I was in for…

Chapter 4

Knights in Black Balaclavas

Romance and the Army Surplus stores. The balaclava problem in relationships. The balaclava problem in a life of crime. Too many crooks spoil the bath. No answer to the candelabra mystery. NotNorman is inscrutable.

I climbed aboard Chevvy's motorbike and roared off into Durban to prepare for my night of rape and pillage. It was an unusual experience. Most men with girlfriends need a flower shop, or maybe – for the more risqué – a lingerie shop, or even – for the truly liberated – a sex shop. But when you have a girlfriend like Chevvy, you need a good old-fashioned hardware store.

I don't know if you've ever tried to buy a balaclava for nefarious purposes. Given that all the bad guys you see on *Crimewatch* seem to carry at least one, and coupling that with the general buoyancy of the crime figures these days, I assumed sales would be up and that getting hold of a couple would be simple. Well, it's not. Balaclavas are not ready-made for the purpose. I'd never thought about it before, but a standard balaclava has a dirty big hole for your face to stick out. That's precisely what you are trying to avoid, and it isn't something you can discuss with the bloke behind the counter. I bet that every great robbery in history has been thrown off schedule because the crooks didn't allow any time for the balaclava palaver. Mr Big would, quite understandably, assume that gang members would have their own balaclavas and, upon discovery that Soapy, Knuckles, Trousers and The Reverend were all unprepared in the head-concealment department, would not have counted on it taking a week of frantic knitting by Lenny the Crack before the job could go ahead.

Anyway, the balaclavas in Durban's finest hardware store let my whole face stick out the front – specifically against conventional burglar attire. Back at the ship, my solution was ingenious. I decided to wear it back to front, and cut holes for my eyes and mouth in the back, which could then become the front, if you see what I mean. This left a clump of uncontrolled hair sticking out through the face-hole at the back, which somehow didn't seem right. I do understand that ones tailoring and coiffure should not perhaps be to the fore when planning the crime of the century, but let's not forget, this was also a romantic liaison and I didn't want to give Chevvy the giggles at some critical moment because my hair looked as though someone had blown a bullet out through the back of my head. But I decided to live with it. I had the additional problem that my eye-hole adjustments had restricted my ability to see where I was going, and I also wanted a mouth-hole big enough for getting my entire tongue out without getting bits of wool all over it (if you see the way I'm thinking here), so I cut the three holes in the back much too big and – as it turned out – slightly out of position. How do all those crooks on *Crimewatch* get such perfect balaclavian holeage? It's a nightmare! When I looked in the mirror, staring back at me was what appeared to be a very surprised, one-eyed panda. A very surprised, one-eyed panda who has had a bullet blown out through the back of his head.

Anyway, when you're done with the hardware store, you need a department store for a black roll-neck sweater, black leather gloves and a holdall. Then it's back to the ship and a visit to the rope store in the fo'c'sle head for the bondage gear. All this for one girl. Man, what a girl!

When I got to the rope store I was surprised to find NotNorman there. We were not working that day, so it was odd that he should be up at the fo'c'sle. It was a working environment, so we didn't come out on deck without wearing working clothes if we could avoid it, and here he was looking very dashing in smart black clothes. He had a coil of ratline in his hand – pinched from the secret stash of good stuff – and was busy with a knife. I felt justified in challenging him. We have to look after the ship security first, and worry about personal nicety later.

'What's going on?' I asked, firmly, but not too accusingly.

He didn't look up. No eye contact. He never usually concentrated like that when we were on deck.

'Hold this, will you?'

He passed me one end of the ratline and began fraying a section a few feet along with his blunt knife, his tongue hanging out with the concentration it required. I wanted to scold him for having a blunt knife. First rule of a sailor's life is to have a sharp knife, but I wanted to stick to the point, and he was avoiding the question. I had to push him on it.

'So, what's going on, then?'

'Amazing last night. Really freaky bad, rude woman. I'm going to meet her again for some dead weird stuff she wants to do. I'll see you later.'

He picked up the lengths of rope he had mauled, counted them carefully – five? Why five? – pushed them into a new black holdall and set off with the kind of purpose rarely seen in the Normanless one. He was definitely up to something. I scratched my head as I watched him stride off down the foredeck. There was something strangely – I dunno – familiar about his appearance. I mean, I know that I knew him, and that he *should* be familiar, but there was something odd that I couldn't fathom – like déjà vu. I made a mental note to get to the bottom of it.

I picked up the ratline and measured off four lengths of around two metres each. I looked at them and wondered if it was enough. Two hands, two feet. Then again, was it the done thing to tie a girl's legs together? It could cause more problems than it solved. Still, best carry a spare. I got back down and was halfway through measuring off a fifth, when a sharp voice caused me to jump out of my skin.

'Oi! Windy. What's going on? What're you doing up here on your day off?'

MoneyBox was standing in the doorway to the rope store. I couldn't see his face properly because of the sun behind him, but I could see he had a bag in one hand, and a knife in the other.

'Oh, hi, MoneyBox. Is that knife sharp? Couldn't borrow it, could I?'

'What are you doing up here?' he asked, a little curtly if you ask me. It was none of his business. I cut the rope and put it into my holdall with two shackles and a bottlescrew, just in case. I proffered the bag at him. 'Bit of a hot date tonight,' I said with a wink. And I left him to it.

But as I made my way down the foredeck, a thought occurred to me: what on earth would a third engineer want from the deckside rope store? And why was he dressed in smart black clothes? Fishy was the word. Definitely fishy. He, too, looked familiar in a déjà vu sort of way. Weird. I made a mental note to get to the bottom of it. Tomorrow.

I set off around 8.30 p.m., giving myself an hour to do a ten-minute journey. I wanted plenty of time to execute the infiltration. I also discovered another thing criminals have to consider. When you set off for work of an evening in your black trousers, black roll-neck, your leather gloves and sporting a black holdall – particularly when it's 30 degrees outside in throbbing sunshine and most people are in beachwear – people feel justified in pointing at you and passing comment. To say one stands out amongst the Hawaiian shirts is something of an understatement, but really, people should show some manners. However, as usual, my SAS brain was swift to find a way for me to blend into the scenery. I decided that, until I was off the city streets and all the way inside the nurses' dormitory, I would take off the balaclava.

I parked two streets away and walked quickly down. I felt a heady mixture of excitement and nerves as I took a few reccies behind the dormitory and psyched myself up for what lay ahead. Moments later, I dropped to the ground on the other side of the wall. This was more like it. Twilight was falling, and now my clothing and attitude made sense. I was undercover, on the spot and deep behind enemy lines. I lifted myself athletically back up to the top of the wall and called to a passerby in a Hawaiian shirt to throw me up my bag. This was to be my last contact with the civilised world. Now it was just me, panther-like and in survival mode as I moved like a shadow through the bushes and made my way up towards the imposing old...

What was that?

I spun round and dropped to the ground. There was a noise from the rhododendrons behind me. Someone had trodden on a branch and broken it. My heart pounded as I lay flat in the lush grass. Was I being followed? Surely not. I had gone miles and miles round Durban on the motorbike on the way here. There was no way anyone followed me on that ride. I'd parked two streets away, hung around on the road, climbed a wall – there simply couldn't be anyone following me. It must be the security guards. So why couldn't I see them now? I lay motionless, scanning the landscaped grounds towards the far wall for any sign of movement. Branches swayed and the wind blew gently. I could detect no movement. Mind you, despite going safe-side with the scissors, my balaclava was cock-eyed and I could only use one peephole at a time. To use both meant dragging the balaclava off to one side and folding my head and nose sideways down towards my left shoulder. That meant I couldn't breathe, but at least I could get a good look round. The coast was still clear. There was nobody about. I looked up at the fire escape. There were three flights of metal staircase. Very exposed. I could see the light at the top. I watched for a couple more minutes. There was no movement. It was time to go for it.

At the top of the fire escape, I paused before trying the door. This was the boundary, and my stomach reminded me of my nerves. This was Big Time. Part of me was hoping that it would be locked shut, and I could go off and play on the motorbike, forget all about this cloak-and-dagger stuff or tussling with a scary woman. I mean, it's one thing to be caught by security guards trying to infiltrate a nurses' dormitory for the purposes of infiltrating a nurse. They wag the finger and go all misty-eyed as they tell you stories about when they were young and tried to infiltrate nurses. It's quite another thing to be caught dressed in black, with a balaclava, leather gloves and a holdall full of ropes and tools, and try to claim that you're just looking for your girlfriend. It's only the clothes that are different, and yet, for some reason, the alibi doesn't hold water in ways that satisfy the authorities. Their eyes don't sparkle with nostalgia as they tell you stories of their younger days when they dropped through skylights and tried to rob diamonds from museums. No, no, no. They sit on your head and tell each other not to take any chances until the police arrive.

For better or for worse, the fire escape was open. I slid inside and padded softly along towards Chevvy's room. She had told me that the bathroom was the door in the corner at the end of the corridor beyond her room. I crept up to the corner, looking anxiously around. There were two doors which could be the corner room. I listened intently at the first. There was no sound. Could be a bathroom; might not be a bathroom. I closed a gloved hand around the door handle and turned it silently. I inched the door open and stuck my head gingerly round the corner. I lifted my left hand over the top of my head and pulled the balaclava across so I could see out of my right eye. It was the bathroom! And there was Chevvy in the bath. She was facing away and hadn't even noticed my arrival. I felt a predator's smile cross my lips as I slid into the steam-filled room and closed the door behind me. I put the bag down gently on the ground and drew out a length of rope. Then took a deep breath.

'Ah haaaaaaarrrrrr!' I cried, pirate-like, and leapt into the centre of the room. As she turned in utter horror, I was already in mid-air, diving headlong into the bath to begin wrestling this fine woman into submission.

It wasn't Chevvy.

I tried to abort my landing, but was already committed to the swallow dive and I landed on top of the poor girl just as her scream was dispatched into every corner of the Transvaal. Despite her fear, she had the presence of mind to pull at my balaclava, which moved about a centimetre and rendered me completely blind. As I pushed to get out of the bath, and tried unsuccessfully to splutter out an apology, she beat me frantically with the shower head and screamed. And screamed. And screamed.

'Rape! Rape! Heeelp! Raaaaaape!'

Eventually, I managed to extricate myself, but she would not be calmed down. I legged it as she chased me wielding an efficient loofah. I managed to squeeze out through the bathroom door and into the corridor, where I held the knob tightly so she couldn't get out after me.

I stood there for a moment, dripping onto the floor, trying to get my heart rate down and think of something brilliant as she loofahed away at the door from the other side, when the strangest of things happened. At the end of the corridor appeared – appeared – well, it was me, I think. Or at least, I had to wave my arm around to be sure I wasn't looking in a mirror.

A one-eyed figure in a mutilated black balaclava, leather gloves and clutching a holdall slid round the corner and began padding down the corridor towards me. I couldn't leave my post, or the girl would get out. I couldn't stay put, or the guy might burgle me. I didn't know what to do. He was waving in a pally sort of way as he approached, but I wasn't interested in any of that honour-amongst-thieves stuff. I abandoned my post and legged it along the next corridor.

I would have loved to have known if he was quicker than me – I doubted it. Fear is an Olympic motivator, but turning my head was pointless. I couldn't see a darned [sic] thing because of the unruly behaviour of my balaclava. However, using only my ears (at least one of which was out in the open via an eye hole) I was able to follow events back at the bathroom. The girl emerged from the steam with the single-minded aim of apprehending the perpetrator of the attempted rape in her bathroom, and ran straight into the path of my poor, innocent lookalike who, by happy coincidence, was perfectly dressed to get the blame for everything. Sure enough, she added two and two, and came up with a perfectly timed whop round the head with a loofah combined with a nifty trip with the toilet brush, bringing the guy to the deck as he tried to run past her. She warmed to her task quickly now that she had slowed him down a bit and he was vulnerable on the floor, gearing up into a state I can only describe as unbridled fury channelled into a string of perfectly delivered wrestling moves. I knew what kinds of moves they were because Ffugg had been teaching me wrestling moves via several intense and interactive tutorials. Her first move was what we wrestlers term a Honeymooner – an admirable choice to get the ball rolling and the head spinning, which led seamlessly into an Oklahoma Slam to weaken and disorientate. He had not put up much of a fight so far, and was barely back on his hands and knees before she went for the final submission move with a horribly well-applied Hudson Spin and Stink Face combination. All I could do was stand and admire her shot selection. It was highly impressive, particularly as she was simultaneously trying to keep a towel around her, and at no time did she stint on her duty to screech continuously for backup. Personally, I didn't think she needed any assistance. It was the masked marauder who was in the most danger here, but I heard others approaching from all angles, including straight ahead. I turned and ran directly back towards my fallen comrade whose legs were kicking from beneath the firmly seated nurse. The couple were obviously getting along famously, so I was able to nip into the other corner room next to them before reinforcements arrived.

Inside it was hot and steamy. Another bathroom. I dropped the bag, pulled round my balaclava and peered with monocular trepidation through the mist. Looking back at me from another bath, naked and flushed with sexual desire was… Chevvy. Thank God. I'd found the right room. She looked surprised to see me. Dumbfounded, even. Speechless was the word. Then she looked down at the black-clad, balaclava'd figure between her knees in the bath and the reason for her surprise became evident. My fellow burglar had yet to notice my arrival, as his top half was deeply engrossed in an energetic submarine assault on Chevvy's honour in the shallow end. Eventually, the crook realised that Chevvy was no longer focused. He sat up and looked at me with an expression of sheer balaclava written all over his face.

'You're on the wrong floor, idiot!' Chevvy hissed. 'Vicky's upstairs. Same room, next floor up.'

Now this was an unexpected turn of events. One expects a little more loyalty from one's girlfriend, even if you have only been together twenty-four hours. I had barely been given half a chance as a burglar-cum-rapist, so to speak, and yet here I was, sent back to the pavilion before I'd even got my pads on. I felt a tad miffed. Chevvy waved her hand at me to send me on my way. The dripping balaclava between her knees nodded damp agreement with her, and I felt as though they expected me to leave.

I picked up the bag and was wondering what Vicky might think – whoever the hell she was – if I chanced my arm with her upstairs, when I remembered the scuffle outside. I couldn't really leave just yet. I turned back to where Chevvy and her burglar were sitting waiting for me to go.

'Em, listen. It's a bit tricky out there at the mo'. Wouldn't mind if I sort of hung about for a minute, would you?' I shifted awkwardly from one foot to the other as they stared back at me. 'You chaps just burgle ahead – pretend I'm not here.'

Chevvy's face had gone – funny. It was the only word for it. Her look of permanent surprise had been upgraded to extra surprised, and her voice was even more orgasmically breathy than ever.

'Windy?' She peered at me quizzically. 'Is that you?'

She looked from me to the other balaclava, which seemed to be sheepishly trying to back out of the bath. 'Then who the hell...?'

The balaclava glowed red, jumped up from the bath and dashed for the door, picking up his bag on the way. This was more like it, so I held the door open. His one wide eye met mine as we passed at the door. I now looked on life rather more optimistically (as well as misty-optically). Apart from the now increased possibility of my burgling a nurse, there was also the delight of knowing that there was a stern reception awaiting this impostor just outside the door. The committee without, having recently witnessed my entrance to this room, would perceive that it was me now leaving. They would forget about the real me within, and focus their attention on the imitation me who had just left. It was becoming rather convenient to have lookalikes following me about and taking all the blame. I shut the door behind him and listened with satisfaction to the rumpus that he ran into outside. He deserved to have six bells beaten out of him by the committee following his outrageous attempt to take advantage of Chevvy. I also changed my mind, from feeling rather pleased that – by some quirk of dormitory policy – these bathrooms had no locks, to feeling that perhaps they might be rather a good idea. Someone should suggest them at the next meeting. Big, strong ones.

The sound of running feet and shouting from outside indicated that a general runabout involving all personnel had been suggested, agreed and commenced, and the participants seemed to be heading off in all directions at the double. Excellent.

I was about to tell Chevvy what a weird time I'd had getting here, when she placed her hand dramatically across her chest, and announced theatrically (for the second time that evening):

'Oh, me, oh, my! A big nasty burglar! And me, alone and naked in the bath! Alas and alack, whatever shall I do?'

She blinked those huge blue eyes at me. I stood for a moment watching her, wondering whatever shall she do, until her face began to register a degree of anger, and I realised with a start that this was my cue! I was on! I leapt into action, dived enthusiastically into the bath and began the nontrivial task of trying to subdue this fine young lady whilst simultaneously arranging a sexual union. No easy task when I additionally had to subdue a wayward balaclava and keep getting out of the bath to fetch equipment from the bag in a one-eyed and damp sort of way. Indeed, I think it somewhat disturbed Chevvy's vibe when I had to ask her to just put her finger Here for a mo' or the knot would go wrong. Anyway, on balance, we were proceeding admirably on all fronts, and I began to think that this was a superb way to go about the business of arousal, when the door suddenly burst open. A dark figure shot in, threw a black holdall down and fell back against the door to hold it shut. He was breathing heavily and wearing a cock-eyed black balaclava and leather gloves. I sat up in the traditional position between Chevvy's knees and pulled my balaclava round to get a better view as Chevvy spoke for both of us.

'Could you sod off, please? Vicky is upstairs. Same room, next floor, OK?'

Well said, I thought. And I nodded the balaclava in support.

'You two just keep quiet,' said the shadowy shape menacingly.

Chevvy was looking all weird again. 'Barry? Is that you?' She leaned round to look at him, and all my careful knot work came undone. 'Was that you in the bath with me just now, you bastard? I can't believe you just did that to me. I thought you were – '

'Just… just shut up, Chevvy, all right? You're supposed to call me Bill.' He came storming over and pointed into Chevvy's face. 'I'm tellin' you now. If I don't get out of this, I'm taking you down with me!'

There was the sound of pounding feet leaving the vicinity outside. He turned away and seemed to make his decision. 'Right. I'm out of here.'

He picked up his bag, opened the door a slice, took in the lay of the corridor, then slid out. A cry went up, and once more there came the sound of pounding feet and shouts from without. This was getting kind of unnerving. I know this may sound a little paranoid, but I began to get a fuzzy idea that something was going on. There were underworld figures lurking round every corner and just beneath the surface in every bath, and any upstanding member of some future jury may well come to the conclusion that, given my attire, I was a fully paid-up member of the gang myself. I suddenly remembered that NotNorman's girlfriend was also a nurse in this home. And he had stayed here last night. Maybe he was in the rope store because... because... and maybe... No. That guy definitely wasn't NotNorman. Not even close. I knew he wasn't Bill. Good chance on Barry. And just because he was not NotNorman, if you see what I mean, didn't *not* mean that the other one wasn't not NotNorman. Didn't it? My head was spinning. Another cry. More pounding feet. I needed to think this through. I tried to round up the facts by enumerating balaclavas on my fingers: as I arrived in the building, we know for sure that Burglar A, was in Position Alpha with Nurse X – now positively identified as Chevvy – in bathroom one. We can safely assume that Burglar B must have simultaneously been on his way to bathroom two where Wrestling Nurse Y lifted him up and, through the medium of a Honeymooner and an Oklahoma Slam, placed Burglar B into Position Beta, followed rapidly into Gamma and finally folding him horribly into position Kappa Omigod for the application of the Stink Face. After I left bathroom one and headed west, Burglar C must have been...

'Oh me, oh my! A big strong burglar, and me all alone and naked and partly tied up already, with nothing to protect me from...'

I looked at Chevvy, all vulnerable and naked and wet in the bath as she recited her lines once more. She would like nothing more than to be forced into good old Position Delta, but I was losing my appetite. If that other bloke was scared – and he seemed to have some inside information – there was probably every reason why I should be too. I knew what had to be done.

'I'll call you tomorrow. Bye!'

'... and me, a helpless maiden with no protection from the big, bad man invading my...'

I left her blinking largely, her hand across her chest, and ran from bathroom one... headlong into a large man dressed in black, with one frightened eye staring at me through a comprehensively mutilated balaclava and a holdall in his hand. We fell to the floor on top of each other and – I guess through sheer panic – began to roll and struggle together until we got a grip on each other's balaclavas and...

'Aaaaah – HA!'

'AAAAAh – HA, HAR ha HAAA!'

Off they came.

NotNorman and I sat in each others laps, looking a little confused, when at the top end of the corridor a black-clad burglar skidded round the corner on one leg, then flew off down a middle corridor, hotly pursued by a posse of nurses and security guards. We were spotted. A couple of guards peeled off to come after us.

'The fire escape! Quick!' NotNorman was swift to see sense.

We leapt to our feet and galloped off in the other direction, up a flight of stairs and round to the right towards the fire exit. Little did we know that the other parties had gone around the other side of the block, also up a flight of stairs, and, as we turned into the final corridor, we saw the other black-clad gentleman approaching at high speed from the other end pursued by the posse. NotNorman and I reached the fire escape first and scrambled down it to the ground. Our impersonator followed with the cast of extras close behind him.

The three of us legged it across the garden. I heard shouts and a thud. I looked back and saw one of the gang had been rugby tackled and sat upon by the authorities. I knew it wasn't NotNorman, so I dropped over the wall with some relief, made it to the motorbike and was out of sight before you could say Big Vern.

The next day, after a conversation with MoneyBox and NotNorman, it transpired that each of our girlfriends had made the same request of us, namely to dress all in black and burgle them soundly. Why on earth would they do that? We couldn't work out what we had been part of. MoneyBox had been unable to attend the midnight run on the nurses due to pressure of work, so we knew that the other burglar couldn't have been him. It fell to Chevvy to provide me with the answers when she turned up later. Chevvy and I sat in my cabin. She looked embarrassed.

'The dressing up thing was my idea,' she said. No surprises there. 'But the robbery was Vicky's plan,' she explained. 'There are some 200-year-old candelabras in the dining room. They are left over from when the home was a palace or something. Worth a fortune, they are. Barry – Vicky's real boyfriend – was going to steal them. The idea was that if we got you guys to dress the same as him, then he would have an alibi if it all went wrong. He was just part of a sexy night of dressing up, and that would match with what you guys and us nurses would all say.'

'Wow! And did he get away with it?'

Chevvy dropped her head. 'Yeah. Trouble is, he's telling us he didn't. The candelabras have gone, but he's pretending he didn't take them.'

'Oh, that's ridiculous! Nobody else even knew they were there, did they?'

'That's right. He must have got the gear, but there's nothing we can do.'

I looked at her incredulously. She came and put her arms around me. 'I'm sorry about the deception, Windy. But I honestly really loved it when you wore those clothes, you know.'

I felt uneasy. How could this girl be trusted when she'd put me through all that? I decided to get away from her to think things through.

'Gracious, is that the time? Listen, Chevvy, I have work to do, and…'

'Is there any way I can make it up to you?' she pouted. She pushed me back into the chair then hitched up her mini skirt, straddled across my lap, grabbed a handful of my hair and kissed me full on the lips. Yes, I would definitely make an excuse and get out there on deck. Yes, right away.

Two hours later, with my doeskin uniform torn to shreds and with teeth-marks in my cap and skull, I was having a beer with NotNorman in a bar in Durban. We came to our conclusions.

'Well,' said the Normanly Denied, leaning back in his chair, 'there's nothing we can do now.'

'Don't you think we should talk to the police or something? They must be looking for information.'

He shook the bean sagely. 'Don't go near, matey. We leave town soon and that will be that.'

'I don't think that's right, Notters. We should do the right thing.' I couldn't tell him that my motivation was purely to keep in contact with Chevvy. I couldn't stand the thought of never seeing her again. She was really special, and my uniform probably had another two sessions in it before it would have to be binned. 'Can't you think of a way we can track Barry down?'

'Nope. And I'm Not Interested.' He put down his drink and moved on to another subject. 'I was thinking. I bet balaclavas are the only item on earth that never get stolen. If you steal one without wearing one, you're going to get caught. If you wear one to steal one, then you've already got one, so why would you take a risk like that when you are –'

He suddenly stopped talking. I looked at him, wondering why he had ceased to ruminate on crooked sartorial dilemmas. He was looking past me with his beer stopped halfway to his mouth. I turned to follow his gaze. There was nothing unusual in the scene, no sport on the TV, and no beautiful women arriving through the door.

'What? What is it?' I asked.

NotNorman ducked his head and tried to hide behind his beer. His head was too big, but it was a valiant effort.

'It's him! It's Barry! Don'tlookdon'tlookdon'tlook!' There was no point in looking. I'd never met Barry, unless of course we had shared a bath together. Even so, I wasn't sure I would recognise him again. 'Whaddawedo? Whaddawedo?'

I didn't know whaddawedo, so I ducked my head and hid next to NotNorman. Barry had to walk past us to get to the bar, but he didn't pass.

'NotNorman! How ya doing?' he sang. 'I thought I'd never see you again after that dog-and-pony show up the nurses' home!'

'Oh, er, hi, Baz. Yeah, I, em, I heard you got away with the stuff.'

Barry looked hurt. 'I didn't take anything! I'm tellin' you. Vicky won't see me any more, and I didn't steal anything!'

I pricked my ears up. 'Really? Who took it then? That stuff was worth a fortune, you know.'

He sighed as if he'd told his story enough times already. 'Look, I did take them, OK? It was me that took them in the first place, but this is the bit nobody believes: when the guards arrested me in the garden I thought I was bang to rights, but they opened the bag and sod me, the stuff wasn't in there! I'd only put it in two minutes before and it had gone!'

'Gone? How do you mean, gone?'

'Someone must have stolen the candelabras from me! The bag had nothing in it but a load of ropes and shackles! Thank God we'd set you guys up, 'cos it made my story about kinky sex hang together, so they let me go, but I have absolutely no idea how they got there! I put the candelabras into the bag personally not two minutes before and there they were, gone!'

I looked at NotNorman, mystified. This was obviously rubbish.

'Oh, come on now, Barry,' I said with the kind of withering delivery employed by top barristers. 'You don't seriously expect us to believe that, do you? Why on earth would you fill your bag with ropes and shackles? Only sailors would do that!'

NotNorman rolled his eyes. 'Windy, you are such a clod sometimes. Barry, you didn't by any chance, find yourself alone in a bathroom with Chevvy did you?'

Barry sniggered, 'Huh! Yeah! I did! Magic it was. She thought I was someone else and invited me to join her in the bath. I've always wanted to have a pop at her, so – hur, hur – I got stuck in! Then some dog turned up and I had to leg it.'

'Right, right,' said Notters. 'And was this dog carrying a bag like yours?'

Barry shrugged. 'Dunno. I just left 'em to it.'

'Ha! That's incredible!' I said. 'You'll never believe this, but I was in the bathroom with Chevvy too! And there was some dog in there before me as well! Ha! He put himself about, didn't he?'

'Right,' said NotNorman. 'And you did have a bag, right?'

'Yip! And you know what? Mine was full of ropes and shackles too! I mean, you gotta admit, as coincidences go, this is pretty amazing, eh?'

'What's amazing,' said Notters with a strange degree of venom, 'is how you get through the day without adult help. Did you say Chevvy was on the ship earlier today?'

I shrugged. 'Yeah, I left her asleep in my cabin. She'd love to hear this stuff.'

NotNorman nodded and stood up. 'I'll bet we're too late, but let's go check anyway.'

And he was off. I slugged down the last of my beer and headed off after him back towards the ship. He wouldn't tell me what was on his mind, but when we got there, NotNorman led us directly into my cabin.

'So,' said Notters. 'I'll bet you there's no Chevvy.'

Sure enough, my bunk was empty.

'She must have gone home,' I said. 'I'll call her if you like.'

'Where's your black bag then, oh master criminal?'

'My bag? Well, it's just… Oh! It was just here. Now isn't that the strangest thing? It was here just this morning. I saw it myself – Chevvy and I talked about it – and now it's gone.'

I began looking under the beds and in the cupboards.

'Let me make a bet with you,' said NotNorman, grinning a strange grin. 'I bet you a twenty that you won't ever find that bag. Make it a hundred. And I bet you another that you won't ever find Chevvy again. You want to bet?' He held out his hand to shake on the deal.

'What on earth are you talking about, man? She was here just now! I'm going to see her tomorrow. Besides, I want to ring her and tell her that Barry is innocent. A man shouldn't have to go through life with that kind of thing hanging over – Oh!' I gasped with realisation as I saw what NotNorman was getting at. 'Noooo! NotNorman! Are you trying to tell me that… that Barry took my bag by accident?'

'Well done, Bullet! I knew you had it in you!'

'NotNorman, what is the matter with you?' I rolled my eyes, shook my head at him and spoke slowly so he could get up to speed. 'They caught Barry *yesterday*! My bag was here today! Barry wasn't even on the ship today – he was in the pub with us! Duuur! You really do get in a muddle with this kind of thing, don't you? Ha, ha, ha! Poor, silly old Notters!'

I clapped him paternally on the shoulder as he left my cabin. He had his head in his hands and I think he was even crying a bit. Poor lad must have been embarrassed. He just never quite managed to keep up with the programme like the rest of us. He was lucky to have me around to look after him.

But I'll tell you what's strange: he was right about the other stuff. I never did find that bag. And Chevvy had already left the nurses' dormitory and cleared out her room when I rang to talk to her. How weird is that? Oh well, I guess we'll never know what really happened. Life's like that sometimes.

Chapter 5

Rock and Roll

The ups and downs of high southerly latitudes. Giewy gets wired.

As you approach latitudes around 40-degrees south, you are exposed to some of the biggest seas on earth. The southern oceans have almost the entire circumference of the world to puff their chests up and feel good about themselves, so the waves build and build until they become moving mountains. For the average teenage sailor, the experience is unique, breathtaking… and scary as hell.

As we bumped our way south-west around the Cape of Good Hope, we were heading diagonally across the teeth of the prevailing sea and storms, and the ship was pitching and rolling in a highly-uncomfortable corkscrew motion. I clung to my bed and tried to ignore it. I determined that I would be a good, solid sailor and absorb it all manfully as part of the life I had chosen. What I hadn't realised was that we hadn't even started yet.

As the night wore on, the pitch and roll got worse and worse to the point where I was expending energy continuously just to stay on the bed. The idea of actually getting any sleep was farcical. But it didn't stop there. It continued to get worse. And when it got to the point beyond which any reasonable man would have given the ship the green light to simply sink and have done with all this trying-to-stay-upright nonsense, it still got worse.

Life was like this: for ten seconds in every thirty, the ship was tipped up on its end; my face was squeezed into the corner where the bed met the bulkhead, my body was concertinaed up onto my face and my feet kicked around in the sky above my bed as if I'd been thrown into the corner by a Ffugg Honeymooner. Things juddered angrily for a while, then the bed jumped up, swung over my head and back round the other way. I spent the next ten seconds clinging to the corners of my bunk with my fingers and toes as my body was pulled towards the deck head, until I found myself looking down between my own legs at the cupboards and bookshelves, apparently now relocated to the floor far beneath me. It was as much as I could do to avoid leaving the bed altogether and disappearing into the wardrobe on the other side of the cabin.

Throughout the night, it continued to get worse – and worse and worse – until I could bear it no more. As dawn broke, I gave up ever getting to sleep, got up and struggled up onto the bridge, bouncing heavily from bulkhead to bulkhead all the way up. I wanted to avoid being trapped in the accommodation when the ship went down. The bridge was closer to the open air and I would be ready to abandon ship just as soon as the shout went up for us to man the lifeboats.

Up until this day, I had always found a bit of pitch and roll to be something of a laugh. It made unusual things happen. I loved to watch the captain's steward trying to carry a tray of tea to the old man's cabin. He would track sideways like a drunk as he tried to walk towards the companionway and keep his precious cargo level, then he would pick up lots and lots of unwanted speed in the wrong direction and find himself with his hair blown back, running flat out down a dangerously steep hill towards a bulkhead at the far end of a corridor he never intended entering in the first place. Before he knew it, he would just as quickly find himself desperately clawing his way up a sheer incline. All this back and forth just to make it to the bottom of the stairs, which seemed to endlessly slew sideways, leaving him high and dry and off to one side again. When he eventually got a fingernail into the banister, it was always touch and go whether he would cling on through the latest roll. I once saw the brave man turn a complete back-somersault, returning to square one from this position, and still keep the tray level. That one elicited huge applause from all of us in the gallery.

And similar wars were being waged all over the ship. Every roll of the ship was accompanied by a distant sound of crockery crashing to the floor somewhere, or the beers in the fridge crowding gleefully out onto the deck like happy children piling out through the school gates for the holidays. I assumed that the ship would be geared up for such weather, but it was only truly prepared for modest movement compared to this. There is, for example, a ridge all the way around every table, supposedly to keep cups and plates on the top when the sea starts pushing them around. But when your lunch picks up enough speed, this ridge simply serves to trip it up, and ensure that the contents of the plate are thrown all down someone's shirt, instead of simply falling to the floor.

What I also found fun was the way people went about their normal day without necessarily remembering that gravity is not the only force in play. I was struggling along in the accommodation once when the mate appeared at the other end of the corridor. He pointed at me and opened his mouth, about to give me a job to do. However, the ship playfully tipped him up so that he wasn't able to make the turn, and he continued shoulder first into the toilets to his left. Still pointing at me and with his mouth open, he disappeared from sight. For a moment or two, I could see his fingers clinging on to the door frame, and I could hear his grunts as he did battle with the angles. Indeed, he might have kept a presence in the corridor if he wasn't being followed by the second mate and the chief engineer who, against all the efforts of their arms and legs, piled across my line of vision from left to right at chaotic and unwanted speed and joined the mate in the toilet. The mate's fingers disappeared and there were some shouts and a flushing sound (which I hoped involved the mate's head). I didn't get to see the resultant pile-up of senior officers because that same roll of the ship sent me clattering into MegaWatt's cabin. So when the mate, chief and second mate eventually clambered back up, I was unavailable for one of the mates 'nice little jobs to do'. Mind you, whatever the job was, it might have been more pleasant than trying to explain to an indignant MegaWatt why I had joined him in his bed.

So the laughs are there for a few hours, but as the ship continues to roll, the novelty wanes. After a while it becomes wearisome, and after days and days, it becomes a Chinese torture.

When I got to the bridge, a part of me regretted coming because I experienced for myself, and with all my senses, the full extent of the lethal forces at work on the ship and wished I had stayed hidden under my pillow. We were struggling along due west now, so were battling head-on into the prevailing seas. A force-nine gale was buffeting the ship. Dark, turgid clouds loomed close over our heads and, coming towards us, darkly menacing in the early morning half-light, were a series of angry, grey hills. These were waves born out of a 40-foot swell, with deep, deep valleys between them; valleys big enough for the entire ship to disappear into. As a new wave came barrelling towards us, the bows and fo'c'sle – still picking up speed from our journey down the back of the previous wave – disappeared with a rivet-shattering thud into its front face. The ship seemed unable to respond to the need for a sudden change in vertical direction, and she shuddered violently as if she was as scared as we were. The wave kept coming, absorbing the ship, eating up the foredeck, until only the tops of the forward mast houses could be seen. The wave loomed over us – even at our elevated position on the bridge – threatening to engulf us forever. I held my breath and prayed for the prows to lift, but it seemed to take an age for all that weight and momentum to pull itself up and for the response to kick in. Gradually, the poor old girl lifted and rose up, and the stress amidships as she did so announced itself in loud groans and creaks from the plates, rivets and transverse bulkheads. It was awful. The stern was now deep in the valley, and the prows were rising fast. The ship reached an impossible angle as the fo'c'sle shot up from the belly of the wave. Tons and tons of water cascaded down the foredeck and she began to battle her way directly uphill towards the crest looming above us. There was more juddering as the propeller tried forlornly to push the ship upwards and the wave began to move us backwards. As the wave passed underneath amidships, the ship flattened out on the crest of the wave. For a few elevated seconds, we saw the terrifying line of hills coming towards us behind this one, and then the wave lifted the aft end. The prows began to fall, and we headed off down the steep back side of the wave and into the valley below. We were arrowing downwards, picking up an awful amount of speed, and we were back round to the worst bit again. As the next wave arrived, we were pointing downwards, and the front half of the ship went crashing into its rising bulk once more. I couldn't bear it. I found myself holding my breath every time. As the wave advanced along the foredeck, the ship seemed to remain pointing towards the sea bed for far, far too long. Just when it seemed impossible to escape, the ship would slowly – ever so painfully slowly – begin to rise, and the whole ghastly process would begin again.

Into these impossible conditions, the mate turned us out at 7.30 a.m. for an important job. We were to go and secure a container that was moving about on the foredeck. It was only moving a few inches with each pitch of the ship, but it had to be secured. We were going to have to go… Out There.

Giewy, NotNorman and I pulled on our wet-weather gear and gathered unhappily by the huge metal doors to the outside world. We were armed with the marlin spikes we needed to tighten the bottle screws. This would be a two-minute job in normal conditions, but today it was hard work just to stand still, even inside the accommodation. It was just about impossible to stand still on the foredeck, let alone undertake physical work out there. My brain told me that this was the time to admit to being the Big Chicken and ask if we could stop now and go home to mummy. But there was no way out of this one.

'Keep hold at all times!' shouted the mate in preparation for our task. 'One hand for yourself, and one for the ship. Clear?' He unsealed the door, looked out into the storm, and it did me no good at all to see the trepidation on his face. I saw him blinking rapidly, as if trying to find better options. In the end, he steeled himself, took a deep breath and then, timing his move to the pitching of the ship, he shouted: 'Go, go, go!'

We bent double against the weather and struggled out, turning inboard as soon as we got onto the foredeck. The first thing to hit us was the wind, making me gasp as it pinned us back against the main accommodation bulkhead; second was the rain and spray, which whipped our faces angrily from every direction;

third was the biting cold. Winter in the South Atlantic is simply intolerable. The fourth thing to hit us was the water on deck. With each wave came a torrent rushing along the foredeck which, if we did not keep clear of it, would sweep us to certain injury and possibly out to sea, never to be seen again. Death under these conditions was a regular occurrence amongst sailors on the old barques, where they had to work the sails the whole time the ship was facing big seas and high winds. We timed our run to get up past hatch three in between the waves. The water still rushing off the deck from the previous wave was up to our knees, pulling at our lower legs as we tried to walk against it. It would not have been possible to even visit hatch one. At least the container we were trying to reach was just next to the mast house at the far corner of hatch three, the nearest hatch to the accommodation. We clung on to the coaming of hatch three and worked our way like a string of mountaineers up to the midships mast house between hatch three and hatch two. As the ship rolled, I knew without any doubt whatsoever that, had I not been holding on with both hands, I would have been unable to keep my footing. I would fall to port, down to the bulwarks, and the passing wave would carry me out to sea. No doubt about it. It was terrifying. I pulled my way up, trying to see through the rain beating into my eyes. We got to the mast house in time to hide in its lee, pressing ourselves against the back of it like soldiers avoiding gunfire, as the next wave piled along the foredeck. The mate opened the mast house and we crowded inside and caught our breath in the relative sanctuary. Another torrent of water piled down the foredeck either side of us, and the wind and rain whipped around the mast house trying to find us out.

'OK. We go in two groups,' said the mate, wiping the water from his face. We were all soaked through and shivering from the cold of a mere 20-second exposure. The mate was shouting to get himself heard over the noise of the rushing water, the wind howling through the rigging and the groans of the ship structure as she hogged and sagged through the storm. 'You and me, Baboulene, in one team, and you two in the other. Never forget: one hand for yourself, one for the ship. Work with one hand only. With the other one, grab the chain of the bottlescrew and hang on. That hand will keep you alive, OK? With each of your free hands, work together. Use one hand to tighten up the screw, the other to resist the whole thing turning. On my shout, come back here to let the next wave go by. Then we'll go back and do the other two. OK?'

We nodded unhappily. He looked out into the pulsating storm. I saw him breathing deeply as he let another wave go crashing by. Then another. I was expecting him to give the word to go, but he waited again, as if plagued by doubt. The next one came by and I saw him take a deep breath. This was it. He waited his moment, took one last look at us all, then shouted: 'OK. GO!'

We crouched and ran along to the port side of the mast house. The container was right in front of us, but I was shocked to find myself doing about 30 mph when we arrived at it. I caught hold of the first chain and clung on for dear life as the weather beat on me like some punishment from Hell. I knelt down and held on to the chain and the lower half of the bottle screw as the mate set about tightening it with a marlin spike with such urgent effort that he grunted and groaned as loudly as the ship structure. I strained myself as well to prevent the bottle screw from turning, but I couldn't hold it. With only one hand and with the bottle screw being wet, and with the unbalancing effect of the…

'Hold it tighter!' screamed the mate, the spit from his mouth at least doubling the effects of the rain in my face.

Despite his threat and my best efforts to keep it still, the whole screw and chain turned with the spike. I wasn't strong enough to stop it from turning. I thought the mate was going to hit me with the spike if I didn't stop it from turning. There was a now-familiar thud as the prows pounded into the next wave, and I knew the next torrent would be along any second. It was time for us to run, or we would be washed away. The ship heaved and groaned, and began to heel back up. I was desperate to run for it, but the mate seemed to have forgotten. He leaned on his lever, and I used all my body weight to prevent him from simply turning the bottom half with it, but it was hopeless. I just wasn't strong enough.

'Out!' shouted the mate. 'Out, out, out!' and the four of us worked our way back to the mast house, where we stood, drenched and breathing heavily from the exertion, as the next flood piled by on all sides. My heart was pounding.

'OK, ours was tight,' said the mate. I was relieved to realise that I hadn't failed. It was simply already done up as tight as it could go. 'But there's a wire gone from the lower-fixing point.'

'Ours was loose,' said Giewy. Even he had lost his idiot grin. We'd finally found some circumstances which wiped the smile off his face. 'We gave it half a dozen turns.'

'Good,' said the mate. 'That should do it. Let's take a look.'

The container had been moving an inch or two with each cycle of pitching of the ship. We stood peering gingerly out of the mast house, and soon it became apparent that the movement had stopped. Giewy's bottle screw had been the problem and they had fixed it. However, the wire to which the mate referred was whipping loosely on the deck.

'OK. Giew. That wire has a clamp on the end. You and NotNorman go make it fast to the lower corner of the container. Don't go mad. Just loosely will do. Just to stop it from slashing around.'

Giewy was the senior apprentice, so he got the job. I was well pleased. And NotNorman had been his partner in the previous mission, so he had to go with him. I felt for Notters – it seemed logical to me that the mate should go out there with Giewy, but either way, I could hardly hide my relief that I got to stay in the safety of the mast house.

Giewy and NotNorman waited for the mate's signal, then ran back out into the storm. Their timing was fine in terms of the roll of the ship, but not in terms of the wire. As they arrived, out of nowhere it seemed to strike like an angry snake. It whipped around and slashed Giewy viciously across his face. He was lifted clear off his feet and fell backwards, losing his grip on the safe hand hold. He fell onto the deck and was now freely exposed to the elements. I heard NotNorman shout for help. The mate and I ran out. As we got closer we could see that Giewy wasn't getting up. He was moving, but he wasn't holding on. I saw NotNorman wrap his legs around the chain that secured the container and grab Giewy's legs, hugging him to his chest and shouting for help the whole time. The mate and I rushed out, but we didn't have a plan and the next wave was coming. I couldn't see Giewy's eyes, but there was blood on the deck. Lots of it. We didn't have time to carry Giewy back. The water was on its way.

'Brace yourselves! NOW!' yelled the mate. He wrapped himself around NotNorman, and lay across Giewy's legs, hooking his own leg around the chain we had been tightening. I had no better ideas, so I did the same, leaping on top of both the mate – gripping him with my legs – and lying across Giewy as he lay on the deck. I hooked my elbow round the chain and grabbed Giewy's coat with my hand. Then the water hit. I buried my head into Giewy's stomach and shut my eyes as a wall of water, carrying massive power, whacked the breath out of me. Something gave way and the four of us turned through 90 degrees. Somehow we were still holding on. But we couldn't hang on for long. The torrent was tearing at me to take me away forever. My elbow was going to come out of its joint and give way, but I grabbed the chain with my right hand

and clung on for dear life. With my left arm around Giewy, I tried to flatten myself against his and the mate's bodies. The rush continued – I didn't think it would ever end – and I could feel my strength leaving me quicker than I could ever have imagined. On and on went the siege, leaving me no quarter to breathe. I felt another jolt as someone's grip was lost. It was too much for me now, and I let go of the chain. The four of us began to move and turn. The water was getting in between our bodies and separating us. The mate seemed to pull me away from Giewy, and the stresses were too much. Suddenly, I found myself flung backwards and rolling down the deck. I felt a whack in my midriff and was pinned against something solid as the wave passed over. Fortunately, we were only exposed to this extent to the tail end of the torrent. The others had let go too, and we floundered around like fish in the shallows as we tried to find our feet and run for safety. I had been stopped from being washed away by the corner of hatch three, and although I was winded and disorientated, I was able to crawl back up to the safety of the lee of the mast house. People were shouting – not just Giewy, NotNorman and the mate, but people on the bridge wing.

Back in the mast house Giewy clutched his face. The wire had cut him badly, across one cheek and up across his ear. Streams of blood ran down his face, and he was disorientated. I stood in the doorway watching the waves and lethal chaos outside. What I couldn't believe was that my predecessors on the old sailing ships used to work out here in these conditions as a matter of routine necessity. The ships were smaller and less stable so the sails needed trimming to maintain control, and to ensure there were still some sails left for the rest of the passage. The crew had to work out here the whole time. They had 'jump lines' above their heads, and when the seas came piling down the deck, they would grab the lines and lift themselves up until the flood had passed under their feet. It goes without saying that many men were lost to the seas on those passages. It really wasn't that long ago.

Soon Giewy had composed himself, and we prepared ourselves for the journey to get him back into the accommodation. We picked our moment and went for it. I looked across as we worked our way back along the side of hatch three. The wire continued to flail. We headed anxiously back to the accommodation.

I got cleaned up and went around to the ship's hospital where the second mate was tending to Giewy's wounds. Mercifully, because the blood had been diluted by the water, it had looked much worse than it turned out to be, but it was still a nasty scare.

The waves and wind kept buffeting us for two whole days, in which we made slow, slow progress. I understood nature's enormous powers and I felt irrelevant and humble. Giewy's journey was even more humbling. He had to go beyond what even nature could throw at him and endure a tetanus injection in his backside administered by the second mate who had never done it before. Now that must have been the stuff of nightmares for both of them.

Chapter 6

The Pirates
of Zen Pants

Windy goes a-pirating. Rocky relationships with cement. The cockney language barrier. Caught by the Kojaks and a Queen tribute band. Franglais in a Douala jail. A dog falls in love. All bets are off… and on… and off… and on…

We arrived in Douala, the main port of Cameroon in French West Africa, where nobody was expecting us, nobody knew anything about us and nobody seemed particularly interested in finding out. We were left at anchor for several days, waiting to get alongside and load cement for Europe. To make up for our apparent lack of appeal, the captain shouted into a radio telephone and banged the handset on the desk until the agent finally left his drugs den and brought us our mail. In amongst the good stuff from family and friends, we each received a letter from head office containing stern warnings about the ports we were visiting next. The letter told us in darkly portentous terms that in West Africa we were likely to come under attack from desperados trying to get control of the ship. In a word: pirates! However, these were not the romantic, fashionable swashbucklers you see at the Odeon. The paperwork left us in no doubt that these pirates were ruthless and fearsome, with speedboats and AK47 assault rifles. They would not hesitate to kill, and we were to defend ourselves with whatever force was necessary. In addition, the company had arranged for local security firms to place soldiers and machine-gun nests on the bridge wings to ensure our safety at some of the ports.

For the next day or two, the talk in the bar rarely budged from the subject of pirates. It was exciting and dangerous, and somewhat all-consuming. After a while, it seemed to get on Jinx's nerves.

'Look here, they aren't so great, these pirates. I bet you – any of you – that Windy and I can steal a whole ship out of this very anchorage. It's no big deal.'

There was a stunned silence as the lads absorbed what he had said, but Jinx was not one for sitting about being stunned and silent. 'Come along then, let's see your money! We'll steal a ship – me and Windy.'

Everyone looked at me. 'Yeah. No probs.' I tried to stifle a yawn. 'Which one do you want?'

There was more stun and more silence as their eyes widened and their heads reeled.

'Pick one, then,' said Jinx to our loser friends. 'Go on. You choose one, we'll steal it.' He moved across to the porthole and surveyed the ships across the anchorage. 'I'll tell you what. See those two bulkies out there? The two from the same company? Our bet is that we can take control of the one at the front and move it so it is behind the other one before this time tomorrow. That's the bet. No silly tricks about swinging at anchor – we'll take control, fire up the engines and move it across the anchorage by tomorrow afternoon. Pirates! Pah!'

'Pah!' I agreed. 'Pirates, schmirates, that's what I say!'

The lads all stared across the bay at the two huge, modern bulk carriers. Sparky, seeing opportunities of his own, opened a betting shop, and one by one, the lads were tempted into an investment. Even though we weren't expecting any piracy in Douala (it was Nigeria, we were assured, that was Blackbeard Central), the shipping fraternity was on alert and stealing a ship was just about impossible, even for sharp operators like Jinx and me. It simply wasn't credible that we could pull it off. After a while, just about everyone had placed a bet. Only two young gentlemen smelt a rat and bet on our success, so we instantly recruited them. That placed Giewy and Payphone on the roll call alongside Jinx and me as the pirate gang, and left everyone else wondering what the trick was going to be. Well, there was no trick. It was going to be easy. Let me explain my confidence.

I had been on anchor watch for the last two days in Douala. The anchorage was off Pelican Point, and there must have been twenty other ships out there. A twenty-four-hour watch is kept when the ship is at anchor to ensure that she doesn't drag. As the ship isn't moving, this is a boring role, often farmed out to apprentices, who can at least be trusted to call an officer if anything at all ever happens – which it doesn't.

Whilst on watch, I had noticed that the two bulk carriers across the anchorage from us were not following correct maritime etiquette. It is required, when at anchor, for a ship to show one large black ball during the day, and two white lights – one forward and one aft – during the hours of darkness.

These ships were both doing both at all times. Jinx had come up from the engine room for a break, and I told him of my findings.

'You mean, they leave the ball up all night, and the lights on all day?' he said, his curiosity aroused. 'Do you see any accommodation or working lights at night?'

'No,' I confirmed. 'But what is on, they leave on all day! They can't be arsed to flick a switch! I mean, it's ridiculous when your professional standards drop to a point of such idleness that...'

'Have you signalled them?'

'Eh?'

'Signal them. Go on.'

'Who, me?'

'Yes, you.'

'What, now?'

'Yes, now!' Jinx picked up the Aldis lamp and placed it in my hands, before shoving me out onto the bridge wing.

'Ah, right, well. You see, we had a brief course on Morse code during the induction, but I can't say I found it very easy to keep up. It was awfully dull, you see, and I was sort of distracted by this girl in the window of the secretarial college opposite, you see, because she used to wave at –'

'Just do it, Windy, and stop whining. Go on!'

I stood hopelessly on the bridge wing. The Aldis lamp gave a powerful beam with a 'trigger' which allowed it to flash and thus send Morse code. I didn't know what to do, but I lifted it up, pointed it like a ray gun at the first of the two ships and began flashing away furiously. Had there been anyone watching from the bulk carriers, I might well have been insulting them, or declaring war or proposing marriage – I had no idea. Fortunately, neither did they, because it became evident over the next day or so that there was nobody on board. There was never anybody on the bridge and there was never anybody on deck. Ships are never left unmanned. Ever. And yet these were unmanned. Ghost ships.

'OK,' said Jinx, twirling his moustache. 'Keep this under your hat, Windy. We're going to make some money out of this…'

And so it was that the bet was made. We stood to make a tidy sum, as did the other two who bet on us winning: Payphone who, by his own admittance – if his impenetrable cockney verbiage could count as admittance – was 'partial to a Glen Campbell[2] now and then'; and Giewy, who said he had forgotten what 'on' and 'against' meant and was mightily peeved that Sparky wouldn't let him swap to the other team once he'd realised what he'd done.

That afternoon, we met on the boat deck, unshipped a lifeboat and began to lower it down to the water. To some extent, we were dressed for the occasion – big boots, headbands, knives – so although we didn't quite look like Calico Jack and his buccaneers, we did do lots of 'Arrrr, ha-harrr-harr-harr'ing. I'm proud to say that my nickname changed to 'Cut-throat Dave' for a while. I rather liked that – shame it didn't stick. A crowd of onlookers, tense with investment, watched us with suspicion. I had already heard a rumour claiming that we had armed ourselves with pots of black paint in order to sneak over and switch the names and leave the ships where they were. I'd heard another rumour that claimed we knew about planned movements of the ships that were going to happen anyway and we were going to claim the credit for an existing process. The last rumour involved Jinx and me making the ships disappear and reappear using giant mirrors. Nobody had worked out the truth, so a crowd of money-haemorrhaging souls looked sadly at us as we made our descent in the lifeboat. The tiniest hint of a scam and they would be on us like a flash, but we weren't concerned. The 'trick' was much simpler than

2   Glen Campbell = Gamble

they could imagine. Jinx and his hearties were going to climb on board, walk onto the bridge and drive the thing. Ships don't have keys like a car does. Security is based on the fact that continuous watches are kept from the moment a ship is launched to the moment it sinks. A ship does require expertise to make it move, in the form of navigators and engineers, but otherwise, it's a doddle to trot off with one. We were baffled as to why these ships were not manned, but were not really interested in the whys and why nots. There was money to be made, so we adjusted our headbands, gripped our knives, adopted menacing expressions and dropped slowly down the side of the *Global Princess*.

The lifeboat hit the clear blue waters of the Bight of Biafra. I felt that sense of vulnerability I experienced every time I found myself adrift atop a huge depth of water. Jinx fired up the engine and we headed off towards our quarry. The crew of the *Global Princess* moved around the rail as they trained their binoculars on to us.

The bulkie we were targeting looked very close, but – as I knew from the radar – it was a good 2 miles away. Indeed, this is very close in shipping terms, but it took us the best part of an hour to get all the way across and make a circumnavigation of the whole vessel, calling up and trying to attract attention. The ship was huge and we were dwarfed under her impressive flanks. We were very cautious – and yes, a bit scared – but it was clear that there was nobody on board.

On the far side of the ship we found a conveniently located ratline attached to a pulley, and when we released it, the gangway began to lower towards us. This was ridiculously easy. It was also confirmation that there was no one on board. They had left the gangway in this way, presumably, to facilitate their own access when it was next required. But what was going on? I looked around for fear of being watched, but there was nothing for miles, except for other ships, whose personnel had no reason to suspect we were up to anything.

We tied the lifeboat at the bottom and mounted the unsteady gangway. It rose steeply up the sheer, cliff-like side of this colossal vessel. A silence descended upon us. The enormity of what we were attempting suddenly hit home quite hard. This was illegal. Highly illegal. It had seemed like a bit of a lark from back on our ship, but now that it was real, it seemed like a swift route to prison. The feeling of nervousness was exacerbated by the sheer size of the ship. She must have been three times larger than the *Global Princess*. The effect was overpowering.

At the top of the gangway, we scampered aft towards the main accommodation block. The huge weather doors were locked from the inside. We carried on around the back of the accommodation and began to work our way up from one deck to the next – up and up and up – but everything was battened down. That was, until we got onto the bridge wing. The door into the bridge was not just unlocked – it was wide open. At first it seemed there must be someone there, but it was evident from the splintered wood that someone had forced the door. We walked onto the bridge with a certain degree of awe. This was the nerve centre. Mission control. This must be what it felt like for a conquering leader to walk into his vanquished enemy's headquarters. Had Adolf Hitler ever crossed Westminster Bridge and walked into the House of Lords, he would have felt exactly as I did right then: really, really naughty.

Inside the bridge all the navigation equipment and controls were covered in polythene sheets. The ship was very new. Everything was shiny and technological and it all looked fantastic. The bridge was an enormous open space – more like a New York penthouse. It was a world away from the bridge of the *Global Princess* – half the technology on this beastie wasn't even invented when our old girl first put to sea.

'There's a generator running,' said Jinx, looking at some dials. 'That means either someone is down there, or else they must be visiting at least once a day. We need to crack on. Come on.'

We followed him down through the accommodation. Now this was really naughty. Every internal door and room was wide open; the captain's quarters, the officers' cabins, the mess, galley and bar. Everything was clean, and efforts made towards preservation and safe storage. All of the valuables had been removed, and although there were some signs of looting and pilfering, the whole ship was completely accessible. It seemed to have been deliberately left this way, presumably so any inevitable crooked activity didn't cause further damage to the ship. Down we went into the engine room, then down and down, all the way to the bottom plates.

Jinx was a senior engineer. He knew what he was doing and seemed very much at home in this environment. The engine room control centre was inside an air-conditioned and sound-proofed room – again, a far cry from the conditions on the *Global Princess*. Jinx twiddled this, and primed that, and adjusted the other, and the main engine hissed and wooshed obediently. It was all very impressive.

'Right. I'll need some time to warm her through, then we're ready to go.' Jinx was sweating despite the coolness of the room. 'Go do your thing, guys.'

'Geddin!' said Payphone, his cockney knees and elbows flexing in and out as if they were connected to his vocal cords. I'd never seen him so excited. He'd be getting the spoons out again in a minute. 'I'll need a bit of lager 'n lime to give Windy the leaflet up on the bonnet. Then I'll give you a tinkle on the dog from the roof garden soon as we're jiggly.'[3]

We weren't sure what he had said, but we got the message that he was in agreement, so Payphone, Giewy and I worked

---

3   'I shall require a period of time to get Windy organised on the forecastle head. I will subsequently contact you via the telephone from the bridge when our preparations are complete.'

our way back out and along the miles to the fo'c'sle head. This ship dwarfed the *Global Princess*. It was enormous. As we arrived on the fo'c'sle, Payphone seemed pleased.

'Sweet a-a-aaaas! Al Capone!'[4] Payphone indicated a small panel with a speaker. 'Ere, Windows. Noodle on the knobbit to give it some rabbit, and I can give it some of tha-aa-aat back when I'm up the city centre, aw-wight, mate? When I say Naaarrr!, you lift the jimmy spanker 'til we nick the legs – two shackles up, yeah? I'll give it proper welly 'til we done matey over there, then you drop the jimmy back to four shackles and Robert's yer muvver's bruvver. Gottit?'[5]

I looked at Payphone. 'Who, me?' I said, mystified. I hadn't understood the specific words, but I got the distinct impression that he was trying to show me how to do something. Then I realised that Giewy was heading off towards the bridge with Payphone He was leaving me in charge. I was the junior here. Giewy should be doing the responsible stuff. In fact, I'd never been given any responsibility since I nearly sunk the *Global Wanderer* a few months previously, and I didn't want any now.

'Payphone, I really don't think it would be wise to leave me alone up here with…'

'Lissen, mush. I need a fridge freezer wiv me on the roof, so Giewy's me oppo. Cor blimey, it's a doddle up ere, even on yer Jack Jones!'[6]

I stared back at him, partly dumbstruck by the responsibility, and partly amazed that Payphone could count his language as English. He looked at me. He was becoming concerned that I might be jeopardising the project.

---

4   'Oh, Jolly good! There is a communications system.'

5   Erm... didn't get a word of that...

6   'I need an assistant with good understanding of bridge protocol with me during manoeuvres, so that will be Master Giew. Heavens above, you should be able to handle matters on the fo'c'sle by yourself by now.'

'Lissen, mushtie. We're tryin' to arf-inch a nanny goat ere. You can't go up the pictures on me narr. Geddit?'[7]

Well, that was hard to argue against for many reasons. I shrugged and took the job. I understood enough about the fo'c'sle standby to know that a shackle was 15 fathoms – about 90 feet. There was nearly 400 feet of cable out there. If I'd understood him right, I was to pull up half of it, the ship would move, then I'd drop it back down again. He was all eyebrows and whistles as he ran through how to work the windlass and the brake again, then he and Giewy left. I was on my own – a complete fo'c'sle standby. I was in charge of the front half-mile of a strange vessel the size of the Starship Enterprise. This would normally be the first mate's role, carried out with an assistant or two, several crew and about ten years of experience.

So very, very naughty.

Soon enough, I saw a huge puff of dark smoke billow out of the funnel. The engines were running. The speaker on the dog 'n' bone – I mean, phone – crackled into life and Payphone's voice filled the air.

'Oi, oi, Windows. Give it big licks!'[8]

I released the brake, turned the lever to set the windlass pulling and the anchor began its journey towards me from the depths. The cable clunked slowly over the gypsy and coiled itself down into the anchor locker below. It was all going very smoothly, but it was loud! The smoke, the windlass, the anchor – everything was so big and industrial and noisy. We needed to do this secretively if we weren't going to attract attention. So far it was about as secret as a cheap wig. Others were sure to notice the movement; we could only hope they would see nothing suspicious in that.

---

7   'Please pay attention. We are attempting to steal a ship. We cannot afford for your concentration to wonder at this important juncture. Do you understand my contention?'

8   'The hour cometh! Weight the anchor!'

The ship began to vibrate and come slowly astern. The anchor cable was coming up nicely, but the angle of it as it left the ship showed that the anchor was still on the sea bed. Each shackle of measurement was marked in paint on the anchor cable. As I watched the two-shackle marker come over the gypsy, the cable straightened and I knew the anchor was off the sea bed. I let a little more come up, then put the brake on and stopped the windlass.

I pressed the button and reported in. 'Anchor up, Payphone! She's clear!'

He said something about rabbits and cushty mushties, and I got the impression that things were going well. The ship began to progress astern, and a few minutes later we were in position a safe distance behind the sister ship. This was amazing. We were actually going to do it. The speaker crackled loudly into life again, and Payphone said something indecipherable. I spun the huge brake off, and the anchor dropped quickly and loudly back into the water. I watched the shackle markers go, and applied the brake as soon as the fourth shackle was out there.

Before the ship had come back up on the anchor, Payphone and Giewy had joined me. Payphone looked around at the result of our work.

'Cock on!' he said for some reason, but I didn't let it upset me.

When Jinx arrived – along with his big, money-winner's grin – he actually shook our hands. He probably felt as I did, that this was a much bigger deal than we'd realised from the safety of the *Global Princess*. We felt elated. The job was done and we could relax.

'So why is this ship abandoned?' I asked. 'Couldn't we salvage it for money? Isn't there like a finders-keepers rule regarding this sort of thing?'

'Must be some bugs bunny in it,' Payphone nodded. 'Let's have a butcher's 'ook.'[9]

We found the problem when we got inside the holds. It was incredible. Inside every hold there was cement. West Africa trades a good deal of cement, but for some unknown reason, the cement on board this ship had gone hard. It was rock, not cement. Tens of thousands of tons of rock-solid cement occupied all the holds. We could only speculate on how it had solidified, but there it was. We puzzled this over for a while, wondering what the shipping line would do to fix things, but we couldn't think of an answer. What would you do? What could you do? You can't move it. You can't unload it. You can't dump it. You can't change its constitution. It's effectively become a part of the ship. You can't do anything! We assumed there were discussions going on in shipping offices somewhere in the world, and that the ships had been put on ice until a solution presented itself. It appeared that these two huge, modern, expensive ships might be write-offs, dumped in Douala. We tried to think of a strategy the owners might employ to get something out of this situation, but there was nothing obvious that could be done. Perhaps they had left the ships unmanned in the hope that pirates might do enough damage to allow an insurance write-off, but they would have quite a job to hide all the concrete from the loss adjusters. There was evidence that insurgents had been on board, but what could they do? The pirates wanted money and the personal effects from the officers and crew. They wanted tools and instruments, along with the brass and other mildly valuable items. They wanted cargo only if it was nickable and valuable, and they wanted the entire ship only if it could be used to hold the shipping line to ransom. None of these things were available to the looters. Our contemplations were cut short by Payphone.

---

9   'This vessel could be at the root of a financial opportunity. Let's make a
careful appraisal of the situation.'

'Oi, oi, lads! Company! 'Ave it on yer dancers!'[10]

A prickly sweat rolled over me as I looked over the side. A speedboat was cutting a fast line towards us from the mainland. We ran along the foredeck, fell down the gangway and leaped into our lifeboat. But the speedboat was upon us. We had barely got on board before it snaked up, cut its engines and landed softly in the water beside us. Two black guys with shaved heads, dark shades and Nazi uniforms stood up at the back of the speedboat and pointed guns at us. Another large black man with a skinhead haircut and sunglasses was standing commandingly at the wheel. He looked like a black Kojak. He shouted at us in deep, aggressive, French tones.

'Sterp! On jeans off! Sterp!'

I was unbuttoning my trousers as quickly as I could when Jinx obeyed Kojak's instruction and turned the engine off. He held his hands out to the sides to show he wasn't up to any tricks. I looked at the automatic weapons trained on me from the back of the boat and felt my breathing stutter. This was not good. The speedboat pulled up beside us and Black Kojak grabbed the side of our boat.

'Inzebert!' he barked. 'Get inzebert!'

There was no point in arguing. The guards kept their guns trained on us as we climbed into ze bert.

'Look, there seems to be some mistake. We were just coming over to… '

'Shudderp!' roared Kojak, waggling his tonsils at us. He pushed Jinx roughly into a seat.

The guards kept their guns pointed unnervingly at our heads as the speedboat's on-jeans roared and she wheeled away for the mainland, towing our lifeboat behind it. Now we were in real trouble. I did notice one thing, though, as we were driven towards our fate. The starboard lifeboat on board *Global Princess* had been dropped into the sea. I was pleased to see that, despite

---

10   'Someone's coming! Best we make off!'

our winning the bet, a rough-looking payload of my colleagues was coming to help us.

'It's no use,' said Giewy. 'They'll never catch up with this thing!'

'I think I know what they are planning,' said Jinx, and although he didn't reveal the nature of his conjecture, it was clear that it didn't give him encouragement. I was beginning to think this was yet another day when I should have just stayed in bed.

The speedboat came alongside a deserted, industrial wharf. We were marched up onto a hot concrete dock with our hands behind our heads like prisoners in a movie, and herded on to a rusty, green bus with no windows. The guards and Kojak climbed on behind us and the bus pulled away to take us off into the depths of West Africa. I looked back longingly for one last time at the *Global Princess* far out in the anchorage. I had a horrible premonition that I may never see her again.

At the end of the dock, there was a gate in a fence. A guard got out, took off a large padlock and chain and opened the gate. The instant we left, we seemed to be immersed in a crowded, bustling market place. But it wasn't a market place, it was the city. Douala was like this everywhere. Under different circumstances, this would have been a fascinating West African adventure. It was like driving directly into a travel documentary. The roads were dusty. The buildings were low, and made of mud and corrugated iron. All the cars were old and mostly piled high with impossible numbers of unexpected items – tables and chairs, cages of chickens stacked twenty high. I saw one pickup with innumerable sheep standing in the back like commuters on the tube, and at least five sitting in the front with the driver.

Pavements did not exist in Douala. They had been replaced by a continuous line of jerry-rigged market stalls selling everything from unrecognisable fruits and wood carvings to monkey's heads and the voodoo spells with which to use them. Sheep seemed to outnumber people at the roadside (this takes some doing in such an overcrowded city). The sheep were all sheared so they looked like goats. Maybe they were undercover sheep. Vehicular progress was slow as people walked in the road. They were all jet black and tall, their height being exaggerated by the goods carried on their heads. The women were elegant and beautiful. They wore jewellery, gold piercings and brightly-coloured, intricately-patterned clothes and headwear. The men were straight faced, aggressive and intimidating. Children stood and stared as we went past. The air tasted hot and dry. It was laden with a dust that made you gag for water as the sun beat down and made everything slow despite the feeling of bustle. The whole place had an air of isolation to it; not surprising really, with the Atlantic Ocean to the west, some of the world's largest rain forests to the east, and to cap it all off, the Sahara Desert to the north. Had we not been under arrest by what appeared to be armed Nazis, it would have been an exhilarating and wondrous journey.

The bus drove through a gate between high concrete walls that had barbed wire along the top, and pulled into a parched, dusty compound that looked like a Third World prison. Numerous fully-armed soldiers sat with their feet on the desks in windowless, concrete offices. Those who weren't in full uniform wore green vests and combat trousers with sunglasses and long boots. It was like being in a San Francisco nightclub. Two Dobermans, chained to a tree, pulled against their chains and barked loudly. Despite the heat, they seemed keen to get their teeth into us. The place felt unauthorised, as if we'd been arrested by a criminal gang, not police. I didn't like it. Not one bit. I particularly didn't like the guns. It came home very starkly to me that guns mean death. That's what they are for. To some, they mean 'respect,' or 'power' or even 'sport.' No. Here guns meant death.

We were marched off the bus, and one of the Nazis pulled us roughly into a line whilst the other kept his gun up to his eye and trained directly on us. As the first Nazi grabbed my shoulder and pushed me backwards and to one side, I looked into his face. His mirrored sunglasses meant I couldn't see his eyes, but I could see he was young. Probably no older than me. Far too young to be in charge of a loaded semi-automatic. He was sweating lightly, the beads sparkling against his jet-black skin like jewels in molten chocolate. I wondered what training he had had, and how many American movies he'd enjoyed in which someone like him got a starring role wiping out nameless extras like me. I wondered if this would be the man to take my life.

Another bus clattered into the compound. It contained another half-dozen soldiers, all looking down at us with something approaching hatred in their expressions. They didn't look like people who cared too much about human rights or Geneva conventions; they looked like bored vigilantes turning up to watch a Christians-and-lions show. But the thing that heightened my fear was not just their demeanour, or even their guns, but the state of their bus. It was rusty green, with no windows and half the bonnet missing. The door was opened by the driver pulling on a large lever, and it creaked and complained as it fell out of its hole and flopped down to the side. I had no previous experience of the Cameroon police force, but this seemed all wrong. Surely, they had enough government money – even if it was French government money – to get some decent transport and mark it clearly? And why hadn't we been taken to a proper jail or court house? There was no evidence here of other prisoners, let alone a judge. I didn't feel confident that we were about to be part of a controlled legal process.

I didn't have much time to consider what all this meant before another officer appeared from the second bus. This guy looked very pleased with himself. Dressed up like Hitler, with an oversized cap, immaculate uniform, sunglasses and shiny long boots, this was the Big Cheese himself. He was also sporting a dog on a lead; one of those stocky, black things, with an all-body crew cut, short, powerful jaws and a steely look in his eye which betrayed the fact that he liked his job. There wasn't much trouble that these two couldn't handle.

Hitler was armed with a pistol on his belt. The dog was armed with an enquiring nose, and was charged with the unenviable task of sniffing a line of unwashed sailors, presumably with the aim of detecting drugs, bombs, weapons or contraband. Had the target of the search been body odour, they could have achieved their quarterly targets in one go without risking the life of a perfectly good dog. As it was, the dog became excited from a great distance, presumably because the Smell of Fear – particularly in this airless heat – would have been palpable even to a dead dog, let alone this one. The two Dobermans joined in the singing contest, so it was all fun and games in the loud-barking and teeth-baring stakes. The dog pulled on its lead with every stride, frantic to get at us, and Hitler jerked him back with every other stride, strangling his barks as he did so. The dog was moving in a vertical circle, as if the Nazi was playing with some kind of yelping yoyo as they progressed towards us.

The officer could see that we were somewhat anxious, and this brought a smile of satisfaction to the corner of his thin lips. He coiled the leash around his wrist to pull the dog in short, and started his investigations by giving Payphone the once over. The dog decided instantly that he was massively guilty of something or other. It went berserk, spinning like The Tasmanian Devil on the end of its lead and yelling its head off. The handler pulled the dog back, gave his victim a sadistic grin and two soldiers dragged Payphone off somewhere private, presumably to undergo an unthinkable interrogation. Payphone looked back at us with fear in his eyes as they frogmarched him away. All the jolly Cockney knee and eyebrow work was gone from his demeanour. I felt my own fear grow at the prospect of what might be about to take place behind closed doors.

'We were moving the ship for safety,' shouted Jinx to no one in particular. 'It was dragging its anchor so we felt it was our duty to get out there and…'

'Sterp!' yelled Kojak, marching towards Jinx, who swallowed hard and stared dead ahead. 'Sterp steel!'

Jinx stopped still, as bidden, and I realised what he was doing. This was to be our story, and he wanted to let Payphone know what to say under interrogation. It was good. We saw the ship was unsafe at its anchor, tried to signal them and then went to make it safe ourselves. We were simply being good Samaritans. Perfect.

Kojak seemed angry now. He grabbed the dog's lead and dragged both dog and Hitler towards Jinx. The dog took two sniffs and instantly went off like an alarm clock at Jinx. Kojak pulled the lead forwards to allow the dog to get right up close to Jinx. He stared into Jinx's face, enjoying his discomfort. The dog was going absolutely haywire.

'Emmenez-le!' Kojak yelled at his men to take Jinx away, before spinning on his heel and marching off in disgust.

The guards who were heading off with Payphone came back to add Jinx to the chain gang. They were just marching their duo off when the dog caught wind of me, and that set him off as if someone had thrown the switch again. He leapt at me, yelping and howling his knowledge of my guilt as if his life depended on it. I don't know what the blasted pooch had on me, but whatever it was, the Gestapo in the shacks around us were now looking out of the windows in amazement that three of us in a row must have some stuff on us. They lifted their sunglasses as if checking their eyesight, and talked to each other in urgent tones. A stream of them began to file out to help as I was dragged over to make up a trio to be taken away to the interrogation room; a room presumably equipped with handcuffs on the walls, electric probes and a sacrificial pair of Marigolds for the purpose of – as Payphone so succinctly put it – 'a rummage up yer Kingdom Come'. I really didn't relish a rummage at all. In fact, I could think of nothing I would relish less. Even the word 'relish' started to sound unsettling.

But before my colonic away-day could begin, the dog got to Giewy. But instead of screaming its head off and spinning like a hooked fish at the end of its lead, the dog went quiet and started to whine as if he'd just got a whiff of something so utterly unspeakable that it didn't know what to do. Everybody stopped to look. It wasn't giving Giewy the all clear, and yet it wasn't making accusations either. Giewy was evidently an entirely new nasal experience for a dog who thought he had smelled it all. I looked at Giewy, who was wriggling as if he had fleas, and his fear was doing nothing to improve the aroma that was having such a profound effect on Fido.

The dog edged forwards, took a sniff and then backed off as if unsure. It was interested in Giewy, but in a different way than it was interested in the rest of us. It seemed to have lost all its aggression, so the handler let it have some rein to investigate. The dog went straight round behind Giewy, wagging his tail and sniffing his bum like one dog finding nasal nirvana in the nether regions of a new friend in the park. With a high-pitched, 'Geiiieeeeew! Gerroff!' Giewy arched his back and tried to get away. But this dog was not one to give up. Anything that could pong as beautifully as this was worth going the extra mile for. As Giewy tried to protect his bottom from nasal analysis, the dog decided to skip the chocolates and flowers and began humping Giewy's leg with such grim determination that the handler, pulling with all his might on the leash and shouting at the dog to obey orders, could do nothing to stop it. Hitler was not used to being defied, and took decisive action. He drew his pistol, pointed it at the dogs head, and roared at it in French to stop humping Giewy this minute before it caught something horrid. The dog was young and carefree. For him, affairs of the heart came ahead of his career, so he kept banging away with a singularity of purpose that could only be admired. The birth control mechanisms were stepped up to their highest level: the dog had a gun trained on its head, a desperately struggling lover and now a guard with jack-boots kicking it unremittingly in the ribs, and yet still his ardour was not dampened. In a climax that sounded like Scooby Doo when the criminal has been unmasked and the 12-decker sandwich is ready for consumption, the dog's victorious mating call echoed around West Africa.

With its mission over, and with the combined strength of two further guards, the dog was brought back under control. I felt happy for Giewy. At least he had finally had sex. Even if it was with a dog which was obviously wired up wrong. It certainly had no taste. Maybe it had a thing for sailors (but that would make it no different from half the Freddie Mercury lookalikes around here). The dog handler was anxious to establish just what the bloody hell the dog thought he was doing, and was berating it in French on the subject of professional standards and basic hygiene. But Romeo didn't care. He was basking in the afterglow, enjoying a post-coital cigarette and didn't give a fig for his job any more. The dog was in love, and nothing else mattered. As soon as it was off work, it would be skipping through the fields casting buttercups lovingly left and right without a care in the world.

Eventually, we were marched off to a concrete room containing a couple of benches and a table. It was darker and cooler than it was outside. We were sat in a line on the benches then, one at a time, we were stripped of our belongings and searched. Mercifully, there were no rubber gloves involved. They found nothing more than the tools and knives we had on us. As each of us was frisked, Kojak seemed unhappy. An agitated conversation took place between him and his guards as he looked through the contents of our pockets with disappointment. Kojak came to a decision. He walked along slowly in front of us, nodding in the silence before speaking slowly through gritted teeth.

'Mornay,' said Kojak, announcing the title of a fish dish threateningly. 'You merst geev mornay.' He rubbed his fingers and thumb together to make the point clear.

Ah. Now I got it. He wanted cash. We looked at each other and shrugged. A mission to raid ships in an anchorage isn't the kind of thing that involves shopping, so we hadn't got a bean between us.

'You wheel geev mornay!' Kojak banged the table in a sudden outburst of anger, and we all jumped. One of the hard-looking guards was so shocked that he dropped his gun, and when he went to pick it up his sunglasses fell off onto the floor. He must have been the Giewy of the gang.

Kojak began to fizz visibly. He stood up, snorting like a bull. 'I am a nappy!' he pronounced, and seemed pleased to get it off his chest.

'He's a what?' said Jinx, a little fazed. I shrugged back, unable to throw any light.

'I am very a-nappy,' Kojak continued. 'You merst geev mornay or is bad news for you!'

Jinx got it now and shook his head. 'Captain,' he explained in that slow, loud voice that the English save specially for patronising foreigners. 'Ship Capitano. Mornay – he give.' And I've never quite understood why we think speaking backwards might help foreigners understand. They spend years learning English at school, then they meet someone British and we start speaking really bad English slowly, loudly and backwards.

There was a silence as Kojak considered Jinx's words. Then he nodded slowly.

'Globule print cease capitano mornay?' he enquired.

Now I was fogged again. Between this guy and Payphone it was becoming a headache trying to understand anyone at all. I looked around at the guards to see what they made of it. They all drew a blank, but Jinx was up to it.

'Yes, yes! *Global Princess*! You read it on the lifeboat, right? Capitano *Global Princess*. He have mornay!'

Kojak considered this for a while. He then reeled off a machine-gun burst of French which had all but two of the soldiers running into each other and out through the doors like Keystone Cops.

Now, it's probably worth mentioning at this point that I have a curious relationship with the French language. My grandfather was French, and he lived in our house when I was small. A good deal of the language was delivered into my subconscious. Unfortunately, none was delivered into my conscious, so I barely passed the O-level, but the fact remains, a good deal of it is in there somewhere. The point is this: I have this uncanny ability to understand what is being said in French when I hear it, without any idea of what the actual words were. It all sounds like gobbledegook to me, and I couldn't string a sentence together to save my life and yet somehow I seem to understand. It's like a weird sort of magic that goes on, and that's what happened now. I knew what Kojak had said – or at least, I was pretty sure – so I tucked the information away carefully in the conscious area of my brain; a nice, roomy area, totally uncluttered by formal French understanding.

We were marched along a corridor and into another concrete room with a single, barred window. The door was slammed and locked behind us. There was nothing in the room except a couple of benches, a hole in the ground patrolled by flies and a nauseating smell of shit that hung in the concrete dust we were breathing and made me gag. We established quickly that the hole was not suitable for escape purposes (the stench alone would require a genuine warrior to make it past first base). Instead, we employed the benches for their intended purpose, and tried not to breathe as we watched the flies fly in slow squares.

And that was it for the day. We were left alone with our thoughts and no idea what was going to happen to us. We were given no food or water, so we just sat quiet and dejected as the sun went down and night fell. There was no light in the room, so we were soon sitting in pitch darkness with nothing but the sounds of the local insect life sucking our blood, the odd car or motorbike spluttering along on the nearby roads and Giewy grumbling endlessly about the lack of appropriate dog control legislation in West Africa.

After a strange and sleepless night, the sunrise found us tired and hungry. You could say we were all a nappy, but I don't think any of us would have enjoyed the joke. We talked things through, trying to find a straw to cling to. Occasionally we would get up and walk around to stretch, but nothing changed. The room became hot as the sun rose and the discomfort grew. This must be what it is like in one of those narrow-minded Bangkok prisons you hear about. It was no life, I can tell you.

It must have been mid-morning when there was the sound of a key in the lock. The door swung open and – to our utmost surprise – in walked Captain Benchmerson looking furious. He was followed by Kojak, also looking furious. Two guards stood on the door with their guns all primed.

'Tombing newts,' said Kojak decisively, giving the captain the V-sign. It was a strong opening gambit in negotiations, if possibly a little rude.

'I beg your pardon?' said the captain, wondering what he was being accused of.

'You have tombing newts,' said Kojak, unrepentantly giving him another V-sign.

The captain's fury was momentarily replaced by a reeling sensation as he got a picture of pond dwellers being mummified. Fortunately, Kojak expanded enough for us get a grip. 'I geev you tombing newts, then we make bees knees.'

Ah. Two minutes. But now it was bees knees. Fortunately, the captain was made of stern stuff and was not to be thrown from his purpose by any number of newts or bees.

'You have no right to hold these men here,' said the captain, firmly moving the subject away from livestock. 'No right at all.'

Kojak reeled round on him and spat out his words. 'You sink I have no rat?' he spat. 'Of course I have a rat! My sheep, Capitan? *Peut-être*, you forget my sheep?'

The captain was already trying to forget about newts and bees. He hadn't even begun to make space in his life for any rats or sheep. Not even undercover sheep that looked like goats. It was probably just as well that Kojak turned his attention to Jinx. 'Zis man!' he spun round and poked his baton into Jinx's chest. 'He try to steal my sheep!'

'Here! I never touched your… '

'And you!' he turned suddenly and gave Payphone some sword work with his baton. 'Eez it zat you is a terroreest?' He snarled as he approached the captain. He walked up to him so they were nose to nose and continued to make plain his suspicions in a low, threatening growl. 'Even you, mon capitan, viz your vera nice cloves et votre smart talking. Are you a bummerre?'

'Eh?'

'A bummerre, mon capitan. I sink maybe you 'ave a plan to bum all ze people in ze city, eh?'

'I say!' said the captain, somewhat taken aback. 'There's no call for that!'

'Eet is my jerb to call for zat! *Peut être* you 'ave a dangereux bum in your trouserres right now, eh, Capitan?'

'You leave my trousers out of this! I shall be calling the British consul the moment I leave zis beelding. I mean, building.'

Kojak nodded knowingly. 'I can taste ze geelty secrets zat you 'ave, Capitan. I can see ze drugs 'owever good you 'ide zem. I can smell ze bums.' And with that he left the room, leaving the captain clutching the doorframe to steady himself.

I don't know whether it was because a truth had been exposed about his secret intention to bum the Cameroon population, or just because he was angry, but the captain was flushed red as he turned on us.

'What the bloody hell did you think you were doing?' he hissed through gritted teeth. 'This is international law you are breaking here! We could be in all sorts of trouble!' He seemed concerned to keep a lid on his anger, if only for the impression given to our captors, but he was clearly fearful for the outcome. 'You lads are in deep,' he continued. 'This government likes to use this sort of situation for political capital. I don't have the kind of money the police are demanding to buy them off, and we might have to involve the embassy. Once it gets to that level, we are really in the mire.'

'Excuse me,' I said meekly. 'I might be able to help. I overheard a conversation between the grand fromage out there, as we say in French, and his men, and I think it might be useful.'

The captain's eyes burned into mine. He didn't have time for pointless distraction and his face did not look like one which had found a saviour. 'So, you speak French now, do you, Baboulene?'

'Well, it's all very interesting, you see, because I have this curious relationship with the French language. It stems from when I was very small, you follow, and my grandfather used to chat around the house, you understand, and my subconscious mind, you see, must have taken some of what he said aboard, and – did I mention he was from Toulouse? He was French, you see – sorry, should have mentioned that at the beginning. Anyway, the thing is…'

The captain rolled his eyes and his fingers curled around an imagined throat. 'Will you get to the point, or I swear…'

'Ah. Yes. Right. I don't think these are police, Captain. That bloke out there told his guards not to tell the police about us, not to tell their friends and not to tell the mechanic. It seems he wants to keep us here in secret.'

'It makes sense to me,' said Jinx. 'I think the mechanic he means must be the engineer – the guy who keeps the genny running on the ship.'

'Mmmmm,' said the captain, deep in thought. 'That tells us two things. Firstly, that this is a private security firm, and secondly, that they don't want their paymasters to find out that security was breached. They are probably supposed to have someone on that ship at all times and they haven't been doing it. OK, their paymasters must be the shipping line. We know who that is, so we have a lever.' He got up suddenly and called for the guard to let him out.

An hour later, we emerged from our prison, blinking in the blinding sunlight. The captain walked us back to the dockside where two *Global Princess* lifeboats were waiting to take us back to the ship. As we walked, the captain explained how he'd threatened to contact the shipping line and tell them that Kojak's security firm wasn't doing its job. Kojak had pretended not to care, and held out for a reduced bribe. The captain had apparently set us free for one thousand cigarettes, two bottles of whiskey and a favour. The captain didn't tell us what the favour was, but he said that we had a task to perform when we got back to the ship that would complete the payment.

We were all mightily relieved to get back on board. I looked at Giewy as we got onto the ship, and we were nothing short of emotional about it. Good grief, we nearly had a hug. The experience had made me appreciative of the British approach to policing, and extremely wary of the anarchy we would meet throughout West Africa.

Giewy and I went through to the bar. There was an argument in full flow. Of course! The bet! I had to collect my winnings from the bet!

'Ahaaa!' I cried cheerfully as I made my entrance. 'How is everybody?'

'We're all fine, thanks!' said The Famous Dick Wrigley, equally cheerfully. I was immediately hit by his good cheer. He should have been whining and complaining and handing over bank notes.

'Look what they did!' said Jinx angrily, pointing out across the bay. 'They went and moved the other one!'

I looked out of the porthole across the anchorage. When we had seen them dropping another lifeboat, they weren't coming to rescue us at all. The lads who stood to lose the bet had such skewed priorities that they had gone out after us, fired up the other bulk carrier, just as we had done with the first one, and whilst we were distracting the security firm for them, placed it even further back behind the one we'd gone through all that trouble to move.

'Do me a lemon!' spat Payphone. 'I punted a monkey on this knees-up! You're 'avin' a giraffe, incha?'[11]

'Fair's fair!' said The Famous Dick Wrigley smugly. 'The bet wasn't that you could move it. The bet was that it would be in place behind the other one by this afternoon. And it isn't! Now just pay up and stop whinging!'

Jinx's moustache flapped up and down like a demented divining fork. There was no doubt about it, we had lost the bet. This was seriously bad news for me. The odds had ended up such that I stood to win or lose a fortune. And I couldn't afford it. I would be paying this one off for a year.

The door opened and the captain walked in. He pointed at the four of us ex-cons.

'Right, lads. Time for you to pay your dues and do that favour. I have a job for you.'

This was going from bad to worse. I knew the nature of 'punishment work' all too well from previous experience. I had

---

11   'Heavens above! I wagered a significant sum of money on this event.
      Verily, someone is leading me a merry dance.'

lost my shirt on this bet, was up to my eyeballs in debt, as tired as I could ever remember being in my life and in desperate, desperate need of a shower. Now I was going to have to risk life and limb in the double bottoms cleaning out crap, or something equally delightful.

'To get you free I made those guys a promise, and now you must deliver. I want you to drop a lifeboat, get yourself across the anchorage and put that ship back where you found it. Quickly and quietly. No fuss, no nonsense. Just get it back in front of the other one and no more will be said.'

We sat looking in disbelief at the captain. A grin grew slowly across Jinx's face.

'But… but… but…' flapped The Famous Dick Wrigley as the meaning sunk in.

'What is it, three-oh?' asked the captain, looking irritated with The Famous Dick Loser. 'Stop flapping your jaw at me and spit it out.'

'It's just that… well, there's no need to… to… I mean, we've already… Surely, it's too risky to… to… to…'

He couldn't tell the captain that the right ship was already in front of the other one. He would have to reveal his own illegal activities to do that and the captain had promised sackings if he heard of any further ship invasions.

'Well, if we've got to do it, then we've got to do it!' announced Jinx, slapping his thighs and getting to his feet. 'Who's coming to help?'

As the sun set that evening, I was back on anchor watch. Jinx, Giewy, Payphone and I counted out the winnings and split them evenly between us. Not a bad haul for a day's work, a night in a West African cell and, in Giewy's case, a rough shag with a mad Bull Terrier. We looked across at the two bulkies. They were now completely the opposite way around from where they'd started, and yet all the authorities were happy. We wondered what would happen when the shipping line eventually came back. Would they even notice? We doubted it. Then again, would they ever come back? The captain had told us that he couldn't see any way they could rescue those ships. The best they could do would be to break them up and salvage the parts. Given my windfall, I could probably afford them myself.

★ ★ ★

As a postscript to this chapter, it may be interesting to note that the shipping line did take action to cure their apparently intractable problem. It seems that both those ships somehow contrived to get themselves run aground in another West African country not too far away. A country which provided their own legal experts, loss adjusters and salvage experts to investigate the circumstances. Indeed, a country whose politics and legal system did not allow foreign legal experts, loss adjusters and salvage experts to even visit their land, let alone board stranded ships and provide formal reports.

I cannot say for sure, of course, and it was thoroughly unfortunate for those ships to be compromised in such circumstances and in such a country. However, I imagine those reports were just what the shipping line needed to deliver to the insurers at Lloyd's in order to be compensated handsomely for their unfortunate losses. I somehow suspect that no mention of solid concrete would have been necessary anywhere at all.

Chapter 7

Pickaxe Watch

Of bold and fearless travel writers. The night of the pickaxe watch. Pirates aren't fun any more.

Following the fun and games in Douala, our next trip found us chuffing north along the coast to Abidjan on the Ivory Coast, up the Congo to Matadi, to Takoradi in Ghana, Lagos in Nigeria, Freetown in Sierra Leone and Dakar in Senegal. Of course, all these places were quite extraordinary to visit, and awesome as far as the natural beauty of it all goes, but to be perfectly frank with you, it wasn't all fun. West Africa was dangerous – really properly dangerous. What we might call a 'civilised' presence had but a toehold in a place where the gun and the gang ruled. It was very easy to get hurt or even killed if you got your sums wrong in some areas. There was this continuously unsettling feeling that you were never absolutely in charge of your own destiny. Danger constantly stalked the unwary, and if you let your guard down for a second you could get into deep trouble. It was a bit like going out after dark in Nottingham.

These days, people actually crave this sense of danger and flood West Africa trying to find it. You can't throw a stone in the Congo Basin without beaning a brave and fearless travel writer on the noggin as he annoys wildlife in the name of natural history. Sorry to go off on a tangent, but I have to tell you this. I know an intrepid, American TV travel presenter. We meet sometimes when he comes to London. In the early 1990s, he was bitten by a snake on live TV and became an instant success. Since then, his ratings went way down. That was until a spider injected venom into his face, making one side of his head go all funny on live TV. His ratings skyrocketed once more. Then came a few barren years when, despite all the efforts of the production company to get him into small spaces with trapped predators, he couldn't even get himself admitted to Out Patients. His popularity plummeted. Last time we met, he told me he was off to infuriate bears in Canada, where the chances of being mutilated were promising. He would have preferred to sit on salt-water crocodiles in Australia, but this was the high season. During the hours of daylight around the inlets of the Northern Territories there isn't a vacant crocodile from November round to March. They are all booked-up: busy being sat upon by intrepid adventurers and having their snouts wrapped up in duct tape. No, no. The Canadian bear-infuriation season was in full flow and he was confident he could get himself mauled within a fortnight. I wasn't so sure. When the salmon are jumping it runs at around three film crews per grizzly along the most scenic stretches of river all the way up to Alaska.

He told me sadly that he had written his last Brave and Fearless wildlife book from an internet cafe on the Tottenham Court Road. Probably the best way to do it.

The point I'm failing to make is that a brief spell spent at anchor just outside Lagos in September 1978 was easily the most terrifying experience of all my years at sea. We arrived at night, and a boat load of officials came out to greet us and do the clipboard thing. However, as usual, they were not ready for us. We were told we would have to wait in the anchorage, possibly for a couple of days, and that the advanced security arrangements we were supposed to have would not be ready for at least another twenty-four hours. I didn't see any real reason to care. It was not unusual for us to have to wait, and it was not unusual for the shoreside support we were supposed to receive to be late and inefficient. However, this was to be a wait like no other.

The officials on the boats brought machine guns with them. Two machine guns, to be precise. They took them up onto the bridge wings and mounted them, one on each side. They were just for show, for the moment, because the ammunition would only arrive with the trained soldiers the next day, but they might work as a deterrent until then. The mate ordered Ffugg, NotNorman, Giewy and me out onto the foredeck and gave us the bad news.

'OK, guys. Pickaxe watch for you. You're going to have to patrol the ship through the night, and you're going to have to keep sharp. This place is lethal. Until the soldiers arrive tomorrow to secure the ship and man the machine guns, it's down to us to repel boarders.'

And he handed us a pickaxe handle each.

'Work in pairs and use the radios to keep in touch. Walk round the ship keeping a good lookout over the side at all times. Try to keep visible and act tough. Watch for people sneaking up and trying to get on board. If they do, hit them. Hit them hard.'

We looked at each other in amazement.

I tried to smile, but it wouldn't work. 'This – this is a joke, right? A wind up?'

The mate looked at me and considered his response with a look of undiluted disgust in his eyes.

'Mr Baboulene, if you don't want to die tonight, you'd better listen good. The pirates round here have no qualms about murdering people in their beds to get control of a ship like this. It happens all too often up here and we have to defend ourselves without compromise if we don't want to be next. Kill or be killed. Which is it to be?'

We gulped and looked at our pickaxe handles. From what I had seen of West Africans, they were not the type to start annoying with sticks. I had the strangest feeling that someone of my age wielding a pickaxe handle would not serve to subdue a West African pirate and bring him smartly into line, but my preference for diplomacy and frank discussion between the parties was not going to win this day. The mate took us through a tutorial.

'Phase one defence: be on the lookout for small boats and dugout canoes. When you see one, shout and swear and brandish the pick handles at them to let them know you are here.

'Phase two defence: if they continue to advance, when they get near enough, throw pots of paint at them. This will cause injury if you hit a pirate, and if you miss, it will go clean through the bottom of their boat and give them other things to think about. OK?'

I was aghast. 'But – but – won't they drown if we sink their boats way out here?'

'Yes, they will,' said the mate. 'And you make sure of it. If you pussy around I guarantee they will kill you if they possibly can. So don't think twice. The second mate will be on watch on the bridge. Keep him up to speed and use him to raise the alarm. I've posted seacunnies on the bridge wings to make it look like the machine guns are manned, but once these bastards realise there are no soldiers on board, they'll try to get up over the sides. Phase three defence assumes we're engaged with the enemy. Raise the alarm via the bridge. The pirates use four-pronged hooks on ropes to come over the bulwark. Try to cut the ropes and keep the hooks so they can't throw them again. If you feel weight on the rope, that means they are coming up and they are quick. Damn quick. Don't try to cut the rope – you're too late. Wait for the heads to pop up, then go for the horizon.' He swung his pickaxe handle like a baseball player winding up for a biggie. 'If we get to phase three, you will be literally fighting for your life. So please, Windy. No fannying around.'

Fannying around? What the hell kind of language was that in a situation like this?

'OK, I'm off to my pit. Don't call me every time you hear a fish squeak, or I'll be hitting you with that thing. Get patrolling and keep your eyes peeled. And don't go off wanking. This is really, really serious.'

The four of us split numbly into two pairs and checked the walkie-talkies. This was so weird. We knew it wasn't a joke – even this crowd wouldn't organise warning letters from London and machine gun nests on the bridge wings just for a laugh.

We split across the foredeck amidships at around hold three. NotNorman and I went to port, Ffugg and Giewy to starboard. We headed aft. They headed for'd. We agreed to meet back here at every circuit. By following a prescribed route from the middle, we would always know the others approximate location, and we would regularly cross paths and check in with each other.

NotNorman and I headed off in silence. It was approaching midnight. It was hot. It was quiet. The sea lapped lazily at the sides of the ship. The ship was deliberately lit brightly with accommodation and cargo lights. Beyond the lights from the ship, it was pitch dark out there. It was eerie.

The hours passed. The ship slept. Round and round we walked. Nothing happened. We became a little more relaxed – blasé, even. Surely, nobody was going to paddle, what, two miles to get out to us at the anchorage? Even so, we looked out over the side of the ship, peering into the blackness as we headed past the gangway and out onto the after deck once more. It was going to be a long night.

Suddenly, the radio crackled into life. The sounds of a panicking Giewy filled our ears.

'Gieeeee-eee-uw! There's a boat! We got one! Starboard side of hatch two. Get up here!'

I felt my stomach churn. NotNorman and I looked at each other with horror in our eyes. Were we really going to have to fight with strange foreign people who wanted to kill us? We ran up to the foredeck and across to the starboard side where Giewy was shouting at a small boat with a light about 50 yards away. Ffugg was pogoing up and down, nutting imaginary marauders on the foredeck with his teeth bared, and growling: 'Come on, ven! Come oooon! You wanna piece of me, do ya? Eh? Eh?'

NotNorman and I joined Giewy, shouting over the side at them to let them know that they'd been spotted. To stop Ffugg from attacking me again, we sent him off to get the mate whilst we picked up paint cans and continued to shout as loud as we could.

Now, there is nothing in it for me to describe in detail what happened next. Suffice to say that we had been, shall we say, on a hair-trigger and, as the mate put it, a fish had squeaked. Officers and crew began emerging from their beds and out onto the foredeck, sporting wrenches, piping, knives, clubs and rapidly beating hearts, ready to fight pirates. The little boat continued on its way, however, never coming any closer and never looking exactly threatening. It could have been homicidal marauders out to slaughter us in our beds. On the other hand, as the mate warmly pointed out, it could have been a couple of old boys on their way home from a fishing trip. Perhaps not every passing vessel needed a gallon can of emulsion through the clinkers.

We apologised for Giewy's over-reaction, and Giewy blamed me, and I blamed Ffugg, and the ship's company drifted away back to their beds. The mate accepted our apology, but warned us, with carefully chosen words, that if we were to wake him once more without good reason, he would kick us each up the backside with such vigour that we would never see our hats again. The accommodation dropped back into a sleepy silence broken only by the loud Essex-tones of Ffugg, bouncing around the foredeck with me in a half-nelson asking me if I wanted some. I knew it was a bad idea to blame him in front of the mate.

Once Ffugg had been calmed, NotNorman and I headed off once more in the other direction. From then until around 3.00 a.m. life was fairly uneventful. We passed the other two every ten minutes or so. They called us rude names and made rude signs, and we called them rude names and made rude signs. Then Giewy led Ffugg away furiously swinging like a champ at me for calling him names and making rude signs, and so the night wore on. We began to feel that maybe we weren't going to be murdered by Cap'n Hook and his mates after all, and it gave us confidence. Even when we did see small boats, it wasn't a worry. We shone searchlights at them, and made our presence known, and we shepherded them until they moved on, and they obeyed us. We slapped the pick-axe handles into our palms and felt that, yes, maybe we could defend the ship. We had what it took. We did indeed fancy ourselves. At one point there was a hefty burst of machine-gun fire from across the bay that brought us back to reality with a bump (and perhaps a little bit of wee-wee leakage). But generally, we began to feel that daylight would be piped safely aboard, followed later in the morning by some nice big soldiers and our bravery would not be tested.

Then it all went horribly, horribly wrong.

We were checking in with Ffugg and Giewy on the foredeck when the seacunnie watching from the bridge wing shone his torch down to attract our attention. We went to the bulwark and looked over. A small light could be seen heading for the afterdeck. We trotted down towards it. Sure enough, it was coming towards the ship. We shouted and waved, and the powerful Aldis lamp, used as a searchlight from the bridge, picked them out clearly. The light showed that we were being confronted by three tall, skinny black guys in a dugout. They had some rope and tools on board. No doubt about it, these were pirates! They continued towards us despite our remonstrations, and we felt that perhaps we'd finally found some people worth a can of paint or two. They shouted back at us, standing up in the boat and swearing. They looked decidedly dodgy and they shook their fists aggressively. It was quite unnerving, even though we were clearly winning the battle before it started. Even so, they continued their approach.

We lifted a few pots of paint onto the gunwale. Surely they wouldn't come closer, would they? I couldn't understand what they were trying to achieve. Surely we looked scary enough for them, didn't we? I mean, Ffugg and Giewy were already with us. We even outnumbered them! Why weren't they having second thoughts? They could see they weren't going to get on board, couldn't they?

'Shall I, like, throw a pot at them?' shrugged NotNorman. They were frustratingly just out of range, but it seemed like a logical next step in the battle of brinkmanship. Now that we could clearly see their faces, I was beginning to feel decidedly uneasy about our lack of progress.

Suddenly, the radio crackled into life and there was a cry from the bridge wing. The second mate was shouting into the radio, and the seacunnie, who had been watching our progress with idle interest, was suddenly highly animated.

We looked up and were struck by a realisation that turned my blood to ice.

There was a second point of attack.

'Oh, Jesus, Mary and Joseph,' cried Giewy. 'These guys are a decoy!'

We left Ffugg fffreatening them in his own inimitable fashion and ran as hard and fast as we could out onto the foredeck and up towards the fo'c'sle head, shouting at the second mate to raise the alarm. Just as I arrived by hatch one, there was a clang and a hook landed on the deck in front of me. It jumped up as if it had a life of its own and lodged under the bulwark. NotNorman ran to it, but he couldn't unhook it. It was under pressure already. Someone was coming up. I felt the most enormous adrenalin rush. I was in fear for my life. NotNorman ignored the mate's instructions and began sawing away at the rope beneath the hook, even as a line of pirates with knives in their teeth were climbing up towards him. Never, ever, ever again would NotNorman fail to keep a sharp knife.

Another hook came over. I grabbed it off the deck, even before it was pulled tight, and threw it away as if it was red hot.

'Cut the hook off, you jerk!' shouted Giewy. 'Don't give it back to 'em!'

I looked around to have a go at him. How dare that jerk call me a jerk, even when justified. To my utter horror I saw a large, shadowy figure emerging from the hawse pipe on the fo'c'sle head. You will remember from the earlier lesson that the anchor cable runs from the anchor locker beneath the fo'c'sle, up onto the gypsy, across the deck and down through the hawse pipe to the sea below. The anchor was at the bottom of the sea and these guys were coming up the anchor cable and entering the ship through the hawse pipe.

'Giewy! Behind you!'

I ran towards the danger. Note this carefully because I'd never done it before or since in my entire life, but the sheer terror combined with the adrenalin and the orders we'd been given caused me to act. I remembered what the mate said: it was us or them, and we had to fight for our lives. I liked my life. I wanted to keep it. The first guy was still mostly inside the hawse pipe. By some miracle, it seems he had his foot caught because he was failing to emerge onto the fo'c'sle. Thank God.

It is with absolute shame that I admit now, in the cold light of day many years later, that Giewy and I set about him with our pickaxe handles. With massive, panic-fuelled blows, we whacked out at his head, again and again. And again and again. We shouted and screamed, and he shouted and screamed as the relentless attack rained down on him. We were in a frenzy of pure panic and we just carried right on hitting him. He couldn't come up because we were clouting him. He couldn't go down, because of the line of pirates on the cable behind him trying to follow him up. There was blood everywhere, and we just kept whacking and whacking. There were cries and shouts, then there was an enormous roaring sound… and a blood-curdling scream as the man suddenly disappeared rapidly back down into the hawse pipe as if he'd been flushed down a toilet. I turned to see the mate standing at the windlass. He had taken the brake off and let the anchor go. The chain ran out, and the man was whipped back down the hawse pipe with it. If he wasn't dead already, being dragged down the hawse pipe with the anchor cable must have crushed him. I turned to see some hands appear on the bulwark where NotNorman had failed to sever the rope in time. NotNorman smashed his pickaxe handle down on the fingers – Bam! Bam! Bam! The fingers disappeared, and didn't come back.

The mate wound the brake on and the anchor cable stopped. There was suddenly no more action to take. As I jumped round in circles, looking for the next point of attack, my heart beat so hard in the back of my throat that it shook my entire body. We heard several splashes as bodies (and possibly body parts) hit the water. There were shouts and cries from below, but no more hooks or invaders. I ran to the bulwark.

'Don't look over the side!' roared the mate. 'Stay right where you are!'

I took the mate's order and didn't look. Part of me wishes I had, not out of morbid interest, but to be sure that we had the situation under control. Anyway, I did what I was told and stayed away from the bulwark.

By now, the entire ship was awake. The foredeck was alive once more with officers and crew brandishing weapons and looking for pirates to fight. But it was all over. I looked down the hawse pipe, half-expecting the guy to pop back up and start fighting again, like the zombies do in those movies. There was blood smeared all around. There was no way he could have survived. Had I killed him? I can't have killed him. He'd had his arms over his head, so I mostly hit his arms. But I had hit him dozens of times – full blooded, desperate whacks with a pickaxe handle. Giewy had done the same. I knew that the pirate couldn't have fended us both off through such a sustained attack. I stood numbly on the fo'c'sle, shaking and confused, rapidly entering a state of deep shock.

The mate shouted across at us: 'Go! Go! Come on, Windy, get it together! You've got a job to do and there may be more down aft. In your pairs now, port and starboard. Get yourselves on patrol. Giewy! Go support Ffugg. Now! Don't think about it! Go! Noow!'

I could hear in the mate's voice that he was shaken too. He was saying all the right things but he was scared as hell. We went off on jellied legs, still stunned with fear, coursing with adrenalin and terrified that it might not yet be over.

The next day, the security forces came aboard. We were properly protected and now I was able to fully appreciate what had happened. I lay in my bed shivering and even crying. The second mate came to talk to me, but I wanted to be alone and locked myself in the toilet. What we had been through was not right. Nobody should have to do anything like that as part of their job. I felt sick. Unclean. I felt violated in the sense that I had been changed forever by this experience. And I was very, very scared. More than anything else on earth, I wanted to go home.

The mate called us to his dayroom and we talked it through. He said he'd seen everything, and that we had done well. He told us that the army had picked up some injured men in the sea. They had arrested and imprisoned them. Nobody was killed.

At the time, I believed him and it helped enormously to hear from an authority figure that we'd done nothing wrong and that everything was fine. Looking back now, it was utterly implausible that the man survived, but I guess I wanted desperately to believe it. I can easily find and indulge comforting words: it wasn't me; nobody was hurt; it was their own fault; I was just obeying orders; everyone was accounted for; it was self defence. Whatever, whatever, whatever. The facts are different and they haunt my sleep to this day. They probably always will. I helped to kill at least one human being that night and no number of clever words or justification can ever change that.

Chapter 8

Symphony for a
Knifed Spacehopper

The Congo body swerve. A bottom-dwelling revenge.

We weren't scheduled to stop in Greece. It wasn't supposed to happen. However, an interesting fact I forgot to mention about West Africa is that the River Congo dodges about. It sways and it shimmies and it congas to its own beat. We were all dancing along with it when it threw us such a body swerve that it sent us reeling into Athens. Mmmm. I think I need to explain a little further.

We took a trip around 80 miles up the River Congo to a place called Matadi, in the Democratic Republic of Congo. The

Congo has got to be one of the most amazing rivers on earth, and not one up which you would expect to find yourself sailing a 20,000 ton ship. The first indication that you are arriving in its estuary is that the sea changes colour – from the usual sun-spangled aqua-blues to a yellowy grey. The river delivers a quite staggering quantity of water down to the ocean, along with its accompanying silt, and it never stops. The current flows one way only, at a frightening speed, and the scale of the river makes the whole thing unreal. I'm not sure how wide the river is in its early stages, but you can't see the banks from the middle. We are talking sizable here.

The key fact from a sailor's point of view is that the river changes where it is. It cannot be charted, because it is never in the same place twice. It presents a totally different course every time you visit. The droughts, the rains, the shifting silts from a deluge… not only does the depth vary, but the main navigable channels snake around like salsa dancers from one day to the next. There are sand bars, sharp bends and twirly whirlpools. This makes it absolutely treacherous for navigation. We took on a pilot, of course, who had local and recent knowledge, but from the moment he arrived we knew from his demeanour that he was winging it. He was a short, black man with large empire-builder shorts and shoes four sizes too big. He looked like a child who had been sent along instead of his dad. The captain was naturally concerned about the potential for running aground – if only because the kid wasn't tall enough to see out of the windows – and asked him searching questions.

'So, Pilot, what do you estimate to be the minimum acceptable depth sounding for this passage, bearing in mind recent rainfall and the draft of the vessel?'

'Oh, yes, Captain. Absolutely,' replied our pilot, nodding for all he was worth in order to inspire confidence.

'So, Pilot, given that we are slightly down by the stern, moving ballast might level the ship and, we estimate, could even reduce our draft by around three feet. Would that be advisable in your opinion?'

'Oh, no, Captain. Absolutely, yes.' He shook his head sagely, then, seeing the captain's expression, changed to more decisive nodding.

'Sooooo, Pilot, why are you out here on a boat when it's a school day? Do you want us to drop you off in time for PE?'

Well, he didn't really say that, but whatever he did say, all he got back was more confident nodding. To change the subject, the man kept giving two-degree helm orders and sending us to get him tea. Here we were, working our way gingerly up the Congo, and the pilot was ad-libbing. As the river narrowed we could see his strategy. He was aiming for dark patches of water and hoping they were the deeper bits. I mean to say, we could have done that much by ourselves. Fortunately, the river was flowing towards us, so the ship was manoeuvrable because of the flow of water past the rudder, and rapid changes in position were possible with the ship effectively standing still in the water whilst proceeding at quarter-speed. This was just as well, because rapid changes were regularly required with this clown. The captain spent most of his time wincing as the pilot took us forwards at four knots – a walking pace – for 80 miles. Good grief, what a yawn.

After more than twenty-four hours of tense navigation, we got to Matadi. We came alongside a fantastically shaky wooden wharf and looked out on to a wonderful, bustling town carved into the jungle. There wasn't really a port area, the gangway just dropped down into a bustling town centre. I loved it. Absolutely loved it. It was colourful and sunny, and the people were jet black and smiley. They all seemed to be seven-feet tall, and they wore brightly-coloured cotton clothes. I don't know what Matadi had that other parts of West Africa did not, but this town was cheerful and happy, not threatening at all. Maybe we'd just been unlucky before.

The shoreside crew gathered noisily. Hundreds of them. As always in these countries, about ten times more men undertook the work than were strictly needed. There were generally so many that they got in each others way, and the job took far longer than it would have done with half the men. We opened the hatch to unload the cargo. We looked inside and… there was nothing there. The cargo wasn't where it was supposed to be. We checked the other holds and the 'tweendecks. We patted our pockets and checked down behind the dresser. Nothing. Several hundred tons of cargo weren't there. That much stuff, as you might imagine, is a tad difficult to lose, so some frankly-worded exchanges warmed the telephone lines around the world. This was followed by an embarrassing exchange with the far-too-many-men who had gathered to unload all the nothing we'd brought for them to deal with. We had to explain just how far-too-many of them there were.

The mystery was eventually solved. We had, swiftly and with almost blinding efficiency, unloaded it all in Cape Town.

We shut up the holds, waved the flag and left with egg on our faces to begin the journey back towards the ocean and complete a delightful, but utterly pointless 160-mile round trip. However, things were different on the way back. I thought navigation had been about as tricky as it gets coming up river, and was relieved when it was over, but it only took ten minutes to realise that coming up had been the easy bit. Things were going to be significantly worse on the return journey because now the river was flowing in the same direction as us. This meant we were moving forwards at a full seven knots just by virtue of sitting still in moving water. Turning the rudder made absolutely no difference to our direction whatsoever. The ship was moving with the water, so there was no flow over the rudder, and therefore no steerage. The only way to get any steerage was to go faster – which was much too dangerous – or to go astern. This worked to an extent, but a rudder is under the stern of the ship and is designed to change the ship's direction from water flowing from forward to aft. It simply doesn't work that well if you try steering in reverse. It's a bit like trying to push a piece of string rather than pull it; it just doesn't oblige. Modern ships have bow thrusters and stern thrusters – often a dozen of them: small motors that jet water out to the sides and allow the ship to pirouette like Rudolf Nureyev in his prime, without using the propeller or the rudder at all. We had but a single propeller and a lonely, fairly pointless rudder. We could only spin and pirouette like Nureyev would if they dug him up and put him on stage today.

As the ship scudded down stream, held in mid-river by natural forces and a good deal of luck, and as the pilot leaped, just like Nureyev, from one end of the bridge to the other chewing his hat, I could tell from my sailor's instinct and experience that we were in grave danger of running aground. Either that, or it was because the captain kept shouting at the pilot:

'What's the matter with you, man? We are in grave danger of running aground!'

The pilot was in a panic that easily matched the captain's panic, and the engine room was in a panic that matched both of them. It was quite a ballet, and as the Captain moved *cabriole* (an allegro step in which the extended legs are beaten in the air) across to the radar, and the second mate ran *elance* (in a darting style, as if searching without hope) from corner to corner of the chartroom with his forearm draped dramatically across his forehead, and the pilot did three *grands jetés* (that pointy-toed running, jump-like-a-stag thing) out onto the bridge wing, the feeling was that the underlying story was going to be a tragedy. Every time the engineers were once again requested for an instant 'full astern' to get some leverage on the water, we all crossed our fingers and hoped they could make it happen in time. These old ships were not really made for regular starting and stopping, but so far, our princess had gamely performed a ballet of her own, in many ways reminiscent of that classic performance, made legendary by Anna Pavlova's infamous display in Moscow in 1912, known as the *pas de glissade smashée dans les rocks.*

As we drifted rapidly towards the outside of a long bend, the captain shoved the telegraph to 'half astern' to get some steerage to bring us across to the short side.

The engine coughed and burped and... nothing happened. It coughed and burped again, and we drifted closer and closer to the edge, and... nothing happened. The captain shouted into the telephone at the chief engineer. The chief engineer roared at the second engineer. The second engineer boggled his eyes and bellowed at the engine, and a small white flag emerged from piston number three and waved apologetically.

'No engines! No engines!' the engineers sang operatically from the engine room.

The captain ran across the bridge, grabbed the radio and called in a dramatic basso profundo to the mate on the fo'c'sle: 'Drop anchors! We're going aground! Drop anchooooors! La, la-la, LAAAAA!'

The mate and his crew on the fo'c'sle were frantic. They spun round and round *fouetté* (to spin on one leg propelling the body with the whipping motion of the free leg) but they had been caught by surprise and it was too late for all that.

The ship ran gracefully aground. I braced myself for the full orchestra to fall over itself in a chaotic heap from the impact, but there was no jolt. No whack. No bump at all. It was a long, slow, surprisingly smooth glide inland. The weight of the ship gave it such momentum that it just kept on going and going and going. It was an unreal feeling. I felt a little rise, like the way a surprise wave lifts one from the seabed, but that was it. On, and on and on we sailed, smoothly up the road. It was also strangely silent. I reasonably expected an accident of this magnitude to be accompanied by straining metal and rivets popping, but there was nothing. No crashing, no crunching – not even the ever present engine noise. The silence just added to the incongruity of the grounding. Eventually she came to a halt, and the ballet on board got itself into top gear, involving the entire cast. People were running dramatically in all directions, leaping and pointing with tragic looks on their faces.

The ship was embedded in a sandy, silty mud. This was relatively good news for several reasons. Firstly, a ship will crush itself on dry land, particularly when laden with cargo. The muddy bottom was supportive, and it was generally agreed that the ship was probably – by which I mean, hopefully – undamaged structurally. The other good news was that the back-third of the ship – including the propeller – was still in the water. We gathered from the pilot that the water level was rising, and that if we sat tight for a few hours (like we had a choice) we could probably back ourselves off the sand bank. Great. So now that the pilot had stacked the ship on the bank, at least he was going to be some use in getting us off. I watched as the captain, becoming increasingly angry with him, stood staring at the pilot, puffing and snorting like a tethered bull. Suddenly, he seemed to decide on a course of action. He took NotNorman to one side and began to whisper in his ear. NotNorman's eyes got wider and wider with every word the captain spoke. The two of them furtively looked at the pilot, then they went back into their huddle and the captain continued to talk out of the side of his mouth. I watched from afar, curious to know the contents of the conversation. Judging from the captain's hand movements, he was imparting to NotNorman the dark art of strangling rabbits.

NotNorman waved me over.

'… and this job takes priority over all others, understand?' said the captain.

'What job?' I said. 'What do we have to do now?'

'You boys,' said the captain in a conspiratorial whisper, 'have my permission to muck about. Understand?' He nodded sideways at the pilot and touched the side of his nose.

From the look on my face, the captain could tell that I didn't understand. He rolled his eyes and then pointed more directly towards the pilot. 'That idiot over there,' he said. 'One of your stupid acts of mindless inconvenience towards other people, just this once, will be acceptable. NotNorman has all the details.'

The captain gnashed his teeth, strangled one more rabbit and left us alone. I looked at NotNorman in amazement. After nearly a year of getting up the captain's nose through my involvement in tomfoolery, here he was giving us the green light to cause mayhem and bedlam to an honoured guest.

'We're allowed to muck about,' grinned NotNorman. 'Provided that whatever we do removes the pilot from the bridge.'

We sprouted the kind of grins that instantly had the captain thinking he might have been a little rash. But he was too late to change his mind. We were gone.

First, though, there was a ship to re-float. It was all supposed to be a terrible problem, but as with most terrible problems, I found it all highly exciting. The engineers spent their time working on the engine, while up on deck we set about organising the anchors to help pull the ship off the sand bank. This involved a process of lifting the anchors (using the wires on the cargo derricks) from their traditional places under the fo'c'sle head and passing them along the side of the ship to drop them in the water as far aft of the ship as we could manage. Once they were in place, pulling on the anchors, combined with a full astern on the rejuvenated engine, along with a higher water line, would hopefully be enough to get us off.

We climbed over the side of the ship on the fo'c'sle head and dropped down on Bosun's chairs (like a trapeze hung on ropes) to attach the cargo derrick runners by huge shackles to the anchors. One at a time we then swung the derricks out over the side of the ship and slowly let out the anchor whilst simultaneously pulling with the derrick. It was quite an operation. The anchor swung along the side of the ship until it was beneath the head of the derrick. The focus then moved to the next hatch down, where the next derrick was swung out over the side and its runner wire was paid out and shackled to the anchor. Now we had to pull with the midships derrick, let out the wire from the first derrick and simultaneously run out more anchor cable from the fo'c'sle.

We then moved to the third derrick, working with the second one, repositioning the first one to support a length of anchor cable to take some of the weight. Then all three derricks and the cable all worked together again to move the anchor down to the next set of derricks, and so on, passing the huge anchor slowly past the accommodation to hatch four and on again to hatch five down aft.

When the anchor was finally in position abaft the poop deck, with its chain looping from derrick to derrick as if it were pegged to a washing line all the way along the side of the ship, we started on the port side anchor, and began the same operation to bring a second anchor down to the same position, but on the other side of the ship. When they were both there, we lowered them into the water, using the after derricks to lower and the other derricks to run out cable, and we watched as the anchor headed for the silty bottom. We then went to each derrick and let go of the cable until it was completely released. The ship began to move backwards simply from the weight of the anchor and cable, and by pulling on the anchors from the fo'c'sle, and with very little engine power, we were dragged slowly and smoothly off the sand bank. It was brilliant, and elicited a cheer from the sweating personnel who had made it happen. And as soon as we were refloated, we had control because the anchors kept us in position as the engines took us upstream at roughly the same speed that the current was flowing against us. Beautiful.

The captain tracked the ship across to the short side of the bend and hid in the lee, where the water eddied and was relatively calm. We lowered lifeboats and went around the ship looking for damage. She seemed fine. We took stability readings in order to detect signs of internal leaks into the double bottoms. Eventually, the decision was taken to set sail. The lifeboats were stowed and everyone went back to their positions.

As we prepared to set sail, the mood aboard was very positive. On the bridge, the captain visibly inflated his chest on the clean air of freedom and an expression of deep satisfaction crossed his face. Then he realised why he was so happy, and the brow furrowed. The clouds gathered over his head.

'Cadets?' he called, approaching us and trying to keep his voice calm. 'I'm almost scared to ask, but: where is our pilot?'

'We, em, undermined his position,' said NotNorman.

'To the point where he didn't feel he could honestly continue,' I added.

'Oh, Lord, what have you done? I hope you didn't go too far. I didn't mean for you chaps to…' Suddenly he was interrupted by the most terrifying noise from just outside the chartroom. 'What in the name of sweet Jesus was that?' said the captain, his anxiety getting the better of his upbringing.

I knew what the noise was. So did NotNorman. And we couldn't believe what we were hearing.

Imagine, if you will, a man fighting for his life in a small, humid room with an endless supply of sweaty, wet spacehoppers inflating around him and crowding him out. As they get bigger and bigger, with their smiley faces and their handlebar ears, he is knifing them so that they deflate with an angry roar of rushing air. But for every one he knifes, another one is inflating. The situation is so nightmarish for the chap, that as he knifes them he releases cries; cries for help; cries of anguish; cries of anger and cries of revenge as he stabs and wails, and wails and stabs at the endless supply of sweaty spacehoppers. Just to top it off, as he struggles, his fingers gripping on marauding spacehoppers produce a squeal all of their own. If you can imagine these roars of deflation accompanied by anguished cries, topped off with the squeals of fingers on wet rubber, then you'll be getting somewhere close to the extraordinary noise we were hearing. And if you can imagine that sound accurately, and imagine that it was all coming from the bottom of just one man, then you will know what we did to him.

NotNorman and I had paid a visit to the kitchens. We donned our chef's uniforms and joined in with the preparations for the meal the pilot enjoyed whilst we refloated the vessel. With a gourmet flourish we augmented the man's dinner with a delicate soupçon, a gourmet dash – OK, we heaped a ladle full – of laxatives onto his meal. This, we felt, would provide a subtle energy to his metabolism that would not only undermine his abilities as a navigator, but would be likely to undermine his bottom as well.

The cries of anguish, the roars of rapid flappy deflation and the somewhat alarming wet rubbery squeals coming from the chartroom toilet seemed to indicate that the spacehoppers were currently on top. However, this man was a professional who was not easily going to give up his position of authority. In between cries, he could be heard trying to shout orders that he presumed we would all be obeying out here on the bridge. Unfortunately, he was drowned out by his own extraordinary background noise, but it was a brave effort on his part, and it added substantially to just how very funny it all was. To hear a helm order interrupted halfway through by a tormented cry and the roar of deflating spacehopper was almost too scary to be bearable.

Despite the distraction the pilot now posed, we did much better without him. The mate and two seacunnies were posted on the fo'c'sle to watch for shallow water and feed back information regarding the best route forwards. They were ready at a moment's notice to drop the anchors again should the ship decide to go sightseeing up the road once more. The pilot did appear on the bridge once or twice, trying to look dignified, but it never lasted long. The perspiration on his brow would be the first clue. Then the sound of running feet and the slam of the chartroom door indicated he was now engaged in hand-to-hand combat with another spacehopper.

Nearly four days after beginning our totally pointless run up to Matadi, we found ourselves back at the Congo estuary, and at last the tension dropped. A dry dock was booked which would give us an unscheduled stop in Athens, Greece whilst they checked the hull properly. The pilot's launch came out and we waved bye-bye and smiled nicely to him. He looked whiter than me as he trudged off with his bottom in tatters to go to the doctor and have his own hull checked.

Chapter 9

Greeks Bearing Cars

Notes on civilisation. The only customers in the restaurant. An angelic vision interprets. Jesus wants me for a hairdo.

So that's why the *Global Princess* found herself under the doctor in a dry dock near Athens. The captain was so pleased with the quality of our bottom shredding up the Congo, that upon our arrival, NotNorman and I were given the whole week off to roll our sleeves up and get to know Greece. In order to raise the quality of our lives, having been overly involved with toilets and bottoms lately, we decided to immerse our minds in the healthy study of empire, and spend some cultural time drinking in a unique and ancient civilisation.

Athens is a remarkable city, and has the kind of history that simply doesn't exist anywhere else on earth. Greece begins at the beginning. Academics sat in *Thinker* positions on every corner, breaking off only for main meals and essentials. Even then they combined eating with pointing at ruins and marvelling historically at one another. They never got bored with it. Morning, noon and night they were out there, pointing and marvelling. Greece is the birthplace of philosophy, democracy, archaeology and that philosopher who invented the stuff about the square-on-the-thingy being equal to the doodah of the other two wotsits. Oh, you know the bloke. Greece showed the world how it should all be done thousands of years ago. However, whilst the rest of the world clawed its way up, toiling across the millennia to scale Greek heights of civilisation, Greece did not simply stand still. Oh, no. It turned round and started galloping back down the course, passing all the other runners in the opposite direction, trying to be the first to complete the full circuit back to economic crisis, social turmoil and civic meltdown. Greece was chauvinistic, bureaucratic, falling down, difficult, anarchic, perverse... and quite simply my favourite country on earth. I absolutely loved it.

Just the bus ride into town encapsulated the paradox. Barely any building was complete. Those that weren't falling down weren't falling down simply because they were only half way up. None of them was finished, but the people moved in anyway, got themselves another Ouzo, invited some friends round and called their house 'ancient'. Athens had genuine ruins, then they built new ruins to keep the place matching. Good thinking.

There is another interesting aspect to Greece that instantly caught our attention. I don't know if they started it, but in Greece they have girls. Oh, Zeus, the girls. If ever there was a definition for a beautiful woman on this earth, she is a Greek woman. If ever you see a girl who stops you in your tracks, makes you drop what you are carrying and require medical assistance to take your next breath, she is a Greek girl. If ever you find yourself changing your life for a girl; abandoning your home, country, job and family in the blind and passionate pursuit of – but hold on. We must not get tied up with Greek girls, if you see what I mean. It is important not to peak too early in the chapter. We shall return to this element of our studies a little later. For the moment, let us try to be strong and continue our analysis of the rise and fall of empire.

The thing I really liked about Greece was the non-conformity. It's not out-and-out anarchy, but people are left to take responsibility for their own lives. It makes for a crazy place to live, and it isn't always a bowl of cherries, but I much preferred it over the 'nanny state' we have these days in the UK. In Greece, if you don't want to take the government's advice and wear a helmet, that's up to you. In Greece, if your children aren't reading and writing by the time they are three, nobody stresses about it; there's plenty of time for all that nonsense, so let the kids be kids, for goodness' sakes. If you're a policeman and you can't be arsed to enforce any traffic laws, well that's fine by everyone else, because everybody else has their own interpretations of which laws make sense to them. In the more capitalist UK and USA, we see laws as a source of revenue: the more laws you can introduce and the more petty they are and the more rigorously they are enforced, the more money the government makes. (Topic for another day, methinks...)

NotNorman and I walked around Athens for a couple of days, taking in the odd temple and monument and museum and, as sensitive and intellectual young men, we were humbled and enriched by the girls we saw in all these places.

After two days we headed to the passenger docks in Pireaus and took a ferry out through the islands. We went to a couple of larger islands; the staggering volcanic heights and panoramas of Santorini (thought to be the site of the original lost city of Atlantis) being a highlight. But we found heaven on earth on a small island called Sifnos, in the Western Cyclades. It was

October – low season – so although the sun was still hot, everything was very quiet and relaxed. It was good to be away from the craziness of Athens, and we felt a million miles from the life of a merchant sailor. It was wonderful.

The Aegean Sea was warm and beautiful. It had no tide, and was clear and calm. The islands were like artists' creations placed on a blue canvas, and the Greeks set the whole thing off with their white houses, ornate churches and timeless ways.

NotNorman and I rented rooms in the main town of Apolonia, from where we walked the length and breadth of Sifnos. The ancient tracks that allowed the locals to move between villages were our pathways, and the people looked at us as if we were utterly crazy as we set off in the late morning sun each day to take a four-hour walk across the island. 'Mad dogs and Englishmen go out in the midday sun,' is the saying, and there we were proving it for them.

On the mountain passes we would encounter weather-beaten farmers with donkeys carrying enormous loads of hay, or wide baskets of olives. They would shout cheerfully at us in Greek (the farmers, not the donkeys), and we would nod and smile back. Sometimes they gave us lemons, tomatoes or pomegranates. It was wonderful. Wherever we went in the world, I had yet to go to a place where the locals didn't know a single word of English. These people didn't know a single word of English. Most people have an opinion on the British. It would be a love or hate thing. The Greeks in Sifnos didn't have an opinion on the British. They had their own lives to lead and didn't give a fig for the British. Actually, they happily gave many figs to the British, but you get my point. Good people. Excellent people.

We climbed up mountainsides, unshaven and sweating heavily in the late summer heat – we must have looked like bandits – then picked our way down the other side of the mountain and visited remote beaches or tiny white churches.

We drank, ate and swam, then set off in the opposite direction to try and walk a different way home. One evening we were returning from a long, long walk, towards the setting sun. We were dropping down from a high pass into the top of Apolonia. We still had some way to go to get back to our rooms, and the sight of a taverna as we entered the outskirts of the town, with a terrific view across the valley to a glorious strawberry ripple sunset, was too much to pass up. We fell gratefully into the seats on the raised balcony, under a canopy of bougainvillea and grape vines, and removed our backpacks and hats. It was a scene of earthly perfection.

A short lady came out. She put her hands on her ample hips and smiled at us. She didn't speak any English, of course, but her words and smile appeared welcoming, and we were able to sort out some cold beers. It was glorious. So glorious, in fact, that we stayed for another. We were the only customers, so the lady was using the lull in trade to feed her family inside the house, emerging only to pick some oregano from the borders of the balcony. So that was why the air was so fragrant. She took the herbs back indoors. We could see the family eating through the open door, and it had a profound effect on us. I looked at NotNorman. He looked at me. We knew what we were thinking and we called for the lady. It didn't take too much in the way of charades before she brought an enormous tray of food out to show us. She pointed at it and said, 'Yo-vetsi. Yo-vetsi!'

It looked like meat in giant rice (which turned out to be lamb in pasta) baked in a fresh tomato sauce. We nodded enthusiastically, and were soon rolling our sleeves up around huge portions of *yovetsi*, along with Greek salad, zingy olives, *mizithra* (a strong, creamy version of feta), and a local red *retzina* wine. The flavours tumbled and rang and burst together in wonderful ways. The sun turned red, and dropped gloriously into the distant Aegean, leaving its colours to bleed across the horizon and give the clouds orange bottoms. NotNorman and Windy were happy, happy boys.

Eventually, we knew we would have to move. It was a shame, and our feet argued strongly the case against, but it had to be. We called the lady and asked her for the bill. She smiled broadly, happy that we were happy, went into the house, came back with the tray of *yovetsi* and began to load our plates up again. We made the international signal for stopping, and signed our names in the sky to get the bill. She was disheartened that we didn't want any more *yovetsi*, but at least we'd made ourselves clear now.

She went back indoors and returned a few seconds later, but no with the bill. With another carafe of *retzina*. We tried to turn it away, but she wouldn't have it and refilled our glasses. We tried all the hand signals we knew for refusing food and wine and requesting a bill – along with some loud schoolboy French, for some reason – but to no avail. We now had plates full of food again and glasses full of wine, and were unable to get our message across, mainly because the lady was regaling us with a continuous tirade of Greek. We got some drachma out and pointed, but this just seemed to frustrate her all the more. In the end, she threw her arms in the air, went indoors and chiselled her husband from his chair. He came out sighing at having been disturbed. I got the feeling he would rather work with donkeys and chickens than holidaymakers. His hands were gnarled from working the land. His face was hard-baked from the sun, and the children ran round his legs as he harangued us with another tirade of pointless Greek and flamboyant hand signals. We stared back blankly. There was a moment of silence before the lady doubled up laughing at her husband, who threw his arms towards us before turning away so the couple could shout at one another for a while. They were quite a double act, although he seemed to be getting genuinely frustrated. He turned back to us and started rattling off in Greek again. The children gabbled and danced around him like pixies. Six goats arrived at a raised fence on one side of the balcony and turned their heads on one side enquiringly. From the way the couple were going at each other, I would have thought they were having a massive argument. I only knew they weren't from looking at the wife, who shook her head at her man with an extraordinary mixture of affection and mirth in her eyes, which betrayed her feeling that their position with us was hopeless. Neighbours came out and started to join in, shouting their opinions from the windows opposite and from doorways up and down the street, but none of them made any more sense than the goats, who were also singing along by now. Notters and I sat bemused in the middle of it all. We were becoming an attraction. Something was definitely amiss. I couldn't figure it out.

In the end the man seemed to have had enough. He threw his hat on the table and marched off up the street, swearing to himself as the kids danced along behind him. The woman indicated that we should wait. She sat us down again, and poured us fresh glasses of wine. NotNorman and I tried to work out what it was they wanted from us, or that we were doing wrong. It was utterly mystifying. We had no choice but to wait and see.

Then we found out.

Back down the track tramped the husband, muttering to himself in between shouted comments and gesticulations to his neighbours. He was followed down the path by his dancing children and a shimmering ring of white light. It was extraordinary. The light was moving behind him, so bright at its centre that I could not looketh upon it. So unearthly was it, that I could not heareth the sounds around me. So compelling was it that I was rendered powerless and could not move. So glorious was it that I could not close my mouth and stop mine dribblethneth.

The chaos surrounding us continued as the husband arrived back on the balcony. The light pulled up beside us, and smiled. A waterfall of red-brown hair framed an achingly beautiful dormouse face and cascaded down around bronzed shoulders. The rest of the world dropped away to nothing around her.

'Hi,' she said, smiling. 'You got a problem?'

'C-c-c-can I touch your hair?' I said.

Fortunately, my words were so crushed by love that they emerged only as a whimper.

'No, we don't have a problem. At least, I hope not, anyway,' said NotNorman in a put-on posh accent, and then he laughed a girly laugh. Good grief. He fancied her. I felt an instant welling of hatred for the man. What made him think he had any chance with a vision like her? He needed shooting. 'I think we could do with some translation though, if you speako da lingo!'

His appalling Greek accent was patronising and not in the least bit funny. In fact, NotNorman had to go. She would never spend her life with me if I was associated with him. I suddenly realised just what a turkey I'd been hanging about with for the last year. Whatever did I see in him? I would have to take over.

'J-j-j-j-ust one stroke of your hair and I'll be happy forever. I won't ever ask anything more of you ever again if you would just let me touch your hair,' I dribbled.

She kept up her smile through my pathetic display, and held out her hand. 'Hiero poli – pleased to meet you.' she purred. 'My name's Hiftyniftyhoshtiboshtiblimmikos.'

Well, it was something unpronounceable and very, very Greek that sounded a bit like that. The point that hit me hard was that NotNorman shook her hand – I mean, he actually touched her. I just about fainted from being so close to such a moving experience. I heard a whining noise emerge from my throat. It was jealousy. I wanted to kill NotNorman.

'Are you Greek?' asked NotNorman, pathetically. 'You look Greek, but you talk like a flaming southerner!' He laughed again at his desperately unfunny joke. I searched the table for a form of cutlery that could see him off. But WonderGirl was equal to both of us so far.

'My family are from round here,' she explained. 'But I live in England. I'm on holiday from college in London at the moment.'

The Greeks around us were getting louder again, all talking at once and running in circles waving their arms around.

'S'cuse me a minute,' she turned to the Greek couple. She breathed in deeply through flared nostrils. Her face morphed alarmingly into that of a frighteningly angry person. Her hair turned into raging flames, her forehead grew and her veins stuck out on her neck and temples. She shook like a rocket about to take off – and then she launched. A massive, guttural tirade of full-tilt Greek emerged from her throat and her body flexed and gesticulated as if she was mid-exorcism. She was like a completely separate human being, throwing her hair about with all the eye-rolling and back-arching and dismissive facial expressions of a native Greek. And the restaurant family came back strongly at her in similar vein. It was as if someone had just fired the gun to begin a break-dancing competition. Have you seen those kids' toys – Transformers? WonderGirl was like one of those, Transforming from 'Vision of Feminine Excellence' into 'Whirling Greek Mad Woman' as if someone had thrown a switch. She then reached the end of her eruption, turned back to us and melted into perfect smouldering beauty mode once more.

'They say you are trying to pay them,' she said, like we were weird or something. She wrinkled up her nose in a way that gripped me by the testicles, twisted, pulled and enslaved me for life.

'Of course we are!' said NotNorman. 'We've had beers, and wine and dinner and everything but they don't seem to want any money!'

He then slapped my hand down sharply behind her back, where I had been hypnotically getting closer and closer to stroking her hair.

'Why should they?' she said. 'This isn't a restaurant. You're insulting them by offering them money.'

'Not… not a restaurant?' said NotNorman. It was kind of appropriate that NotNorman should attend a NotRestaurant, but the truth was dawning. This was someone's house. We were sitting in their front garden. We had dumped ourselves on the balcony of perfect strangers. They had brought us beers and their personal wine, whilst we snapped our fingers for them to bring us their family meal. Good grief, how embarrassing.

'My God! What amazing people!' said NotNorman. 'We didn't realise! Surely, there's some way we can repay them for their hospitality?'

WonderGirl shrugged. It was a delightful, heart-melting shrug. A shrug so perfect it made you desperate to stroke her hair when she wasn't looking.

'Their son is getting married in the church up the hill there next weekend. You could turn up with a gift. They'd be really touched and you'd get invited to the celebration. It'll be some party.'

'Ach, no good,' said NotNorman. 'We'll be gone before then.'

'Well, there's always the paniheiri – a festival – at the same church. We'll all be there dancing and eating. You should come along to that.'

'Perfect! When is it?'

'September thirteenth,' she smiled – it was early October at the moment, so we'd have to wait a year – and she turned to go. The kind of turn to go that tells a man she might leave his line of vision. This would be the type of disaster that would bring Hercules crumbling to his knees. I hadn't considered life's picture continuing without her being in it.

'No!' I shouted. It was the first fully-formed word I'd spoken since she arrived. She turned back with a start and looked at me for my next golden words. I didn't know what to say. I couldn't see, speak or think. I didn't say anything.

WonderGirl put her head on one side and smiled sweetly, a look of sympathy on her face for whatever mental affliction I was labouring under. Then she turned away again. I went to shout again, but I couldn't. She walked back up the path, and her light blinded me again. I couldn't live a normal life without her near me. In fact, I couldn't live a normal life when she *was* near me either, but it was infinitely better than the dark, harrowing existence foisted upon us everywhere else in all the world where she wasn't.

'Phwoar! D'you see the arse on that?' said NotNorman, crudely adjusting his trousers. 'I'd love to give her one, eh?'

You see what I mean? Dark and harrowing. He needed shooting for the good of civilisation.

We got up to leave, bowing and thanking the wonderful people who had fed us. They nodded and waved with big smiles on their faces, and nodded more when we promised them in slow, patronising English (delivered backwards) that we would be back with a gift sometime soon. We wished them luck with their wedding. The unspoken words spoke volumes. They were fine people who were happy to make us feel welcome. They knew we were grateful and they were pleased by that. It was payment enough. The whole thing was magical.

Early the next morning, NotNorman and I were woken by the sound of a car careering off the road. We ran to the window, but there was nothing to be seen. We went back to our beds in time to hear another car career off the road. And another. By our fourth visit to the window we found the culprit. A cockerel in the field opposite was stretching his neck and screeching his damn head off like he couldn't make the bend. So that was why all the Greeks got up so early. And why they eat cockerels.

We were due to leave that evening, on a small boat from Sifnos to Syros, from where we would get a light aircraft to Athens and make it back to the ship with a good ten minutes to spare before she was due to sail for India. We were cutting it fine because we were rather intrigued by the idea of a paniheiri – the church festival WonderGirl had told us about. Some enquiries at the boat ticket office educated us. Every single church on Sifnos had a paniheiri one day in the year. And there was one tonight at Vathi – an idyllic but remote beach on the far side of the island. We could go there for a while and still get back to the port just in time to connect with the boat that would take us to Syros. As long as we left the paniheiri in good time, everything would be fine, wouldn't it..?

That evening, we got to Vathi with all our bags just in time for the sunset. The scene was idyllic. A church with a courtyard on the water's edge was festooned with flags and flowers. Children took it in turns to pull the ropes that swung the bells to call the people to the festival. The walls of the courtyard were also the jetty, and a line of yachts nodded appreciatively over the wall like horses looking for sugar lumps. To either side of the church were long beaches with restaurants and bars spilling onto the sand. The people at the church welcomed us, fed us, played infectious fiddle and bouzouki music and gave us wine. They dragged us up to join in the Greek dancing, and we spun under a huge moon and a canopy of stars in the warm night air. It was glorious. We were entirely seduced by Sifnos; the *retzina*, the food, the dancing, the people, the music and the wonderful ability that the Greek Islands have to make you forget what time it is. We were going to miss our boat if we were not careful, but we were no longer interested in being careful. We were becoming Greek in attitude. We would enjoy ourselves whilst the moment took us, and leave the other stuff to sort itself out in good time. From the first moment we became aware that we should be leaving or we would miss our boat, we knew, deep down, that we had no chance. They grabbed our arms and dragged us back for one more dance; they refilled our glasses and pushed more food into our mouths. I thought, sod it. I'll wait for NotNorman to take responsibility. Why should I be the sensible one all the time? NotNorman didn't seem to care either. We really, genuinely wanted to get back to rejoin the ship, but the way things were going, there was every chance that by the next time we thought about it, fifty perfect years might have slipped past.

I also had something else on my mind. Indeed, I didn't blink once all evening. I made my eyes sore, scouring the faces and the dancers, hoping and hoping... but WonderGirl didn't turn up. As it got later and later, and more likely that she wasn't coming, I began to feel that maybe we should have caught the boat after all. If we missed it, we wouldn't get the light aircraft. And if we missed that, we would be late to Athens. And if we missed Athens then our ship would sail without us and we would be sacked. WonderGirl thought little enough of me as it was, without my becoming an unemployed vagrant on her island.

My hope that she might turn up turned to disappointment, and the boat we were to catch – the boat we simply had to catch – was due to leave, from several miles away, exactly Now.

The depth of trouble we would be in began to hit home. We had nowhere to stay. We would have to pay for flights home, or maybe if we kept our jobs, we'd have to pay to catch up with the ship at the next port... which was Cochin in Southern India. That would kill us financially, and the company would kill us as employees. So when I saw a taxi wending its way down the road towards the church, it was with a certain urgency that I gathered our bags under my arms, chucked NotNorman over my shoulder and struggled across to collar it.

The driver was as old as the Acropolis and as battered as a pilot's arse, but to my eyes, he was our salvation. If the boat was a little late – and most things were in Greece – we might just make it. I dumped all the stuff, did the deal with the driver, then stretched my back and marvelled at how slowly he managed the traditional Greek taxi driver's job of arranging our belongings so the boot wouldn't shut.

We jumped in. I got in the front and tried to implore the man to go quickly. But he was determined to introduce himself.

'Stavros,' he said, holding out his hand.

'Yes, good. Boat? Ferry? Ferry? Boat? Ferryboat? For Syros? Syros – Ferry boat? Syros? Syros? Ferry boat – Syros?'

'Ha, ha, haaaaarr!' he laughed, as if he fully understood just how much we'd missed it by, then waved our worries away with a dismissive tilt of his head. No Greek was ever worried about someone else's problems. They were always philosophical about other people's problems. Eventually, he turned, at long last, to drive the car. Stavros had a broadsheet newspaper spread out on the dashboard and over the steering wheel. I expected he would fold it up to drive, but he didn't. He blew out his copious white moustache, like someone airing a sheet, then carefully adjusted his glasses halfway down his nose so he could read the thing as we trundled along. As the car began to pull away up the hill, I could not believe what I was seeing. For one second in ten he would peer over his glasses at the road, then he would devote the next nine to improving himself in the business section. To help him focus, he sipped coffee from a cup in his right hand for all the world as if he was in a taverna on a Sunday morning. I looked back at NotNorman and we made faces of disbelief at each other. This wasn't safe. The old boy was drinking coffee… and reading the paper… whilst driving the car. I noticed that the crossword was half done and that there was a pen on the dashboard. Surely, he didn't fill it in whilst driving? Well, not yet. He was too busy – now that the car had achieved a suitably lethal speed – trying to organise a cigarette.

He steered with his knee and took the cigarette out of the packet, but dropped the lighter. This valiant man was not to be kept from his nicotine fix, so he finished the article (an article that clearly amused him), then set about retrieving the lighter. He pushed the newspaper back up onto the dashboard, wedged the coffee in next to the handbrake, placed the cigarette on the newspaper next to the pen, dropped his head between his knees and steered with the back of his neck for a while so he could get his head into the seat-well where he found the privacy he desired to give his lighter a stiff talking to. I was terrified. I reached across and furtively steered for a while as he argued with his Zippo between his feet. I didn't want to upset him, but I didn't want the car to fly off the cliff either. Eventually, he resurfaced, showed me his chastised lighter, pulled a face that told me what a rascal he thought it was, then picked up the steering again as if it was the most natural thing on earth. I guess after years of passengers secretly steering whilst you get down amongst the pedals to discipline your belongings, you become convinced that paying attention to the road isn't necessary. He blew out his moustache again to make space for the cigarette and smiled broadly at me as I nodded encouragingly and begged to all the Gods Greece has given that he would stop smiling at me and look at the road.

As the car built up speed along a straight section, Stavros lost his happy demeanour. He frowned and took a couple of hefty veers across to the wrong side of the road and back. With heavy concentration on his face, he allowed the car to drift gently to the left, then wrenched on the wheel to send us veering back to the right again. I couldn't understand what was going on, until I followed his eyes and it dawned on me. The old buzzard had experienced a moment of inspiration regarding four-across and was trying to get his pen to roll back along the dashboard before he forgot it.

The pen rolled, and it was time for him to reorganise his life so he could fill in the crossword. He shoved the coffee cup between his thighs, grabbed the pen with one hand, the lighter with another, the cigarette with another, marked four-across with the finger of another, then, as he took a long, satisfying drag on his ciggie… his two-way radio crackled into life, calling him to answer. He looked at it with profound sadness in his eyes and his moustache drooped at the ends. He was busy enough already without the office calling. I considered chucking my Rubik's Cube into his lap to see how he would get on, but I didn't want any tears. Anyway, he was now a man on a mission: he had to get himself sorted or he wouldn't be able to answer the radio. He started from the top: clenched the coffee cup between his teeth so he could steer with his knees again, looked at the lighter for a while then chucked it back in the seat-well. He then picked up the radio receiver, squeezing it into the crook of his shoulder in such a way that the cigarette in his now outstretched hand was able to set fire to the ornamental doll figure of Jesus-on-the-cross hanging from the rear-view mirror.

He couldn't deal with the blaze immediately because he was trying to secure some business on the radio. The fire spread quickly to Jesus's hair – giving him a curiously devilish appearance – whilst Stavros had become so engrossed in his shouted conversation that he'd forgotten about the pedals completely. His long-forgotten foot was flat down on the floor and the car was accelerating rapidly towards a ramp in the road. As we got faster and faster, and nearer and nearer to the ramp, NotNorman and I held a big-eyes and wailing competition in the smoke, but it didn't put him off. He had read about customer service in the business section, and his loud negotiations on the radio took top priority.

All of a sudden, Stavros stopped and looked at me, one eye down each side of the coffee cup and with clouds of smoke billowing above his head. He went quiet and looked stunned. The radio slid from his shoulder down between the seats. Stavros was frozen in anticipation and possessed by an overwhelming need. A need that meant the crossword, the radio and even the fire could be forgotten. A need that heeded not for the excessive speed at which we were approaching a ramp. A need which eclipsed all others. A need which made his nose twitch and wrinkle and, unfortunately, a need which required the extraction of a handkerchief from his trouser pocket. He abandoned all other activities, and performed a remarkable manoeuvre too death-defying for me to recount. All I can say is that if you know your yoga, it required him to adopt The Crab position in the driver's seat (with a coffee cup over his nose).

When the sneeze came, I thought we would all die. The coffee cup rifled against the ceiling and his worldly goods went to the four winds as he failed to get the handkerchief into position in time. As the car zoomed over the ramp, the shepherd at the roadside and his bewildered goats were treated to the sight of a vehicle leaving the ground and remaining airborne across the divide, apparently through sheer force of nasal expenditure. They also experienced the remarkable noise of a shouted sneeze as it echoed around the hills, and witnessed a dozen sheets of newspaper and a billow of smoke suddenly shooting out through all the windows at the same time. Then the car was gone, and the goats were left looking blankly at each other. There was no evidence of the visitation in their lives, apart from an unfinished crossword floating serenely to the ground around them and a coffee cup with a hole blown out through the bottom rolling round and round in the middle of the road.

When we got to the port, we were too late for the boat by a good twenty minutes, and yet, by some miracle, it was still there. In fact, the boat was in darkness and there was no sign of an imminent departure. NotNorman and I got out of the car and began to unload our bags, but soon the rush abated and we looked at each other. Where were the captain and crew? Where were the other passengers? Stavros looked knowingly and communicated as only he could. He danced a little Greek dance, with surprising grace for an old man.

'*Capitano! Paniheiri? Vathi!*' he said, pointing to the distant lights and carnival sounds along the coast. He then doubled over and laughed long and hard.

I slapped my forehead and realised. To my left, during the last Greek dance I had indulged back at the church, I had recognised someone. He was a happy Greek guy, two along from me, singing proudly. I couldn't recall where I'd seen him before, but I should have noticed not just the drunken, contented smile, but also the captain's hat set at a jaunty angle by a man secure in the knowledge that the last boat would not leave without him… because he had the keys. I had seen him before when we came across to Sifnos on his boat in the first place. All the other passengers for Syros were watching him for their cue to depart and were still indulging themselves happily at the *paniheiri*.

NotNorman felt sure they would all turn up in the next few hours. We sat on our bags and listened to the water lapping against the sleeping boat.

I looked back at Stavros as he walked bow-leggedly towards his cab, trousering the money we'd just given him, but my lasting memory of that moment was not Stavros, or the old cab, or even the horror of the cab ride itself. What caught my eye was the doll of Jesus on the cross, still swinging under the rear-view mirror. Jesus was eerily lit from above by the cabin light. He looked rather bedraggled and undignified, with a plume of smoke still rising from his scorched hair. He was also dripping and splattered with some sort of goo. Mind you, I guess he should count himself lucky that the sneeze put the fire out.

Chapter 10

The Tale of the QuikFit Chessmen

Thoughts on India. Welcome to Surrey. Mindi is popular. Methods for handling talkative girls. Ahmed The Magnificent. The Chess Masters. NotNorman and Windy become generous. Breaking and entering.

Fourteen days and a Suez Canal later, we could be found in Cochin, Southern India. It was a world away from Europe and another breathtakingly beautiful place. It was also a world away from India as far as my preconceptions were concerned. Stories of war over Kashmir, amputee beggars on skateboards and dead bodies in the Hooghly River seem to provide all the impressions I had. Certainly, when I later visited Calcutta, it was more of an experience than a holiday, and yet Southern India is another world altogether. Why don't we carry with us images of Kipling's India, of Mowgli and *The Jungle Book*? Surely, these images are the first ones into our brains as children, so why aren't they dominant thereafter? Why not images of Goa with its Portuguese architecture and the perfect sunsets over unreal beaches? These images are all familiar to us, and yet they do not stick. To see fisherman casting their nets into the Arabian Sea at sunset, children – healthy children – living uncluttered lives as nature surely intended and to enjoy some of the world's most glorious bounty first hand is a privilege, without then adding the fact that nobody comes here. The whole Kerala region was unspoilt by tourism and yet an endless wonder. Particularly as the price of everything was so ridiculously low that I could practically have retired on the $20 I had in my pocket, and lived like a king into the bargain.

Then there was the odd charming blast from another world as we discovered some remnant of the British imperial past, like a Victorian mansion in the jungle. We were told about such a place by the ship's agent, who said there was some sort of event going on to save a colonial pile that dated back to the time of the Raj. It didn't sound that riveting, it was quite a long way away and we didn't see any fun in visiting a stately home. That was until we made our first major cultural discovery. There are thousands and thousands of tiny, black, three-wheeled scooterish taxis – called 'tuk-tuks' – which look a lot like giant ladybirds, and beetle about the streets throughout India. We rented ourselves a tuk-tuk and driver each, and had a gentle trundle out of the city and about ten miles into the jungle. I was very pleased we did; it was wonderful. The bustle and chaos of Cochin city was replaced by dense jungle. The roads got more remote and narrow, until we were beginning to wonder if we would end up in a dark alley having our kidneys removed, when out of nowhere appeared two huge gateposts, each one a statue of a giant lion menacingly awaiting the postman. Yip, the Brits had been here all right. We sped in through the gates and suddenly we were in Surrey. A carriage driveway led to an imposing Victorian mansion made of large blocks of sandy-coloured stone. The whole effect was nothing short of regal. Already on the driveway was a western style coach, from which a number of well-dressed gentlefolk had emerged and were staring up at the building.

A stout, bearded Asian man came bowing and smiling across to us with his hands in prayer and his turbaned head to one side.

'Thank you, thank you for making such an effort to come here. My name is Anup.'

He shook our hands.

'No problem, matey,' said Benny the Dog, taking charge as our representative. 'What's the score, then?'

'We are starting a trust to rescue this magnificent mansion,' said Anup. 'Queen Victoria stayed here in the nineteenth century, and it is the best remaining example of colonial architecture in the whole Kerala region. We want to rebuild it and open it to the public. You can simply make a donation to the charitable appeal, or if you prefer, for more substantial sums, your investment will buy you an ownership share in future returns, which we believe will be appreciable. Come and look around.'

We looked at each other. He thought we were investors! I looked at Benny the Dog and Ffugg. Anup had more chance of getting off with Queen Victoria than wrestling a quid out of these skinflints. I buttoned my $20 carefully into my best secret pocket, and hid in the middle of the gang in preparation for when they shook a tin at us.

Despite the level of disrepair, the house was impressive. The gardens were pretty wild, of course, although their previously landscaped extent was still distinct from the surrounding jungle. From the outside, two-thirds of the building was still in great shape – perfect, even – but one end had collapsed as if the whole building had simply sat down in the style of the lions at the gate, with one end upright and the other on the floor.

Anup took us up a fan of steps, through some grand pillars to the heavily padlocked door where we joined the other investors, including one more special than the rest.

'This is my daughter, Mindi,' said Anup, bowing us towards Miss World. She didn't smile, but bowed her head demurely to one side. I hadn't noticed her in the crowd, so when she came upon me so suddenly like that, I was just about knocked over. She was dressed in somewhat traditional Indian dress, with a vivid gold and red sarong and plenty of bling. Her jet-black hair was long, brushed over one shoulder and down over her breast. Her eyes were huge and brown, and she had such grace and elegance. She was like a princess from a fairy story. As we entered the house, we lads politely let others pass (in order to contrive to be next to Mindi). She looked haughty in that wonderful, untouchable way girls do that just makes you want to try all the harder. We all wanted to be next to her. I tried to get my defence in first.

'Hi,' I said. 'Look, I'm really sorry about my friends here. They are about to be crass and unbearable. Really, I'm not like them at all, so when they start up, could you please not just assume that I…?'

But my words were lost in the desperate clamouring of NotNorman and Benny the Dog as they tried pathetically to get in her good books. She stopped us all with a raised hand.

'So, are you planning on investing in the trust?' she said.

There was a moment's silence as we looked at each other and decided on the right answer.

'Yes! Yes, certainly!'

'Worthy cause…'

'Serious business, worth every penny…'

'Absolutely! Substantial sums…'

She raised her eyebrows at us and swept away into the house.

We all trooped in behind her. I decided to give the poor girl some space and lagged back. I didn't want to get too far back – I wanted to hear what was going on – but I definitely couldn't be dealing with the scrum going on around her legs. Besides, it seemed the only way this girl would ever come near my trousers would be in order to remove the $20 note. I double-checked the buttons and kept space around me at all times.

I turned my attention to the house. The hallway was enormous. The floor was made of huge solid stones in fine condition. They could have been laid yesterday. There were three types of stone: a slatey white, a rusty red and a coal black. They were laid in a diagonal pattern, giving the appearance of a chess board, and achieved an odd, three-dimensional optical illusion if you stared at them for too long. The ceiling was a mile away, and a great curving staircase seemed to go on forever up towards it. Although everything that could be removed in terms of fixtures and fittings was long since gone, it was still very impressive and well worth preserving as far as my untrained eye could see.

We toured the reception rooms, the library and the safe bits of the upstairs. It was superb. (One door, at the west end of the upstairs, opened on to a 30-foot drop, but we'll let them off the odd scare like that.) I spent my entire time trying to get into Mindi's eye-line. I know it's pathetic, and that there's more to life, but I couldn't help myself. I nodded sagely at Anup's commentary every time I thought she was looking at me, as if I was mentally calculating exactly how much of my fortune I would be investing in the trust fund. I didn't honestly want to break the $20 at all, but if it might provide access to Mindi I would definitely consider it. She was an exceptional woman; I was just wishing I had some smaller change.

Soon enough, I had my strategy in place. I spotted a chap who genuinely seemed to know what he was doing – clearly an architect or something. I followed a safe distance behind him, and did whatever he did: holding my thumb up and staring at it with one eye shut; knocking on the walls and listening intently for… for… someone from 1872 to knock back; wincing and shaking my head as if deeply unhappy about some vital structural implication that nobody else had noticed. It was great, and I felt sure Mindi would eventually ask me about my background in civil engineering. By the time we were all outside again I was quite an expert. I watched my man carefully, then put my hands on my hips, tutted and sucked my teeth as I stared up at the roof line and the intricate (and apparently unique) leadwork. Having read the structural evidence carefully, I looked round. Giewy was standing with his hands on his hips, staring up at the roof line and leadwork, tutting and sucking his teeth as if he knew what he was doing. Benny the Dog was doing the same. So was NotNorman. It was pathetic. Giewy was even adding his own touches – making a square with his fingers to look through with one eye and with his tongue hanging out. Oh, right. Seriously professional you must be. Did he really think he was fooling anyone? Moron.

I had been so drawn into these games that I didn't realise that the others – including Mindi – were getting back on the coach. I saw NotNorman take her hand and kiss it gently. I heard him say: 'I'll see you later, then,' and she nodded her assent before wafting magnificently into the coach. He'd only gone and landed her. Jeeez. I hated it when NotNorman got a girlfriend. He would go all pathetic and talk about her all the time. It would be 'Mindi this' and 'Mindi that'; 'I did this to her' and 'she did that to me' and 'I went all like this when I stroked her hair'. Unbearable. And that was when he wasn't off somewhere with her and completely ignoring me, which he did every time he got a girlfriend – I would be left on my own for days at a time, and when I did see him it would only be so he could quiz me about what I thought of her and how great she was. It was pathetic. And boring. And rubbish. And I didn't care, anyway.

He came trotting over like a puppy that just dug up a bone.

'Did you see her!' he sang through a triumphant smile. 'Did you, eh? I got her number!'

None of us answered him. We all carried on looking intently at the house. It was important to make the most of the time we had here. It was a special and fascinating place.

'I told her I was on the team that designed Kensington Palace. Ha! She believed me! We're going out later!'

'You know what?' I said to Giewy. 'I think those architraves are renaissance, you know?'

'Giew,' said Giewy, nodding sagely in agreement.

'I mean, you gotta admit, she's a seriously good-looking woman, right?'

'I'll tell you what,' said Benny the Dog as we stared at the house. 'Those rooms which have collapsed, yeah?' he waved his arms at the reclined end of the house. 'They have more rooms running underneath them. Not cellars – more like normal rooms. I found the steps down. You can't get in because of the collapse, but I bet the rooms are still there. 'Cos they're underground, they might not have been damaged.'

'Of course they've collapsed,' I said. 'Just look at them!'

'Just look at them – exactly,' said Benny the Dog. 'The collapse is in a big pile, right? Like it's landed on solid ground.'

'I mean, can you imagine getting your hands on that lot? Man, I think she's up for it!'

'If the lower rooms had collapsed then the fallen part of the building would have gone down into the hole. It wouldn't be piled up like that.'

'So what?' said Giewy, screwing up his face like he always did when asking a question.

'You're all just jealous 'cos she's going out with me. I know what's going on.'

'So the whole house has been stripped of all its valuables as far as we've seen,' replied Benny the Dog, 'but they won't have got to those rooms. Stands to reason. The rooms were fine when the collapse happened, and if they'd been entered since then there would be an entry point now. Which there isn't. I bet there's still stuff in them. I'm gonna get some gear up here and find a way in. You wanna play?'

Being an engineer, he understood the way the house was put together, and he had access to the kind of destructive machinery he needed to gain an entrance. It sounded doubtful but exciting. We all agreed that we would help him in any way we could, then we chased off to catch up with Notters, who had stomped off back up to the main road on his own in a huff. I was secretly pleased.

We got a proper taxi this time, and once again a taxi driver surpassed himself in the industry's globally-agreed strategy to frighten the crap out of us. It was dark as we drove back to the city, and the driver turned his lights off whilst driving along – presumably to save on bulbs – for as long as he thought he could remember what the road looked like. I mean, seriously. It was pitch black, but he would memorise the road ahead, then switch off his lights and go as far as he could before turning them back on again. I wanted to ask him if he had an Uncle Stavros on the Greek island of Sifnos, but I was too busy screaming to get the words out. And what made this game doubly exciting was that all the other drivers were doing it too. They couldn't see each other until one or other decided to hang the expense and turn a light on. It was unbelievable. I was pleased to be sitting behind Ffugg, who was in the front. He looked like an airbag with a face, so he might prove useful after all.

The following lunchtime on the ship, I arrived in the bar to be met by a wonderful sight. Mindi had answered NotNorman's invitation, and she had turned up with a couple of friends. Notters was full of himself.

'Ahhaaa, Windy! Good to see you! Now, you've met Mindi, haven't you…?' he gave me long enough to nod an acknowledgement before steering me carefully past, 'And this is Serena, and this is Bhupinda.'

He held me firmly by the shoulders as if to say that I was now in my required position. I shook hands graciously and offered to get some more drinks in. NotNorman and Benny the Dog took up the offer most ungraciously, and sent me off to get them a beer each. I didn't want to get them a drink. I wanted to get them a pilot's dose of laxative so they would leave me in peace with the glorious Mindi. The other girls looked fine too, as proven by the circle of drooling gentlemen surrounding them, but there was only one for me, and that was the one NotNorman was patrolling carefully. Don't for goodness' sakes tell NotNorman I told you this, but Mindi was a genuinely beautiful woman, and becoming more of a knockout every time I saw her. I saw right through NotNorman's plans. He had brought a couple of other girlies along in order to throw me and Benny the Dog off the trail of Mindi, but I wasn't going to fall for that. I looked at him. All big smiles and perfect politeness and a pretend southern accent. Ha! All his northern pride and boorish remarks about southerners went right out of the window now that he wanted to appear intellectual! How insincere was that? How could she fall for it?

Mindi's attention was being dominated by NotMoron and Benny the Tit, so I sat casually nearby and tried to muscle my way into their conversation. Mindi laughed at my jokes, but NotNorman deliberately held his laughter back. He made snide comments through clenched teeth in response. However, the real problem was that I was getting side-tracked by Bhupinda. She had locked on to me when I handed her a drink. I didn't want her attention, and kept trying to see past her to stay involved with Mindi's gang.

I tried to be polite. I pretended to listen to Bhupinda, smiling and nodding as if I was interested whilst actually concentrating hard on keeping up with the others. But every time I made a joke and joined us back into the *interesting* conversation behind her, Bhupinda just saw it as an opportunity to breathe in, then moved across in front of me again and started on and on about some bloke she knew once who had a boat and a sister and a cat and how nothing ever happened but she could still talk continuously about it without hesitation, repetition or deviation and the only interesting point was that these people and their cat were added to an enormous list of people she had known who had moved house without telling her where they'd gone and didn't you just hate it that people did that all the time? I was struck with a similar emotion and began to think she must be sponsored by the guild of removal van companies. It was incredible. Each time she started talking, it quickly became clear that she didn't intend to stop any time soon. NotNorman's plan was working. I was becoming removed from the Mindifest, and was being worn down by this relentless, moon-faced talking machine that moved in front of me every time I tried to get around it.

For a while, I did force a smile and kept at least a tiny bit of polite nodding and eye contact going with Bhupinda but, good grief, she went on. Blah, blah, blah. Drone, drone, drone. Before long, the only words I could hear during her conversation were the ones in my own head, screaming inside, imploring her from behind my clenched smile to 'SHUT UUUPP! SHUT UUUUUP! GO AWAY! NAFF OOFFFFF! LEAVE ME ALONE! SHUT UUUUUUUUUP!'

I kept on clapping my hands together and saying, 'anyway I really must mingle,' or 'well, lovely talking, but I really need the loo', or 'good Lord, look at the time! I really have to throw myself out of this porthole', but there was no let up in the verbal onslaught. I started to hallucinate. Her big round face got bigger and rounder as it kept droning on and on and ooooon. Soon she had six faces, all circling in front of me and talking all at once like some hideous visitation from a 1970s pop video. She didn't even breathe, not once. I wasn't even pretending to listen politely anymore. There was no point. I ruffled her hair up. No change. I pressed her nose in and made a honking sound like a 1940s car horn. She kept talking. I squeezed her mouth together from the sides. Her eyes bugged out but the gabble just kept on coming. I pushed her cheeks right into each other in front of her teeth. It gave her a surprised look and distorted whatever it was she was batting on about, but she just kept on and on and on and on and on and on regardless. I beat her to death with a chair but there was no change in the output from the mutilated corpse on the deck. It was beyond reasonable limits.

I was in the throes of trying to slit my own throat with a beer mat – she had apparently witnessed many tragic suicides in her time as a conversationalist – when there was a bit of a row outside the bar. The door crashed open and an Asian gentleman in a top hat and tails, carrying a fold-up table, a magic wand and a large tray, came falling in, followed hot-foot by the seacunnie who had been trying to stop him.

'He says he invited, Sa'ab. Not true, eh?' cried the seacunnie. It wasn't true, but that wasn't going to stop me. Anything to get away from Bhupinda.

'Yes, yes! He's with me! Come in, come in!' I chanted magnanimously, and waved the seacunnie away. 'Do you want a girl to talk at? I mean, to?'

The visitor, who had been expecting a physical expulsion, found he had a foothold. He straightened his jacket and stood upright and dignified.

'I,' he announced, bowing low, 'am Ahmed the Magnificent.' And he certainly was. He was around 4-feet tall, with a silver beard that almost reached the floor at the front and coat tails which nearly reached the floor at the back. He wore a scraggy white shirt with a bow tie and matching bow-legs, and he had a large jug and an intriguing looking plastic tray with a lid. 'I am here to perform – my performance!'

'Errr… what kind of performance is that?' asked Benny the Dog with suspicion. Given some of the things he had seen around the world, he perhaps thought it best to ask, particularly with ladies present.

'It is a Magnificent show,' said Ahmed, patting the lid of his tray with a reassuring smile. 'You won't have seen anything like it.'

Exactly the problem, I thought, but now we at least had a focus of attention that was not Bhupinda's life story or our battle over Mindi. Benny the Dog asked again what the show was about, and Ahmed replied that if we paid up for the show, we could see what it was all about, couldn't we? An argument ensued concerning whether we should allow him to proceed. I wanted the focus to remain away from Bhupinda and NotNorman, so I cut through the crap. I ran to my cabin, got some money and paid the man his price. I mean, the guy was obviously some sort of magician. He might be a crap magician, but even a crap magician couldn't do any harm, could he?

In my defence, as the sponsor of this event, the first minute and a half couldn't have gone better. Ahmed the Magnificent indulged a theatrical preamble, talking with wide-eyes about the mystical East and the intriguing and inexplicable things that happen when in the presence of magic like his. As he spoke, he removed his jacket, erected the fold-up table and placed the tray carefully on the top. I'm not sure what could be mystical and inexplicable – or even Eastern – about a tupperware tray, but we made ourselves comfortable with our beers, and began heckling from the stalls. I felt pleased with the rise in excitement. I looked around at our lady guests. They were enjoying themselves so far, and I was happy to take the credit. Ahmed the Magnificent then flexed his fingers. The tension rose as he paused dramatically, hovering over the tray... he lifted the lid... and the chaos commenced.

The next few minutes were a bit of a blur, but as far as I remember it went something like this. Inside the tray were half a dozen snakes writhing about in two inches of water. They weren't huge, but they were certainly agitated, bright yellow and looked well worth avoiding. The lid-lifting seemed to be the starting gun for them to begin a race, and they quickly set about legging it over the sides of the tray, their black, beady eyes and flicking tongues betraying their desire to find someone to blame for their imprisonment. I had heard stories of snakes swallowing whole cows, and for an instant I wondered if we would still be able to hear Bhupinda talking from inside a snake. Such happy thoughts were soon overwhelmed by my own desire to avoid a personal encounter with one of these most fearsome of reptiles, over which Ahmed the Magnificent was demonstrating a remarkable lack of control. He had a little crooked stick with which he continuously returned these murderous beasts to the tray each time they made a break for it, but there were lots of them, they were emerging from the container from all sides and he was concentrating more on the spoken part of his act than he was on snake herding. In short, he was losing the battle. I wanted him to forget the spoken part of his act and get the lid back on, and I soon became anxious enough to interrupt his performance.

'Erm, Ahmed, old friend. You couldn't just, erm, pop those chaps back in the old pot there, could you? Maybe do a few card tricks or something? You see, these snakes...'

'Eeeeeeeeeeeeeeek!'

I was interrupted by a corporate scream as one of the snakes made it out of Ahmed's range and headed sou'-west at full ahead. As Ahmed chased it, the others were quick to identify opportunities for a new life that now lay in the nor'-east. They landed noisily on the floor and set off. Things were now officially out of control, and these were not shy or nervous snakes. They did not suffer from stage fright, but seemed keen to play a positive part in the performance. So, whilst the rest of us tried to cling to the ceiling, the snakes lapped the bar and The Magnificent Ahmed busied himself with his act, returning the snakes to the tray with his little crooked stick each time one completed a circuit and came in range.

The distraction of the snakes had led to a certain lack of focus on what Ahmed the Magnificent was saying, so it was something of a surprise to me when he suddenly grabbed a snake, held it up in the air, its head in one hand and body in the other.

'And now... Ahmed the Magnificent... will eat... this... snake alive!' he announced proudly.

The ladies all screamed in unison (OK, OK, I might have let out a small one myself) and a good deal of verbal effort was made to discourage him. But we were not in strong positions to do much about it. Reading from left to right: Benny the Dog was sitting on top of the television with his feet drawn up; the girls were clinging to each other in a line on the back of the sofa; I was standing in the sink behind the bar and had armed myself with a washing-up brush; and NotNorman – where was NotNorman? – Ah! There he was! Clinging octopus-like to Bhupinda's head as she stood on the back of the sofa. I couldn't help but notice that Bhupinda was telling NotNorman about how she met some bloke with a snake once, still managing to squeeze the words out despite NotNorman's arms and legs circling her face. From these vantage points, we tried our hardest to discourage Ahmed the Magnificent as he concertinaed the snake up so its tail was squashed up behind its head, then, to roars of disapproval from all present, he pushed it into his mouth.

As the concertina'd body opened up, the snake visibly slid down his throat until finally, and to passionate condemnation from all present, the tail disappeared. He opened his arms wide to accept his applause, and opened his mouth wide to show us there were no snakes hiding under his tongue or curled up in the rotting cavities of his teeth. But we knew that already. One look at his rolling, pulsating stomach told us where it had gone.

He then picked up another snake.

We all renewed our shouts for him to stop. He concertinaed up the new candidate and adopted the position. Then, recognising the levels of disapproval, told us that, for a small additional fee, he would *not* eat snakes – he would pack up and leave. We agreed frantically to paying him to go away, but we were in the ship's bar. We didn't have any money on us, only ever signing for items taken from the bar. I had been to my cabin to fetch his price the first time round, and we would have to go again to fetch some more.

We tried to explain to the chap that we could get him some more money if he could just give us a clear path to the door and a couple of minutes. But we were too late. Gulp. Slither. Schloop! Another snake snack took its place in Ahmed's intestines. His stomach writhed around and he looked to be in some discomfort as he urged us to produce more cash… and set up a third snake for consumption. When we didn't produce the required money in time… Gulp! Another snake joined his mates inside The Magnificent Belly. At this moment, the chief engineer entered the bar. He was a huge, Northern man who wasn't scared of anything. He was eight feet square, without a single hair on his entire body, but despite his size he had a high voice like Sybil Fawlty.

'Awww, bloody he-eelll,' he sang, irritated that there was no peace to be found in the bar and that he now had another job to do. He looked at me standing in the washing up bowl, then at the damsels in distress, added two and two, then collared Ahmed and dragged him bodily from the room. He then put his head back into the bar and pointed first at me, then at Notters.

'You, and you. Pack up them snakes and follow me. Now!'

Fortunately, three of the snakes were already eaten. One was in Ahmed's hands and the other two were in the tray, so we were able to slam the lid on before we actually had to handle any snakes. Even so, Mindi was shouting abuse at NotNorman, the like of which you would not expect from a lady of good breeding. It seemed, from what I gathered before we left the bar in something of a rush, that he had omitted to prepare her for the presence of snakes and snake digestion artistes in the bar. Man, she was mad! I had the strangest feeling that things might have swung away from NotNorman in the battle for her affections, and try as I might, I didn't seem able to feel sorry for the man.

Outside, Chiefy organised us into a team: I carried the jug of water; Giewy carried the tray of snakes, NotNorman carried the fold-up table, and Chiefy carried Ahmed by the scruff of his neck and booted him Magnificently up the bottom every other step of the way to the port gates. He was deposited remarkably gently at the road – I think deep down it's hard not to find some respect for a man who earns his living getting his arse kicked the length of the harbour with live snakes in his belly.

'And make sure he doesn't come back!' yelled Chiefy, as he stomped off back towards the ship.

NotNorman and I stood and watched Ahmed the Magnificent get himself together. He drank the entire jug of water – must have been a couple of litres – and then, with a noise like a passing 650 Honda, threw up the snakes back into the tray. I can't say if they were happy or not – snakes don't tend to betray their emotions with facial expression – but they were alive and well, and definitely had something unusual to discuss with the family back in the tray. Ahmed picked up his equipment and headed off. He was my precious $20 richer, and had another $20 in his line of sight in the shape of the Scandinavian container ship next along in the dock. I wondered how many ships would see his performance in a day. What a life. Maybe one day I would see him on *Opportunity Knocks*.

I turned to go back to the ship, but NotNorman seemed reluctant.

'Shall we go up the road?' he said a little sheepishly. 'I, ahem, fancy a bit of a walk, don't you?'

'What? But the girls – Mindi. I wouldn't leave her alone with those other sharks if I were you.'

'Yeah, well. I'd rather let things calm down a bit. Let's just go round the block and get some air, eh?'

We set off for a circuit. I was buoyed by this. In the bar it had seemed that the race was over. Now, thanks to Ahmed the Magnificent, things looked much better for my prospects. In the race to win Mindi's affections I appeared to be arriving strongly on the stand side.

'Ah well, can't be helped,' I said, clapping NotNorman matily on the back. 'You're right. Let's go get a beer.'

I knew that I would be able to find Mindi's phone number in NotNorman's cabin, and felt I would have a pretty good chance of talking her into an evening out if I chose the subject of chivalry and the appropriate manner in which ladies of high quality should be treated.

'Don't think you can get your hands on her,' said NotNorman, reading my thoughts. He sounded bitter and twisted. No humility, some people. 'I'm not finished yet. Anyway, she thinks you're an assmunch.'

A what? Never mind. Stick to the subject, Windy. Don't let him throw you with odd abuse.

'Notters, Notters, Notters,' I said, calmly. 'You are the principal, errr, donkey chewer in the neighbourhood, and you've proved it. Now give the poor girl a break and make way. It's only fair.'

We argued about what was right and what was wrong for Mindi in language and tones that were somewhat presumptuous about her plans for her own future, and definitely not the way two good friends should speak to one another. To be honest, NotNorman was beginning to get right on my wick. Why couldn't he back off when he should? He didn't own Mindi. What was his problem? I wanted to give him a piece of my mind. In fact, I would go further. I wanted to teach him a lesson and take him down a peg or two in the good old traditional fashion established by the Marquis of Queensbury. However, Notters was bigger than me. I needed an opportunity to get ahead in the fight. In my experience, if you can clock someone a tasty one round the back of the head with a shovel before declaring your intention to fight them, it tends to give you the required edge. I'd been planning such an approach towards Ffugg for some time. Now I felt a strong desire to give NotNorman the same treatment. However, unless we stumbled across a shovel leaning by the roadside, nothing further in the line of positive action could be taken. We walked in studied silence.

We were crossing a street and I was pondering my predicament, when we were distracted from our mutual loathing by an unusual sight. A line of Indians were sitting respectfully behind tyres laid flat on their sides all along the roadside. They knelt like mystical devotees of the Michelin Man, genuflecting at the sacred symbol of the Great and Inflatable. It was strange. Why would anyone worship tyres? I know there are some strange cults in India, with people making lots of money by starting religions based on fairly flimsy spiritual grounding, but surely someone wasn't making a profit from the saintly qualities of discarded car parts, were they?

We changed direction to investigate further and, as we got closer, I could see that in the centre of every tyre nestled a chess board. So that was it. For a small fee, the guy would take you on!

'Oooo! Notters, look at this! I shouldn't boast, you know, but I'm really rather good at chess.'

'Hate the game,' he said. 'Takes hours and then the oldest bloke wins. I'd rather eat pants.'

'Oh, really? Well, that says a lot about you then, doesn't it? There's no luck involved in chess. It's analogous to the human condition. If you can play chess, you can play Life. Great game.'

'Tell you what,' he said, looking me in the eye. 'If you can beat one of these guys, I'll give you a clear run on Mindi. All yours. What do you reckon?'

'What? You'd stand aside?'

'Yip, I'll stand aside and let you make a fool of yourself – if you can beat one of these guys.'

This was a great plan. It would allow me to get close to Mindi, and it would allow NotNorman a climb-down so he wouldn't have to admit that he was rejected by Mindi and beaten by me. Excellent.

'Maybe I should book a hotel. You know – just in case, eh? What do you think?'

'I think you're a nob.'

'Did you just call me a knob?'

'No. A nob.'

'Oh, right. Nob. I thought you said knob.'

'Nob. I said you're a nob.'

'Ah. With you. Nob. You'll still be friendly when I'm out and about with her, won't you? You can be grown-up about this, can't you?'

'I'll try. Let's see you do one of these blokes first shall we? Who do you fancy?'

Looking down the line, I can't say I fancied any of them exactly. Not in any sense of the word that I could sanction, anyway. They were a fairly rag-tag bunch, although I doubt there's a great hourly rate to be made from playing chess in the street. They mostly wore only loin cloths, and looked skinny and under-nourished. Even so, I chose the sickest-looking one I could find – he had a sunken chest, legs like a budgerigar and was wearing a sling that ran round the top of his head and under his jaw. Toothache. That should slow him down a bit. My entry fee might help him to buy some root work. As I approached, his attempt at a smile was nothing short of heroic.

I settled down opposite him, and NotNorman sat beside us with a broad smirk that I very, very badly wanted to see shovelled off his face. I was all ready for the off when my opponent made an unusual opening move – one that I had rarely encountered before: he began to wail as if the drilling was going ahead without an anaesthetic. Two thoughts immediately raced into my mind: either I hadn't paid a satisfactory amount up front or else he was sitting on a set of rapidly deflating bagpipes under his loincloth. In fact, it was neither of these. It was an opening ceremony of some sort, which we would have to sit through before we could get under way. He picked up what looked like a shoelace from amongst his nappy somewhere and made patterns in the air, howled at the moon, then touched his forehead to the ground in between his crossed legs. He then sat quietly in front of me with his eyes shut. I thought it must be over and was just about to offer him white or black when he opened his eyes and mouth as wide as they would go, screamed massively again and set off round the shoelace and howling circuit once more. After a dozen or so rounds of this, my ears were ringing, but he was ready and we were off.

The first few moves went without drama, but I could see a decent battle might evolve from his opening gambit. He certainly wasn't going to be a pushover. A couple of passers-by had answered the call during the shoelace and singing routine and had stopped to watch. Now we got going in earnest, a few more were looking on. I smiled at them as they looked over NotNorman's shoulder and became absorbed. After half-a-dozen moves each, a few more had gathered on the other side. I became conscious that the game was quickly becoming a spectacle. I was used to playing chess in a room with one other person. If there were more people in the room, it was because they were also playing chess. This crowd of onlookers was not my idea of how it should be done at all, and it was beginning to affect my game. It wasn't the fact that people were watching, more the way they felt entirely comfortable to make comment and point and tut at my moves. It undermined my natural game. As the contest took shape, the numbers built up, but they were not quiet and respectful, as a chess crowd should be. They were opinionated and unhelpful. Before long, people were shoving each other and offering me loud and unwanted advice, then arguing with each other about the moves I made. It became increasingly difficult to concentrate. Each of my moves was met with a comprehensive range of strident criticism from a grandstand of apparent experts. Sometimes I could hardly see the board for pointing fingers. I couldn't understand the language in which my tactics were being pulled to pieces, but they left me in no doubt that they could see disastrous developments looming that I patently could not see. It was disconcerting to the point that I didn't want to make a move at all. I tried to stay in the zone and make sure of my moves. But the longer I took, the more the tension built in the crowd. My opponent seemed unruffled. He found no trouble in focussing on his own moves, and then on my turn he would take the opportunity to harangue back at his critics in high pitched Malayalam. It wasn't fair.

Soon the attention drew the other chess-hustlers round. They abandoned their tyres and put bookies' hats on, and the crowd became even rowdier once a financial interest was established. Not only that, it seemed someone had started a new business bussing opinionated grand masters in from the suburbs. They haggled with the bookies, exchanged impassioned views with each other and money changed hands across the board after every single move. Before long, there were no other matches going on anywhere in the street. Just ours, and I felt the spiky tingle of a cold sweat up and down my back.

Every time someone put money on the game, they would pat me or my opponent on the shoulder to show how confident they were in entrusting their investment with us, and take up position behind their champion. How was one supposed to play chess under these conditions? Gradually, a group of shareholders gathered in support behind me, and another, somewhat larger group, built up behind budgie legs. As we tried to play our game, the two sets of supporters remonstrated with each other across the cauldron in which we sat.

I began to feel distinctly warm around the collar. Given a choice at that moment, mine would have been for Mindi to go stuff herself. There were easier ways to get a girlfriend, and I just wanted out. But it wasn't just about Mindi anymore. Lots of people were going to be angry with me if I lost the match and their money along with it. I couldn't just walk away now, it would be – wait a minute. Suddenly, out of absolutely nowhere, I noticed in front of me – Salvation. It was Salvation in a form I hadn't really considered, but there it was, beaming like a shaft of gold across this scene of misery. Deliverance, in the form of what we chess experts call a 'Good Move'. Oh my goodness, here was my road to glory. I even glimpsed the possibility that I might win. Now, that would change everything! That would be fantastic! I took a deep breath and milked the moment. I knew this would go over big with the gallery. I lifted my hand. The grandstand drew breath. With the flourish of a chess master, I sneaked my Queen onto his back row, bagging his castle on the way in. Geddin, you beauteee!

There was a brief and breathless silence as the implications were absorbed. Then the shouts went up and the place went berserk. It was like the dealer floor of the Bombay Stock Exchange. Massive amounts of money changed hands, torn up betting slips filled the air like confetti and a great tide of fund managers wrote off their last quarter's portfolio. With derisive shouts and hand gestures, they abandoned their former hero and made the journey across the arena to come and sit behind me. I smiled happily. I had united a divided people who were now shaking hands and welcoming each other home with visible relief as they stacked up in rows behind Baboulene: the People's Champion. These guys knew their chess. They knew that there is no luck involved. It is a simple fact that the best man always wins. You see, some people might find this kind of situation hard to deal with, but we Baboulenes are made of steel. Pressure is what we thrive on. Mr Toothache sat looking silly, with one or two wimps shaking pennilessly behind him, knowing they were about to lose their shirts.

Then he moved out his knight, pinning me on to the back row and looking ever so likely to get my queen. It had been a trap. He had sacrificed his castle, knowing that he would get my queen in return, and I'd fallen for it. There was a sharp intake of breath from my side of town, followed by a moment of deathly silence as people realised the disastrous accounting error they had made. They looked at each other for a second, then the world exploded into life again as the shareholders in Me Ltd threw their hands in the air, gathered their stuff, and writing off their losses as they went, made their way, quick as they could, back round to him again. I sat in the wilderness, looking across at a sea of wide eyes stacked ten high behind my opponent on the other side of the tyre, all staring at me in disbelief that a man so criminally lacking in chess skills was allowed to remain at large in the neighbourhood.

The game was hotting up. I attacked his king to prevent him taking my queen, and he countered with a skewer against my castle. This kept my queen vulnerable, but simultaneously let me know that he would pick off my other pieces if I tried to cling on to my queen. The crowd was blocking the street now, and the noise following each move was deafening. Cars were beeping, people were shouting, and our game was causing gridlock all the way up to the Kottayam Road. Tensions were rising. As I considered my position, people leant over, shouting for all they were worth directly into my face and pointing desperately at the pieces they felt required attention. It was intimidating to say the least. Everyone on earth was an expert on chess all of a sudden, but I couldn't understand what any of them was saying. What I did know was that whatever move I made would upset a large number of cash-strapped people. I would be murdered tonight with what the Hindi call 'dracpe' (Dunlop-Retread-and-Chess-Piece Enema), and there would be a run on the bank tomorrow. Things were becoming difficult.

I had to lose my queen – there was no choice – but I wanted to get what I could from the loss. I also needed to assess how much damage he could do towards my king if I tried to cling on to my queen any longer, but I couldn't concentrate for long enough to see more than a couple of moves ahead. It was impossible to maintain a thread of thought, and the longer it took for me to decide what to do, the steadily more ugly the gambling public became. The noise became deafening until the moment when I lifted my hand to make a move. The crowd held its breath and went silent as my hand hovered over the board. The silence washed back through the crowd, over the road, and a swish of a whisper came back like an echo as the wider world and the global television audience received the news that I was about to move something. Then I changed my mind and put my hand back in my lap. Everyone returned to their arguments; poking each other's lapels and throwing each others' hats up on to the rooftops. Until I lifted my hand again – held breath and silence once more.

In the end, I had to move something. I knew it would be controversial, and I knew I hadn't thought it through as I would have liked to have done, but the longer I did nothing, the closer to a corporate cardiac the mob became. I made my move, then adopted crash positions. There was the traditional silence as the onlookers digested the implications. Then off they went their different ways, throwing their arms about, tearing up betting slips and prostrating themselves in front of the traffic. There was a delay as the word was passed across the road concerning what move I had made, then a distant wailing echoed out across the land.

I don't know if you have ever been threatened with physical violence during a chess match, but it is not a nice feeling. I could see a goodish number of fairly unsavoury characters were not pleased that I appeared to be losing. I felt under enormous pressure, but there was nothing I could do about it. The fact was, I *was* losing. I could probably delay things a fair time, but I didn't think I could stand the pressure any more. I wanted it over with and I wanted to be out of there.

'Oi! I've been looking for you!'

These words, delivered at sergeant-majorly volumes from my left, caused everyone to stop their arguing and look round. There, looming over NotNorman's head, stood Mindi. She had a face like thunder and was carrying the array of gifts NotNorman had given her that morning.

'You lie to me about charitable donations. You lie to me about conservation. You lie to me about who you are. You nearly get me KILLED by snakes, and then – THEN – you sod off and leave me alone on a CARGO SHIP. Well you can shove THESE flowers and THESE chocolates where the sun don't shine, and I HOPE – YOU – ROT – IN HELL!'

To give her words appropriate emphasis, every word in capitals above was accompanied by Mindi whapping NotNorman round the ears with a bunch of flowers or boxing him on the head with chocolates. The word 'HELL' saw her raise the ragged remains of the entire symphony of box, chocolates and flowers above her head, leap skywards – her face rivened by fury – then bring the lot down on his head like McEnroe warming up a new racket. The crowd stood in horror as soft centres and battered blooms rained around NotNorman. They called out to Mindi to think again; they tried to explain to her that the path of true love is rarely smooth; they implored her not to be so hasty and they moved to stop her. But it was too late. She had already spun on her heel and stormed off in the classic style of a woman scorned. I looked on the scene and could not help a smile from crossing my face.

Now you may think me a little cruel in revelling in the pain NotNorman was forced so publicly to endure. Maybe you think that even the onerous code upon me as an honest chronicler is no excuse for these levels of sordid detail. Perhaps you are even now reconsidering your views on the nature of the Baboulene you have grown to love so much. Well, keep calm. Stick with the programme. You see, the detail of NotNorman's suffering is essential to the story, and my pleasure was not at his ill-fortune (well, not only that).

Statisticians tell us that somewhere in the world, every minute of every day, a man is being whapped with flowers, pelted with chocolates and – if he isn't lively enough to see the way things are progressing in his love life and get out of there – having his face lit up with a frying pan. When the original chess masters thought the game up, they neglected to cover this area. They didn't take into account the admirable bowling arm that suddenly comes available to a humiliated woman.

The upshot of their short-sightedness is that our bishops and castles, when under attack from a Cadbury's Love Selection coming left arm over the wicket six at a time, tend to skittle off the chessboard and get lost under the rim, or lose themselves in the space where the inner tube goes. Chess pieces are so adorable like that.

So the crowd, in calling for Mindi to take a wider view, were not honestly interested in the fortunes of her love life. They were concerned for their sporting investments. She didn't care. She had felt pained, she had given NotNorman a piece of her mind and, looking at him now, with a mouthful of bedraggled floral remains and his hair full of Caramel Surprise, she felt much better.

So did I. The game could never be completed now, and would have to be called void.

Some argy bargy ensued, in which the bookies were besieged by punters, each of whom felt they had a case for at least a refund, if not some winnings, given that I was so clearly losing on points. The bookies clung manfully to the stake monies and seemed equally convinced that the game was far from a foregone conclusion. A group of gamblers, driven by a nostalgic attachment to their money, were so desperate that they were on all fours, picking up the stricken chess pieces and attempting to put things back as they were in order for the game to continue. NotNorman and I exchanged glances. We crawled out between the legs of the madding crowd, and made our cockroach-like escape from the carnage.

Once we were upright again, and had put some mileage between us and the QuikFit Chessmen, I made a bold, executive decision. I looked at NotNorman and addressed the subject head-on.

'Listen, Notters. I was thinking. That Mindi is a spirited and strong-willed girl, admirable in many, many ways, and I think you deserve her. I know it takes a big man to step aside and make such a sacrifice, but I think you're worth it, old man, and I'd rather we stay friends. You go ahead and nurture your relationship with my blessing.'

NotNorman seemed somehow to have placed an equally high value on our friendship.

'No, no, no. Wouldn't hear of it, matey. All yours,' he said, picking lily stalks out of his ears and opening his trouser fly to shake free a nut cluster. 'You didn't lose the chess match, did you? A deal is a deal, and in a way you are now obliged to take over. Dreadful blow to me, of course. Any girl who can breathe fire like that is pretty special, but I'll give you her number as soon as we get back. You go for it.'

Back at the ship there was a commotion going on. The rumour was that Benny the Dog had made a breakthrough up at Surrey Mansions and there was booty to be plundered by the first to get there. A swarm of tuk-tuks was hailed and soon we found ourselves back amongst our shipmates staring up at Surrey Mansions. Nothing seemed to have changed. All was quiet around this vast, imposing building. It was like turning up for school on a Sunday. Could it really be that Benny the Dog had made some sort of find? We walked up to the front door to find it locked. Even if Benny the Dog had some big idea about accessing unexplored sections of this building, he must have forgotten that the door was padlocked!

'Do you think we're walking into a practical joke of some sort?' asked NotNorman. He looked around at the bushes and back up to the gate. I understood what he meant. The peace and quiet suddenly seemed laden with suspicion. I looked around for signs of a setup. There were no twinkles in the eyes of the others. They all looked as mystified as we were.

'Come on, let's walk round the back,' said MoneyBox, and we began our circumnavigation.

It was a glorious building, and gave off an impressive aura of history and importance. I knew it was deserted, and yet it felt terribly wrong to be trespassing. It is amazing to think what a powerful tool of social control an imposing building is – you just ask the Church. This one felt steeped in authority. It must have seen some stuff during the time of British rule.

We walked around the eastern end of the building – the end that was intact – and continued along its length at the back. As we got past halfway, and approached the western end of the building – the end that was in a heap – there was evidence that some work had taken place, and voices could be heard, apparently coming from underground. As we drew up next to a large pile of rubble, we could see where the voices were coming from. A set of steps had been dug out from beneath the collapsed area, and up those steps was emerging Benny the Dog, stripped to the waist, sweating heavily, carrying a simply colossal hammer, and beaming from ear to ear.

'Hey, dudes! I told you, didn't I? Come and look at this!' He beckoned us to follow him down the steps. I wasn't so sure that moving around underneath an entire wing of a collapsed house was a good idea, but it was too amazing to resist.

'I knew there must be a door under here, see, 'cos the kitchens are just there and you can see from the lintel above ground that this must have been maybe a coal shoot. We dug it all out, and it's a pucker entrance to the building!'

As if to prove his words, we entered the building. Dozens of candles were set out all around the floor at the bottom of the stairs. Despite the candle power, it seemed very dark, but this was mostly down to the brightness of the sunshine outside, and our eyes quickly adjusted. The candles were arranged around a large, square hallway with doors leading off straight ahead and to the right. It was dusty and the air had a stale, unhealthy taste to it, but the hallway was amazingly well preserved.

'I reckon we can get into the main house up there,' said Benny the Dog, indicating a pile of rubble to the left with a casually swung hammer. 'That's stairs, that is.' It didn't seem likely, but he seemed very sure. Benny the Dog led us through to the right. 'We'll get in there later. Come 'ere. Look at this.'

We moved through the doorway to the right. More candles lit the way into a huge space which must once have run under the entire wing. It was surprisingly clean, given the total collapse of the building above. The scene that met my eyes was incredible.

The room was dominated by a full-size snooker table. The walls had racks of cues and a scoreboard. Leaning on the table were Jinx and KiloWatt; the latter was in a tricky snooker behind the yellow and the former, pleased with his work in snookering the latter, smiled at us and made widespread adjustments to his genitals. SmallParcel was turning circles in the middle of the room, staring off at the unseen wonders his own head gave him from the top-grade opium he had ingested continuously throughout our time in Southern India. MegaWatt was sitting on a chair, studiously refurbishing a cue tip, and Corkage was cleaning a picture he had removed from its position hanging on the wall. From the spaces all around, it was a fair guess that other paintings had already received his attention.

It was incredible. The room was almost pristine. The date of manufacture on the snooker scoreboard was 1880. Almost exactly one hundred years previously. Hell knows when the collapse had occurred, but since then, although the rest of the house had been ransacked and stripped, this room had been frozen in time. I know the light wasn't good, but it seemed to be exactly as I imagined the British Viceroy and his colonial staff must have left it when they were finally ousted. The collapse of the building was probably part of the coincidental collapse of British rule. It was reasonable to assume that this place was exactly as it had been in the late 1800s, otherwise the valuables inside would certainly have been taken.

I ran my hand over the snooker table. It was flat, and although the cloth was moth-eaten, the wood surrounds and the slate bed were absolutely perfect. The cues were all straight – probably nicely matured by now – and the balls were excellent. Corkage thought they were made from ivory and were worth a mint. The pictures hanging all around the room were expensively framed, so the paintings within were wonderfully preserved; a complete set of themed illustrations, featuring dogs and cats in pork pie hats playing billiards and poker and smoking cigarettes. Only joking – had you going for a minute though, didn't I? They weren't really. They were all scenes of India – a themed set of watercolours by the same artist: landscapes, fishermen, elephants, jungle rivers, villages. I don't know much about painting, but MegaWatt seemed to think they were one-off originals that would have been commissioned specially at the time of the Raj. They were a unique record of a bygone era, almost certainly lost paintings by a 'name' artist from the nineteenth century, and definitely worth a lot of money. MegaWatt, Benny the Dog and Corkage had made themselves responsible for looking after them…

'Are you going to tell Mindi and Anup about this?' asked NotNorman. 'It all belongs to the trust, doesn't it?'

'Yes, yes, of course,' said Benny the Dog as he unscrewed the scoreboard from the wall. 'Just as soon as we've prepared it all properly.'

Pronounced: 'nicked all the valuables', I thought. I suddenly realised that we were illegal occupants of an historic site, and that I was now officially a member of what was rapidly becoming a criminal gang. I felt a sudden fear that Black Kojak and his Douala security force would arrive down the stairs in a minute, and we'd all be rummaged up the kingdom come.

I looked around for a souvenir of my own. We had already missed the top prizes, which were going to the team that had dug it all out, so there wasn't much left of any great value. I wanted a snooker cue, but that wasn't going to happen unless I was prepared to fight an engineer. I couldn't even get a snooker ball, as Corkage had laid claim to the full set, including the pristine box they lived in. That was a nice prize for him. A day or two later, I actually got a small sword, which had been mounted on the wall in another room. I still have it at home today.

And whilst we're ensuring that this book elevates the soul as well as informs the mind, I can tell you now a pure fact of life, proven empirically that very day: even ten relatively fit and strong young men cannot get a snooker table up a set of narrow, cellar stairs.

Chapter 11

Large William and the Nodders

Thoughts on a sailor's lot. A plot is hatched and an item rigged. A Latin lesson in family planning – some nodders go off pop. The Large William Competition – Windy inverts a sausage field.

As the ship puffed smoothly out into the Arabian Sea, NotNorman and I stood at the rail on the afterdeck and looked back at Cochin, bathed in the fresh light and cool air of a Kerala sunrise. I realised that once again I had become smitten. I was so sad to leave. What a glorious, glorious wonder Southern India is. I felt a pang of grief that I only had one life. I needed at least a dozen to spend a satisfactory length of time with all the people and places I had fallen in love with. We watched the sun explode the city slowly into life, and discussed this sailing lark. Something was bugging me and I wasn't sure what it was.

We decided that if life is a marriage, then a sailor's life is a series of honeymoons. Unique honeymoons that are allowed to go ahead without the hapless attempts to live happily ever after that inevitably goes hand-round-throat with the traditional fun-filled fortnight at the beginning.

Imagine meeting a partner, falling in love, adoring each other with such total devotion that you get married and rush off on the perfect honeymoon together. Then, a fortnight of all-consuming passion later, you thank each other very much, shake hands and go your separate ways. A fortnight after that, you find another perfect partner, fall head over heels in love, and off you go again. That's what a sailor's life is like. And the thing is, I am not trying to glamorise things, because although it might sound ideal, it's not. It becomes unsatisfying. It's like being offered a lifetime of puddings and cakes to eat, and never being allowed another main meal. A sailor's life is an inescapably shallow life, because deep, long-term involvement with anything, any place or anybody is not possible. Sure, this is great for the younger man, who loves all the novelty and welcomes regular change and shallow pleasure. He is prevented from making foolish mistakes and getting too bogged down too early on in his life. But it becomes a problem as the years go by, because it is the natural order of things to want more from life, and to take more responsibility as you mature. A marriage *should* follow a honeymoon. Many of the older mariners with whom I sailed were not happy people. They were stuck at sea because their qualifications meant that they could not easily find work ashore, and there was no joy left for them in what is an anchorless life; a life without the good things that arise from the pain of responsibility and deep involvement. It is a life that is particularly difficult for a father or husband, whose wife and children are strangers to him.

Notters did not appear to share my concerns. 'What is your problem?' he said. 'What can possibly be wrong with a life of endless honeymoons?'

I didn't answer. I didn't know what was wrong with it. I just knew something was bugging me.

'Well, you'd better get used to it,' said Notters, turning back to the view, 'we're going to Bangkok next.'

As the sun rose and the ship woke up to the sea passage across to Bangkok, the dynamics on board changed. Whenever we were deep sea, the doors were all unlocked and replaced by curtains. The guys mooched about the accommodation in slippers. All the defences came down and the smiles came out. It was like the feeling round the house after all the relatives had pushed off after Christmas. The feeling of relaxed camaraderie was refreshing.

The other development once the ship put to sea was that closer relationships were established with the individuals one met or worked with regularly as part of one's particular routine. Working, for instance, the twelve-to-four watch, one became close to the second mate as you shared those dark, deep-sea hours on the bridge whilst the rest of the ship slept. Then at 4.00 a.m., you might go to the bar and share that special unwinding hour with the third and sixth engineers, who have been on watch in the engine room whilst you were on the bridge, so you shared a sense of unity and a certain frame of mind whilst the rest of the world slept.

For this sea passage, I was on the eight-to-twelve watch, on the bridge with The Famous Dick Wrigley. This was a good watch in that it was the closest one to a normal day. You could sleep between midnight and eight in the morning and be awake during your time off in the daytime from noon until eight in the evening. The other watches all involved sleeping in two chunks. However, one of the main advantages of being on the eight-to-twelve with the third officer was that I could draw upon his extensive knowledge in order to get revenge on any Ffuggs that might be hanging around like a skin infection and in need of a lesson about who is in charge.

The Famous Dick Wrigley was a man with a good deal of experience in monkeying with first trippers, and was an excellent resource, not just for ideas but also for equipment. He was in charge of the fire extinguishers. We agreed that he would impart to me some out-of-hours knowledge between noon and 8.00 p.m. that would undoubtedly be of value in my extinguishing a fire, and we spent our time in between watches in earnest preparation of critical safety and fire equipment in advance of a big night that was to occur shortly, during which I planned to put Ffugg out in no uncertain fashion. The night in question was centred around a curiously macho challenge known as the Large William – or perhaps more plainly, the Big Willy – Competition (in which, please note for the formal record, I had absolutely no intention of participating). We knew that the Big Willy Competition would involve a goodish general intake of alcohol, and my revenge upon the naïve and raw young Ffugg would be exacted mercilessly as part of the evening's festivities.

'If you take a foam fire extinguisher apart, you will find two key components,' explained The Famous One, poring over the various parts of a dismantled extinguisher in the private environs of his safety officer's cabinet. 'Firstly, there is the main barrel part full of water. Secondly, there is a small glass phial of chemical which sits in a chamber at the top. When you bash the extinguisher smartly on the head, the phial is smashed, the chemical mixes with the water and bammo! Three hundred cubic metres of foam emerges under pressure and at high speed from the nozzle. Simple, reliable and effective. These are the tools of your revenge.'

I was so pleased I could hug him. 'Thank you, The Famous Dick Wrigley,' I said warmly. 'I shall do you proud.'

Armed with this wonderful combination, I spent a concentrated hour with my tongue poking out the corner of my mouth, dismantling and reassembling this apparatus, along with some additional apparatus, and then reforming them into a new and sporting configuration that we shall meet in more detail shortly. Suffice to say that I locked out sticky thing (E) and carefully cleaned the openy-closey thing (B) of all moisture. I then added the chemical from the phial to handy container (C) just behind the trigger mechanism (A). Working with the meticulous care of a bomb disposal expert, I then conjoined the two into the greater part (D), and covered the whole thing with a neat housing (K), so that any passing, wide-eyed, spanner-brained Ffugg (G) would walk headlong into it without suspecting a thing. I stood back and gazed with pride upon my work. I had done such a good job, even I couldn't see it. Nobody would ever suspect the mayhem within. Except 'everybody', that is, because The Famous Dick Wrigley was out and about warning people of Ffugg's fate so that only he would walk into the trap. Of all the ship's company, only Ffugg did not know. The rest of us were a Band of Brothers. He would be the victim at last and I would be part of The Gang. Please insert a mental picture of me at this point, twirling my moustache and emitting an evil laugh in the style of Dick Dastardly.

The night of the Big Willies began directly after dinner with a couple of beers. The lads passed round bottles of Cobra and we raised a glass to one another happily. Only Ffugg was unaware of the underlying reason for the cheerfulness of his colleagues. He must have thought we were all striding around with match-winning immensement in our trousers. I knew the truth; and he was going to suffer. Not only was my device all ready for him, I had heard a rumour that other merry japes had been organised for the young lad's educational advancement, and I sat back happy in the knowledge that it was going to be a fine night.

For those of us who have ever wondered what on earth a bear garden is, this night gave us the answer before 9.00 p.m. The booze flowed, the chaps became raucous, and the term 'bear garden' was suddenly defined for me with a simple clarity I had never previously achieved. This said, The Big Willy Competition (which I assumed would landscape nicely into a bear garden) seemed, mercifully, to get forgotten as other animal activities, drinking games and sideshow practical jokes somehow became even better ideas. I am sorry to have to report that, even though this was supposed to be my night of glory, I did fall victim to a practical joke or two myself. On one occasion, I nipped around to get our caps from our cabins. NotNorman's cap and my cap and Ffugg's cap were required for a game. I don't remember the details of this game, but it required a pack of cards, a saucer of Branston Pickle, a dead rat from 'tweendeck two, and three officers' caps to be a success. I never got to find out how the game went, for reasons that will become apparent. Whilst collecting my cap from my cabin, I noticed what seemed to be a giant slug in my sink. We had just seen a brand new film called *Alien* so I was understandably put out by this visitation to our ship. I was on a vessel not unlike the one in *Alien*, I was three sheets to the wind on Cobra beer, and here in my sink was the spawn of the monster. It sat there, vibrating with an unearthly life. So large was it that it bulged out above my sink. And so turgid was it that the slightest touch would disgorge its guts all over the room. I bravely went nearer to establish the species. As it turned out, I didn't need Charles Darwin to help me with the identification process.

It was a condom (species Rubberoidicus stopanothermum). A condom filled – indeed, stretched to the very brink of exploding – with water. (Or, as Mr Darwin might have put it, a fine example of Rubberoidicus, from the genus Aqua Fulltoburstium.)

If the sink took, say, three litres of water, this nodder (as they were more commonly known in the maritime field of evolutionary research) was doing its utmost to keep hold of at least six, and it quivered dangerously on the edge of exploding. I had seen condoms used before in this way. A good quality nodder can be filled with water until it is the size of a pillow, and I can tell you that when they go off the effect is far more dramatic than you could ever imagine before you see one for real. They explode, and the resultant tidal wave is mighty powerful. This one was more heavily laden than any I had previously seen. Evidently, the cradling effect of the sink allowed them to fill it some way beyond normal capacity.

My problem was that I had to remove this condom, and keep it from soaking the world around it, but how to do it? This was a puzzle to which my intoxicated brain could not find an answer. I decided, rather sensibly, I thought, to sleep on that one and hope to have a good, clear-headed answer in the morning. I turned to leave and there, on my desk, was another huge, six-litre slug-nodder, also heavily pregnant and throbbing angrily on the edge of rupture. This time, however, it was on my desk, and in grave danger of soaking my correspondence coursework on which it had been placed, as well as the carpet, bulkheads and furnishings. I knew that any attempt to move it would result in a spectacular eruption. I decided to sleep on that one, too, but gingerly edged my correspondence coursework out from under it. Luckily, it came out cleanly. I opened the wardrobe to put the documents safely away on the shelf within.

What I did not know was that there was a towel carefully laid out on the top shelf of the wardrobe. And what else I did not know was that this towel was pinned to the back of the wardrobe door. I was also unaware that laid lovingly on top of this towel on the top shelf was yet another giant and turgid slug-nodder-alien. Now, some things in life follow predictable, logical patterns, and here was a case in point. As I opened the wardrobe door, the towel was given a degree of momentum by virtue of its being attached to the door. This momentum was transferred on to the Rubberoidicus fulltoburstium which, perfectly reasonably, threw itself at me from above. I watched in a kind of poetic slow motion as the slug fell, trembling like a giant raindrop falling through the air, bounced off my chest, rolled down my body, landed at my feet and turned the place instantly into a water park. The outburst wet the ceiling, soaked the walls drenched every inch of Me and took my breath away. I was transformed from Windy into Wet and Windy. My correspondence coursework was transformed from a certain A+ to a moshy mess. The carpet was transformed into a marshy wetland. The rainfall in the cabin lasted a full six minutes. The noise from the bar turned to uproarious laughter, cheers, whoops of delight, a long round of applause and individual helplessness that went on at least as long as the rainfall.

I couldn't believe it. All that setup I had spent days working on for Ffugg, and these sods were still laying traps for me. I pulled the towel down, wiped my face with it and remembered that herein lay the secret to moving a six litre slug-nodder. Cradling it gently in a towel was how the traps were set in the first place, and this was the key to safe removal. The cabin was more like a day out on the Norfolk Broads already, so I reasoned that it was best to handle the other two now rather than have a whole new soaking the next day.

I eyed the remaining two condoms suspiciously as they vibrated gently in time with the ship's engines. The one in the sink was tricky, because it would be difficult to get underneath it, but the one on the desk looked relatively easy to swaddle in a towel. Once embraced thus, it could be taken out and put over the side. I lay the towel out alongside the slug on my desk.

I took a deep breath, then began to roll the condom ever so – ever so – gently on to the towel.

Now, I don't know if you've ever been tricked into buying any of that super glue stuff. I have, and generally found that it isn't really as great as it seems on the TV advertisement. So many times, I have thought to myself that a dab of that super glue – the one that affixes grown men to the ceiling and hangs elephants under helicopters on the TV – is just what the doctor ordered, only to discover that in real situations it works about as well as tap water for sticking things together. Well, this night, it worked fine. Just the teeniest, tiniest dab of super glue had been placed on the desk before the slug was given its home, and it was highly principled, dedicated super glue that was determined to give value for money. The moment I tried to move the slug, the treacherous glue gripped, the condom gave up the unequal struggle, and six litres of water exploded upwards from the desk. The initial splash was of a scale I had only ever experienced on the foredeck of a ship battling through a force ten around the Cape of Good Hope. A cascade flew into my face and a waterfall sloshed up the bulkhead and down my front, instantly raising the local swamp water level from two inches to four.

The cheer from the bar was so loud it went through me like a knife. Why me again? They were really going for it out there. I could hear from Corkage's asthmatic laugh that he was going to need his nebuliser. Every time we'd had a rip-roaring laugh on the trip so far, he'd had to go and stand in the corner with a gas mask on, or die from an asthma attack, which just seemed to make things all the funnier for the rest of us, to have him standing there struggling for life and oxygen in a mask that made him look like a giant mosquito. Tonight there was going to be a queue for the nebuliser. That's how helpless they all were. The worst part was that I could hear Ffugg laughing heartily along with them, and it hurt, I can tell you. It really hurt.

I turned and looked sadly at the slug in the sink. I might just as well try to get a half-nelson on this one now – I mean, how much worse could it get? I couldn't lift the thing – besides, my tormentors had probably decided to hang the expense for the evening and invested another dab of super glue in the bottom of the sink. I got a pin from the desk. If I could slide the pin ever so – *ever so* – gently through the skin of the condom, it would leak slowly and gently into the sink over night, and dribble down the plug-hole. I'd seen it done before, and I knew that if I could penetrate it with a surgeon's precision, everything would be fine.

I doggy-paddled upstream to the sink, brushed the rain out of my eyes and addressed the slug. It was angry and heaving, stretched taut and holding on by a micron width of skin. It was ready to give birth and desperate for its waters to break. I reached over to the back, hoping that the overflow would do its job until the plug became serviceable. I took a deep breath and slowly – ever so, *ever so* slowly – brought the pin down on to the skin of the slug. The pin entered easily. There was no explosion. I was in luck. The pin slid in and I felt, finally, that I was getting somewhere. I removed the pin and still my world remained stable. I stood back with a great deal of satisfaction (for a man who was already knee deep in water), but no water emerged from the pinhole. The thing remained watertight. I was expecting a few drops, or even a light spray, but there was just a tiny drop which stubbornly refused to get any bigger. I looked at the problem. I should probably walk away. The job was done, and nature would take its course. There was a hole. There was pressure. I would give it time. I watched the slug with suspicion. I pretended to walk away, but it didn't fall for it. I kept my eye on it but it wasn't leaking at all. So what would you do? I can tell what you are thinking. You think I'm about to do the wrong thing with inevitable consequences, but what the hell would you do, smarty pants? I decided to place another tiny pinhole near the first one. That might set up some sort of air intake to allow water out the other side. Or something. Or maybe I should just squeeze it a bit and see if water emerged from the existing pinhole. OK, so it might not have been the smartest decision, but I was drunk. And drenched. And it had to be handled now. There was no point in soaking the whole place again in the morning.

It was quite interesting, I suppose, if one is being detached and analytical about it. The shape of the basin seemed to triple the explosive effect of the condom. The eruption was left with only one direction in which it could go, and that was to explode itself upwards. The first wave contained the usual quantity of water as the slug spewed its guts in a swirling up-current into my face and all across the deck head, but then the other half of the total quantity, which would normally have gone downwards and sideways, curled around the bottom of the sink, picking up speed all the way, and came at me in a highly impressive second wave. I know a chap can only get so wet before he is soaked through and can physically get no wetter, but I got significantly wetter than that. I struck out for the shore and headed back miserably towards the bar.

But the uproar I was heading towards got me down; particularly the laughter. Corkage would be increasing the dose in the corner now and I began to feel miffed. Why had they given me the slugs? What was their problem with playing tricks on Ffugg? I mean, he was the first tripper. And if they were scared of Ffugg because he was a thug – or Ffugg, as he pronounced it – then why not do Giewy? He was a numpty, thoroughly deserving of slugs. It just wasn't right to inflict these things on me. Halfway to the bar, I realised that I only had one cap. We needed three for the game, so I went back to our passageway and stopped. Something wasn't right. My inebriated brain couldn't figure out what it was, but something seriously didn't add up. I went back into my cabin and stepped cautiously inside. This time, it was genuinely like entering an alien world… because it was dry. Dry as a bone. There were no slugs. There was no flood water and no bombed out remains of shredded condoms. I tottered in the doorway, unable to comprehend what was going on. My head was spinning with beer and with the mystery of this dark and spooky magic. My correspondence course sat unmolested on the desk. My sink was empty. I felt my heart beat rise. Was I hallucinating? I had a sudden revelation that maybe I was asleep. That was it! I was in a warped and uncomfortable dream. So I spent a fruitless couple of minutes punching, slapping and pinching myself to get me to wake up. It was like one of those dances they do in Austria. I didn't wake up. My cabin was clean, dry and ready for inspection.

I reeled from my cabin and went next door to Ffugg's cabin. It was identical in every way to mine except for the remnants of blown condoms dangled limply from the ceiling and the overall impression was that someone had installed a stagnant village pond in his cabin and then blown it up from beneath to see what it would look like. As I pieced matters together, I couldn't help but feel a little foolish. The lads *had* set Ffugg up, and I'd spent the last twenty minutes saving him from it all by bringing it down around my own ears instead of his. That's why they were laughing so much; it wasn't just my plight that was amusing them – they must have been wetting themselves looking at Ffugg, who must have been sitting there laughing along with them with no idea that it was his cabin I was demolishing for him. I suddenly felt more than a little concerned that there was more bad news in this for me than the simple humiliation I had brought upon myself so far. Once Ffugg became fully appraised of the situation, would he be grateful to me for saving him from this? No, no. He would go mental. He would certainly have trashed his own cabin in slug mismanagement had he been given the chance, but he wouldn't see it that way. He would see only that I had annihilated his home-sweet-home. I had transformed it from a smart, homely cabin so it looked like the wreck of the Hesperus and Ffugg would want to exact a violent retribution.

I headed back towards the bar, my brain desperately trying to work around the alcohol to come up with a good answer to my mounting problems. As I got closer to the bar, I heard some snippets of conversation that confirmed my fears.

'Wot? Soaked everyffffing? I'll tear him limb from limb!'

The cheers rang out once more from the bar, and I heard the fee fi fo fums and felt the ground shaking. No doubt Ffugg was on his way round to inspect the fruits of my labours, and further indication was there that the delighted audience was following close behind him. I dived into the toilet block, slammed and locked the door to a cubicle, sat on the toilet and lifted my feet up in case anyone checked underneath. I sat there trying desperately to decide what to do.

I heard something of a commotion outside as I sat there wracking my brain. I couldn't come up with anything. I must have sat there for five full minutes, listening to raised voices and people stomping round the accommodation. They even checked in the toilets, but I just sat there gnawing anxiously on a toilet roll and feeling terrible. I was a laughing stock. I was going to be beaten up. I didn't know where to go or what to do. I felt like a fool.

Nobody loved me.

After a while, the noises outside calmed down and I decided to face the music. Ffugg would have been ragged by the lads by now and had time to cool off. Maybe he might not directly blame me – it was all their doing, after all. I'd had time to think and this was the best I could do, but I hadn't bargained on making yet another tragic mistake.

You know in that film, where the goodie gets chased through a shopping mall? He thinks he's escaped when he makes it to the lift and the doors shut just before the bad guy gets in, but then he's injected with truth serum by a special agent who was already in the lift. His face turns to anguish as he realises what has happened. Then the scene changes to the view inside the guy's bloodstream, where the serum joins the rushing blood and white corpuscles in a fast-flowing artery and flies off down towards critical organs to cause internal bedlam. Well, that's what happened inside the doings of the toilet when I flushed it. Internal bedlam. In fact, I knew exactly what happened inside the doings of the toilet when I flushed it.

My pulling the chain (A) caused the flush valve (C) to open, and the ball float (F) to drop. The chemical which had been safe and dry in the filler valve (B) rushed down into the main bowl (D). There, the chemical flushed into the water (C). More water arrived from behind as the ballcock (E) opened to ensure all the chemical had plenty of catalyst to react with, and, whilst I stood like a doofus (G) wondering why, oh why, I pulled the chain of the very toilet I had personally rigged for Ffugg, an unearthly yellow growth began to emerge rapidly from the toilet bowl. Before I could take evasive action, I was drowning in a toilet cubicle filled with 300 cubic metres of foam and Corkage was making a dash for it back to his mosquito impersonation. In seconds I was completely engulfed. I couldn't breathe as the stuff filled the entire cubicle, my eyes, nose, ears and mouth, and I found myself thrashing around hoping, with what little mental capacity I had left, that a good old panic would fix all my problems. I heard, through my claustrophobic horror, the cheers and laughter of a bunch of blokes whose evening had gone better than they could ever have dreamed. I was just adding endlessly to their joy by dying in a toilet cubicle filled with foam. It must have looked great from their perspective, with great clouds of foam billowing out over the top and bottom of the cubicle door, which banged and clunked with the flailings of the genius inside who'd set his own trap off and was now choking energetically behind it.

In flat panic, I tried to tear the door open, but it was stuck. The door unlocked, but it wouldn't open, presumably because it was being held shut from the outside (the technique we had agreed earlier in our plans for Ffugg to ensure he got a good long swim). I put my face down my shirt in order to breathe through the material so I wouldn't drown. It was like being trapped in a spider's web. The more I struggled, the worse things got, until suddenly, the door opened and I found myself body surfing across the toilet atop a wave of foam as the lads ran giggling through the exit.

I slid and fell about for a while like some sort of new-born swamp donkey, swearing and shouting until I eventually struggled to my feet. I stood for a while, trying to gain some balance as I slopped off the bubbling crud from my head, face and body, then limped sadly through the sewerage back to my cabin to get changed. I was the laughing stock again, but this time it was entirely my own fault. I had triggered all the pranks that had been so carefully set up for Ffugg, and far from getting my revenge, I'd even walked into the one I had so carefully crafted myself.

Beer. That's what was needed. Beer. And lots of it.

Ten minutes later – and to uproarious applause – I walked into the bar. I feel sure you know something of the old Baboulene spirit by now. If there is a silver lining, you can rely on me to find it, and if there was an up-side, it was this. Ffugg had felt quite strongly, by all accounts, that a violent reprisal should be administered against me for the wholesale damage I had caused to his cabin and worldly possessions. However he – like everyone else on the planet – was laughing far too much about my 'foaming at the mouth' (as it was labelled) to deliver said violence with the required sincerity. I had done such a great job of doing myself up with practical jokes that even he considered that I had been punished more than enough, and I got away with nothing more than the standard wrestle. Indeed, I was welcomed like a celebrity to the bar with cheers and a standing ovation. And here was the silver lining. There in the bar was one last chance of grabbing victory from the jaws of this evening's multiple defeats.

You see, there was still the Big Willy Competition. Now, as I mentioned, I had absolutely no intention of entering the Big Willy Competition. The event was juvenile, and I saw nothing to be gained by patronising it. Indeed, my first instinct upon realising that the other contestants had already made their entries, if you understand me, was relief that I had at least been spared the peer pressure to join in. I should point out, of course, that my reticence to enter was not because I, em, couldn't win, or anything. It just wasn't a grown-up thing to do. I was Officer Material. I was above it. And yet, I couldn't help but notice, as I looked at the results so far, that – dare I say it – a victory on this occasion was not entirely out of my reach. None of the existing measurements was beyond me, so to speak. In fact, I could see instantly that, with what I had in my trousers, I actually genuinely really and definitely had a chance of mounting the podium, if you see what I mean. This was big news. Coming low down the order in a Big Willy competition is not something desirable. If dropping ones trousers serves only to send Corkage rushing for his life support, it can be damaging to the psyche and degrading to the individual so I was a supporter of those who called for Big Willy competitions to be banned from the Merchant Navy as inappropriate practice. However, *winning* a Big Willy competition was a whole different ball game, if you get my meaning. Winning a Big Willy competition was possibly the best thing on earth that could happen to a man. And here, tonight – there was no doubt about it – I was in with a chance of swinging with the big boys.

The Big Willy Competition works like this. At one end of the bar there is a half-width section of surface that is hinged and swings up and down to allow people to get behind the bar to serve beers. It is about the width of a plank and serves as the field of play for the Big Willy Competition. It has various names deriving from its involvement in this most auspicious of contests, most of which are indelicate, so we will refer to it by one of its more acceptable titles: 'Sausage Field'.

Each competitor in turn steps up to Sausage Field and lays himself out across the width of the plank. He can push himself up against the stadium sides, pull with his arms and clench his buttocks as much as he likes, he can think back to favourite episodes of *Baywatch* (although the heckling from the audience tends to put a damper on those sorts of tactics), and when he has extended himself to the point at which the veins are popping (on his forehead), a pencil is employed to make a mark on Sausage Field to indicate the talent of the individual and the magnitude of sausage.

I looked at the marks on Sausage Field, and it was clear that I had more than just a shot at this. I had steadfastly avoided Big Willy Competitions in the past, partly because there were always one or two sailors on board armed with the kind of equipment I half expected to see them use to feed themselves buns. But on this ship, I had stumbled upon a set of colleagues none of whom quite managed to scare the horses. Indeed, there wasn't any doubt about it: I could win. The prize was a dozen cases of beer and, more importantly, the admiration of my fellow man for ever more. I could be That Sailor! I could be The One of whom others were jealous! That could be Me!

But could it be a setup? I took the precaution of asking NotNorman – who had observed the Big Willy Competition whilst I was wrecking Ffugg's cabin and foaming at the mouth – if the measurements on display were genuine. He assured me with hand on heart that they were. I took him to one side and told him I was considering giving it a shot in Sausage Field, and he made a rather unkind comment along the lines that, having shared rooms and showers with me in the past, and as my best friend, these were absolutely genuine measurements and I should be able, if living in the real world, to see for myself that it would be unwise for me to enter the competition. I didn't quite understand what his motivation was for discouraging me. Maybe he was still smarting from the Mindi episode. Maybe he was unhappy with his own button mushroom and didn't want to socialise with me for the rest of our lives knowing what we would both know if I won tonight. It would put an uneasy dynamic into our relationship. But this was no time for such sensitivities. I would still be his friend even if he did have to stand forever in the shadow of my almost deformed monster of an appendage.

I looked again at the paucity of competition and made my decision. I had seen Big Willy competitions before, and I knew this was genuine. There was no trick, and I could win. This could turn things right round; indeed, it could be the making of me for the rest of the trip. I would be The Man they would talk about in hushed whispers in years to come. I would be the guy they couldn't get out of their subconscious when they were struggling to satisfy a girlfriend.

The lads had perhaps thought I had done enough for them this evening, so my announcement that I was entering the Big Willy Competition was greeted firstly with a stunned silence, secondly with a roar of approval and thirdly with a mosquito standing wheezing in the corner. The looks on their faces was one of simple amazement coupled with unbridled delight. I didn't care though. This was going to take me from Zero to Hero in one simple measurement.

Now, I have to admit, that despite my experiences to date – you will remember, of course, the Grand Cranking Competition and the Crossing the Line Ceremony on my first ship to name but two – I was not really the type for this sort of thing. And I can't say I felt totally comfortable as I dropped my trousers and arranged myself for a late entry. I looked around at the guys in the bar and the mosquito in the corner and, to be honest, they didn't look too haunted so far. Well, they were in for quite a shock. In fact, so was I. I flopped myself out and without any real effort, my firehose unfurled directly into first place. I tried to remain cool, but I could barely hide my delight. I was huge. This was fantastic. There were seven or eight pencil marks with the names of the entrants written carefully behind them and, good God, I was at least two inches longer than most of the others. I was a clear inch past second place. I turned and looked for admiration from my inferiors. I would be modest, of course, and show some humility. I mean, I couldn't help owning this beast. It wasn't my fault. I was just born that way, and these poor saps just had to acknowledge the gold medallist and try to get on with their lives as best they could in the knowledge of what I had to look after in my pants. Indeed, it is worth mentioning here that there is a wider, more serious, issue. There are those who think that events like these are wrong and that there should be legislation against them. But I know the Merchant Navy. I have been there as a sailor, and I can tell you that these competitions are character building and important to the history and traditions of the maritime world. People shouldn't interfere with these ancient customs. No sane person could honestly find anything wrong in a bit of harmless fun like this, and there was no doubt in my mind that do-gooders and politically correct namby pambies shouldn't carp on about it just because they have small willies.

I stood there in my moment of glory and soaked it all up. What it meant. What it represented. I felt as if I had finally arrived in life. I mean, you don't get to see a danger to traffic like *this* everyday and surely, as my colleagues imagined the thing from a woman's perspective, they couldn't help but feel a twang of jealousy. They covered their inadequacy very loudly with cheers and hoots of helpless laughter – the spare masks meant there were now three giant mosquitoes in the corner – but that was only to be expected from the insecure. I surreptitiously forced myself forwards and found another quarter-inch over and above second place. It was no contest. I was enormous and the others were nowhere, and for one brief and wonderful moment, I felt like a God. Like a Sex God. I was Mr Firehose, and I wish – oh, how I wish – the story ended here.

I stood up against the bar victoriously, and the crowd cheered and laughed. And laughed. And laughed. I knew they were just covering their own inadequacies, but they were pretending very well. They were falling on each other and rolling about on the floor. I couldn't quite make it out, and began to feel strangely small. If they kept undermining me like this, I might get overtaken by some of the other pencil marks. I stood there, trousers round my ankles and manhood lying across Sausage Field.

'What is it?' I snapped. 'What are you all laughing at? Look, will you? Just look! I'm the winner, aren't I?'

'Windy, Windy,' said Jinx, wiping the tears from his eyes. He put his hand on my shoulder and pointed past my shrivelling willy, across Sausage Field to the area behind the bar. 'We all did it from *that* side…'

Chapter 12

Driving to the City on the Porcelain Bus

The thrills and spills of regurgitating grand locations. Windy feels unwell.

Before we move swiftly on, I did want to tell you about one other thing that happened on the Night of the Big Willies. A quick warning: remember what time of night it was, and the state we were in. This is probably going to be the grossest chapter in the entire book, so please feel free to skip to the next one. Particularly if you have just had lunch.

Following my fabulous humiliation, everyone was keen to celebrate. The Famous Dick Wrigley got up on a chair and made a speech in support of me, during which he pointed out that it normally took a couple of years to gain that much amusement from the ineptitude of a single human being, and having delivered my quota in one evening, I was to be admired. Glasses were raised and raised again as the lads relived the sequence of events and the laughter rang out loud and long as they told one another how it was for them. The upshot was that by about 2.00 a.m., we were more than ready for another sporting endeavour that I only ever met on board ship. It was called 'Driving to the City on the Porcelain Bus', for reasons that will become clear. The game had a pleasing simplicity to it, running a little along the lines of a singing competition. There were no complex rules, no need for years of preparation, no backroom staff. A prospective competitor needed nothing more than copious quantities of Cobra beer bubbling away ominously at the back of his throat to consider himself perfectly prepared to join the choir. This being the case, we had an entire chorus line of artistes ready to roll, so we repaired to the toilet block to let the hallelujahs ring out.

The idea is this: each singer in turn is required to make a formal, spoken introduction outlining the city of the world he intends to recreate. As the murmurs of expectation ripple through the audience, he then tickles his tonsils and throws up a bellyful of Cobra. As he does so, he is obliged to shout out the name of his nominated city as tunefully and succinctly as he can, whilst the rest of the lads, in their capacity as judge and jury, listen on with a critical ear. Once he has vommed up his favoured location, they award marks out of ten for clarity, style and degree of difficulty, and knock points off for hesitation, repetition and sometimes just the smell.

Sparky was first up. He stood in the toilet cubicle entrance, facing us and concentrating hard as the beads of sweat formed on his brow. We could all see he was more than ready to sing his heart out.

'Good evening, judges,' he stuttered, swallowing hard. His face twitched and his cheeks blew as he tried to avoid a false start. 'Tonight I would like to give you my interpretation of "Calcutta". Thank you.'

An appreciative murmur of anticipation ran through those present as Sparks turned, adjusted his collar, closed his eyes and ran through his performance mentally. He then knelt down, took the steering wheel firmly in both hands and there was a pause as he focussed on bringing the essence of West Bengal to the forefront of his thinking.

I was not yet up to speed with the technicalities of this endeavour, but Degree of Difficulty was an important factor in nominating a city. Roaring out an elongated 'Hull' during the act of being sick is really quite easy – almost unavoidable, in fact. Other easy deliveries, such as 'Arkansas' or 'Sumatra' don't fool anybody, so Sparky's brave rendition of 'Calcutta' got the competition off to what you might call a roaring start.

His head disappeared into the bowl as he set off driving to the city.

'CAAAAAAARRRLL!' roared Sparks. Good grief, it was loud, and it certainly had length... but then he stopped. I thought that was it. He tried a few times to get going on the 'Cut' bit, but kept stalling the bus. There was a quick but clear 'Cut,' followed by another 'Cut,' then another, then a more rapid 'cut-cut-cut!' but he couldn't get the bugger started. We were about to give up on him, when he got the idea again, and along came the rest of it:

'TTTAAAAAA-AAAAAAARRGGHH—Ah-HAA-HA-HA-HO-HO-HA–HA-HAAAAAAARRH!'

The overuse of the signature motif, reprised too often in the central aria, lost him marks from the structural purists amongst the judges. Even for those for whom his repetition represented expert use of the rondo form, the impression of evil laughter in the last few 'Ho-ho-ah-ha-haaarr-har's was a little disturbing, and the swear word tacked on the end was largely superfluous to the overall feel of the city, but he still got a creditable six out of ten and a warm round of applause. Personally, I thought this was overly generous. Not simply for the offence to musical sensibilities, but for the presumptuous renaming of one of India's major cities from 'Calcutta' to 'Carl-cut-cut-cutcutcutcut–ah-ha-ho-ho-ha-ha-hahahaaaaarrrghh-bastard'. It didn't seem right to me, but then I was new to the game.

Apparently inspired by Sparky's work, MegaWatt bundled him out of the way, gripped the steering wheel firmly in both hands and enthusiastically delivered up his interpretation of 'Edinburgh', which was extremely good. Indeed, so keen was he that he gave us Scotland's first city no less than three times in a row, each one apparently delivered in a different dialect – I heard Yorkshire and Scottish followed by Cornish – and he enunciated every single letter with Thespian pride. His style was good, with his head well inside the bowl, white knuckles and his feet kicking in the air above him throughout the chorus. An extraordinary performance. Calls for 'More!' were waved away by the exhausted MegaWatt, but still, it was marvellous.

NotNorman was next. He stepped forward, bowed respectfully to the judges, took a deep breath, started snapping his fingers to the groove, shaking his head in time and then he sang cheerfully:

'*Is this the way to –*'

He then turned, dropped to his knees whilst tickling his tonsils and tried manfully to bring 'Amarillo' centre stage. He stuttered and he hiccupped and he snarled. He growled, clenched, gritted and strained, but there was no sign of Amarillo on the map. He stood back up, apologised to the judges for the delay, and began his preparation again in a boyish soprano.

'*Is this the way to –*'

He dropped to his knees again, choked, barked and gagged into the big white telephone, but there was still no one home in Amarillo. He stood back up, composed himself once more, started to snap his fingers and shake his head in time like some desperate pub singer, and began again.

'*Is this the way –*'

'Oh, Jesus!' shouted MoneyBox. 'Get out the wa-hey-hey-heeeeeey!'

MoneyBox barged Notters from the driving seat and set off for the city with no formal introduction whatsoever. His was a muscular performance. He gripped the steering wheel harshly in both hands and drove aggressively with action, volume and veins sticking out all over the place, but his technique was all wrong. Whatever city it was that he was driving at wasn't anywhere I'd ever heard of. Quite frankly, his sick was a mess. He surfaced and looked at us as though we should be impressed.

'What the hell was that?' asked Jinx.

'You know,' said MoneyBox, breathing heavily and wiping his mouth on his sleeve. 'That place in Wales. It was just about perfect, so I don't want any nonsense from you lot.'

We all sighed. There's always someone who claims that what they just deposited in the toilet was, in fact, a famously named town in Snowdonia. MegaWatt, who was Welsh, was quick with the riposte.

'OK then, if you just sicked up somewhere in Wales, say it again now in normal spoken English.'

This put MoneyBox right on the spot, and I have to say, his response was unexpectedly robust. He gritted his teeth, his eyes bulged, and he returned to the bowl for a totally unexpected appreciation of 'Ikea', which was a big surprise to everyone listening and, overall, possibly raised more questions than it answered. MoneyBox really was dominating the proceedings – we just didn't know where he was going to take us next – but this wasn't going well with the judges. Once he'd resurfaced, they informed him that they could only accept his first answer.

So his visit to Ikea, and his argument that it was a town in northern Sweden, were to no avail. He argued that his Welsh opus should count, that he'd sung it once and he wasn't going to do it again. Indeed, he couldn't do it again. In order to allow the judges an opinion, MegaWatt sang out the real name of the place:

'Llanfairpwllgwyngyllgogerychwyrndrobwyllllantysiliogogogoch.'

I have to say, I did feel sorry for MoncyBox. I thought he'd had a damn good stab at it. He'd definitely got that 'gogogoch' bit spot on. An uninvolved passerby would not have thought MoneyBox was being sick, he would have thought he was simply fluent in Welsh. However, it was pointed out that he did also tack a few 'gogogochs' on to the end of 'Ikea' too, so I guess it might have just been a fluke.

And then, to add a wholly unnecessary complication to the knotty problem of MoneyBox's recital, Giewy surprised everyone on the bus – himself included – by being sick on the floor over by the door. He got no points for this (despite clear evidence of 'Herm' in there somewhere, which was nice. I don't think the Channel Islands get the recognition they deserve these days). Indeed, as he croaked out a request for a doctor, he received only admonishment from the other singers, as practising before your official turn was apparently against the rules, and duets had to be agreed with the judges beforehand.

As the arguments grew louder and Payphone declared himself more than ready to be Moby Dick (as he called it), Jinx declared that anywhere in Wales was forbidden as unfair on the judges, the toilet and the people of Wales, so the whole country was declared out of bounds. Similar legislation was passed on anywhere allegedly Russian, and moments later on anything Aboriginal, after Payphone gave us a somewhat unsettling account of 'Woolloomooloo'. It simply wasn't possible to count if there were the right number of 'oomoos' and 'loomoos' in there for it to make absolute sense. They seemed to go on forever.

Having been drowning my sorrows to some goodish extent, I began to get a deep stirring within that told me I was about ready to join in the chorus myself. No doubt about it, I was about to become a bus driver. With a short but dignified introduction, I dropped my head into the steering wheel and delivered a long and, I felt, pleasantly circumspect illumination on 'Perth'. It was held in a well-controlled counter-tenor throughout, and I remember thinking in the middle of the actual elucidation that things were going well. However, my stomach had other ideas. It considered my rather plaintive 'Perth' to be nothing more than a marker to work against, and followed up immediately with a deeply moving and unplanned rendition of 'AUCHTERMUCHTY'. It was delivered in the voice of Chewbacca the Wookie and was thrown, ventriloquist-like, to appear to come from all around us like a message from God. Not that God ever mentioned 'Auchtermuchty' – or, interestingly, anywhere along the A9 – in his documented messages to the Chosen Ones, but if he had, I feel sure it would have sounded all omnipresent, like mine. I was told later that it sounded like a brontosaurus calling for a mate across the plains.

Once the judges – having turned circles in search of the source of this extraordinary visitation from Fife – found out it was me, they just threw away the rule book and began clapping. This was something so unique in my shot selection and tonal colour that continuing with the contest seemed somehow pointless, which was a bit harsh on Corkage, whose astonishing assault on 'Warsaw' in the cubicle next to mine could only ever have been matched for ruthlessness and ferocity by the Germans in 1939.

'I declare Windy to be the winnerrrrr!' sang Jinx.

'ARR-HARRR-HARRRR-AMARILLOOOOOOO-OH-HO-HO-HOOOOH!!' came a cubicle-juddering roar from the one next to Corkage. NotNorman had finally found a gear. He started like Blackbeard and ended like Santa Claus, but it was too late for the also-rans. I was finally a winner and had two cases of beer to prove it! Not that I wanted them. I could imagine nothing more disgusting than more beer. Tonight was to be my porcelain bus driving and brontosaurus impersonation swansong. In fact, I determined that this was not only to be my porcelain bus driving and brontosaurus impersonation swansong, but also my Big Willy Competition swansong and my beer drinking swansong.

I was never, ever, ever going to drink again.

Moving swiftly on...

Chapter 13

Eastern Promise

Sniffing the horizon. Market day. Windy experiences a visitation of angels (and takes them back to his cabin). Windy is scared to go back to his cabin. Giewy saves the day.

For sailors there is nowhere on earth quite like Bangkok, and there is, of course, only one reason for that: Gorgeous Girls. As we rocked up into the Bight of Bangkok, there was palpable excitement radiating from the ship to the extent that, from a distance, she must have been entirely enveloped in a cloud of testosterone. As a teenager already pretty obsessed with the birds and the bees, the feverish atmosphere didn't do me any good whatsoever. I had never been to Thailand before, but I got the message loud and clear that these girls were not just beautiful; they were not just exotic and armed with mystical Eastern ways; and they were not just ready to dedicate themselves to fulfilling my every desire in wonderful oriental ways for weeks on end. Oh no. There was more. Whilst the kind of girl I tended to meet in the UK rather annoyingly seemed to want something more from a relationship than the simple knowledge that they've made me very happy (and could go and make dinner now), these Thai girls would be beautiful, cheap, available, almost depressingly numerous and, in return for their excellence, would demand only a couple of dollars of relationship commitment on my part.

For the entire sea passage, every evening before dinner, we would all gather on the bridge wing. It was a strange ritual involving a collective sniffing of the air for the first signs that our wait was over. These were grown men so excited by the prospect of female companionship that they were joining together in earnest communion trying to smell girls from hundreds of miles away. I joined in the ceremony as best I could, although a nagging part of me thought that if we could smell them from here, they perhaps weren't as desirable as I was being led to believe, but the lads seemed ever so pleased when they apparently caught a whiff. Once one of them had locked on, the rest of us piled over to his area on the bridge wing with their heads back and nostrils flared, climbing over one another to get a fix. As the olfactory mixed with the erotic, the lads would begin to float skywards, sucking hard on the precious aroma, moaning and sighing with nasal delight. As they came back to earth, stories would ensue about previous Thailand conquests that this particular smell had brought rushing back to them. Testosterone-fuelled stories of macho achievement beyond the realms of male capability, and yet told with such wild-eyed conviction that I was actually getting scared.

The evening ritual, coupled with my own unrestrained imagination, drove me completely berserk on that sea passage. If you can put yourself in my place for a while before you read on, and try to think what it was going to be like, you will probably make yourself blind, but then, to find that the reality goes beyond what you even dared to imagine – well, that makes Thailand – at least for blinkered young sailors – absolute heaven on earth.

As the ship drew slowly towards its berth in Bangkok, I got my first glimpse of how far short of the truth my imaginings had been. There were girls in their dozens waiting on the quayside. It was really quite bizarre. Docks are functional, industrial places, generally populated by concrete greyness, miserable pot-bellied stevedores, heavy machinery, cranes, containers, fork-lifts, noise and diesel fumes. But not here. Here, these factors were pushed firmly into the background by brightly coloured silk, makeup, coiffed hair and perfume fumes. There were girls everywhere.

As soon as the first rope went ashore – with the ship still far from alongside and with no gangway down – the invasion began. Girls were climbing up the ropes, arm over arm, with grim determination in their eyes and handbags in their teeth. Girls were arriving expertly by parachute on to the foredeck. Girls were Fosbury-flopping over the bulwarks and dropping from the ceiling tiles by ropes into the accommodation like the SAS in red sarongs. It was unbelievable.

Close behind the girls were the Sales and Marketing departments from a couple of hundred electronics outlets. Small boats (called 'Bum Boats', for some unknown reason) came alongside us on the seaward side, and before you could say 'Citizen Quartz', hundreds of shopkeepers were piling over that side and claiming their pitch. By the time the gangway went down and the first Thai person made his dignified entrance via the orthodox route, the entire foredeck of the ship had been turned into a vibrant market place, with colourful stalls selling cheap watches, pirated music, portable stereos, sports equipment and a summer collection of light cotton clothes. I stood with a few of the lads in the bar and looked down in amazement as a conveyor belt of electronics came over the side from the bum boats and was set up for sale by number three hatch. The ship's security, which was supposed to police all the comings and goings, was utterly pointless. This was some operation. I had to admit that I did fancy a turn around the market. It looked great, and the prices were, by all accounts, irresistible.

The bar door crashed open and four Thai girls came in. They squealed with delight at having found the room they were looking for and came running over. They were young and beautiful, and I felt my tummy go all funny. These didn't look like scary, worldly prostitutes. They looked, well, wonderful. One of them, a girl with shoulder-length, jet black hair, hazel eyes shaped like a cat's and a tiny hourglass figure came to me. She took my arm and looked up into my eyes like a kitten in a pet shop pleading for a home. I couldn't believe it. If what the boys had told me was true, this girl was effectively mine. I could do with her whatever I wished. She would be my obedient servant. My plaything. I could do all the things girls in Britain would hit me for even thinking about, and she was stunning. It didn't seem possible that all this wonderful, wonderful beauty could be mine, all mine.

Oh my God.

My tummy wouldn't stop being all funny. Let's not forget, please, before you judge, that I was not only very young, I was in an environment – an entire culture, both on our side and on theirs – which accepted prostitution. The justification we fed ourselves was that these girls wanted husbands. They did what they did because they wanted a passport out. Indeed, many merchant sailors did marry girls from the Far East. We were doing them a favour by allowing them to test drive some potential British husbands. If the girls did well enough, you might just take them home with you. I made a decision: yes,

I would allow this girl to try me out. Although I wouldn't absolutely write off the possibility that we might one day be married and I could rescue her and make her grateful forever, I wouldn't let on that this was a tad unlikely. She had the choice not to devote herself to me, so it wasn't my fault. I'd let her try her very best first.

The door opened again and half a dozen more Miss Thailands came trotting in. Even though I was already very happily fixed up for the night and was thinking about perhaps turning in early, my tummy went all funny again. All these girls were dazzling. They were so well dressed and they had put so much time and effort into their makeup and hair and skincare. One of the new girls was truly one of the most beautiful girls I had ever seen. She took my breath away and, despite the girl already on my arm, I couldn't take my eyes off the new arrival. I felt a pang of guilt as I looked at her. She was petite, with a tiny, tiny waist – I could have put my hands round her waist and touched my fingers on both sides – and yet curvaceous and so, so graceful and just – just... Wow. This was amazing. And as I stared in disbelief that such a gloriously beautiful girl could be so readily available, she came over to me, lifted my arm, slid underneath, looked up into my eyes and smiled. Oh, my tummy. My tummy, my tummy, my tummy. I was instantly worried about the prospect of losing stunner number one, but then the new arrival released me from her gaze and acknowledged my first new friend. They reached across, smiled, held hands and kissed in fond recognition. They kissed each other. I had a Thai girl under each arm, they had both adopted me as their own and they were kissing each other. And you expect me to find this bad and unacceptable? As I excused myself for a moment and went to join the queue for a quick hit on Corkage's nebuliser, I could see no wrong...

A week later, I was standing on deck with NotNorman, watching the Bangkok workforce loading sugar with teaspoons into cups that they poured into baskets that they carried up and poured slowly into the holds.

'Man alive, these guys take an age to load cargo, don't they?' said Notters with a hollow misery in his voice. 'Can't they get on with it so we can go somewhere else?'

'It's ridiculous, isn't it?' I agreed, bitterly. 'How is a shipping line supposed to make money when these people take so damn long?'

NotNorman sighed deeply. 'We're gonna be stuck here forever.'

I was about to expand on the specific nature of my own depression, when MoneyBox came stomping up.

'When the hell are we going to get out of this God-forsaken Hell hole?' he moaned. 'Can't you make them work any faster? I can't bear it any more!'

I knew what he meant. I had seven girls living in my cabin. I mean, *seven*. I was scared to go near the place because they would all be pleased to see me. They would start touching me again. They thought I wanted another massage. They were under the misapprehension that I might enjoy more special oils. They thought it would make me happy to have more personal attention. They were wrong. They were going to kill me and it was a nightmare. I had moved out of my cabin and was sleeping with NotNorman on the boat deck. With me going missing for long periods, the girls were left with nothing to do but prepare their bodies and stand guard over two hi-fi systems, a dozen watches, three personally tailored, hand made cheesecloth suits and a library of pirated music so big you could run a radio station for a year without playing the same song twice.

As we stood complaining and comparing the physical symptoms from which we were suffering due to over-exposure to pleasure, Giewy came gangling along the deck. Even he had had enough. I mean, even Giewy had had enough. Think about it.

'Giew! It's all sorted, lads! Mate's given us two days off and I've organised a trip to the Bridge on the River Kwai. We leave this afternoon.'

I fell on Giewy's neck and wept. He was my saviour. A true friend in a time of need. I made a note to include him in my will. If I could leave the ship now, I might not have to go through any more of that sex nonsense. Praise the Lord.

I promised myself that Bangkok would be my sexual swansong. I never, ever wanted to see another pert breast or wiggly bottom or soft belly again as long as I lived. No more. Just the thought of a sarong dropping to the floor made me shudder. From now on, I'd have girls as friends only, none of that sweaty, pointless nonsense to worry about. Me and girls, we'd just be mates. I'd be the one bloke who could see beyond the physical side and connect with girls on a more spiritual level. I was relieved to have found a Finer Me. One with control over his animal drives. One who could dedicate himself to higher things. My life would be better from now on. More worthy. It was a lesson learnt, and a difficult, life-changing decision. Still, no pain no gain, and I would value the gain.

We Baboulenes are like that. We make a decision and that's final.

I would like to leave myself for a moment, if I may, bouncing along on a coach, watching the beautiful Thai countryside waft by on my trip to the Bridge on the River Kwai, in order to present you with one serious thought. The way we handle prostitution in the UK is all wrong, and, given that there may be some of you thinking of booking tickets to Thailand after what you just read, I think it is well worth a mention.

It is total and utter naïvety for the authorities to think that criminalising prostitutes will ever get rid of the problem. It won't. There will always be prostitutes and there will always be customers for prostitutes. We need to live in the real world, and legislate for reality rather than for some idealistic belief that one day we will live in a society in which nobody will bully the vulnerable; that in future no women will need to turn to prostitution; that people will be so fulfilled that they won't get addicted to heroine; that the sex industry is somehow going to fade away. We would like to think that one day all men – husbands, drunks, politicians, celebrities, the lonely and disfigured – all men – will be so socially advanced that they will not create the market for prostitution. Get real. Not only is the sex industry a necessary service, it is here to stay anyway. It should be treated as a living reality, regulated and made safe, not brushed under the carpet and ignored.

Even if you don't accept this, and steadfastly believe that a prostitute is a criminal, try to see it from this angle: criminalising prostitution punishes the victims of crime, not the criminals. This is the most exasperating aspect for anyone who really understands it. Most prostitutes are addicted to drugs and controlled by organised crime, and yet it is the prostitute that is targeted by the law. It is like saying that if you have your car stolen, you are involved in car crime – which you undoubtedly are – and if you are involved in car crime then you should be punished for it. That's how it works for prostitutes. The criminals are the people traffickers, the drug dealers, the money launderers, the Mafioso, the pimps and criminals who run the trade. The girls are left with no safe place to go. They are punished by the underworld if they try to escape their chains, and punished by the law if they do as they are forced to do.

Because prostitution is illegal, it operates underground in a black market and so the law as it is actually empowers the scum who run it. And the downside of legalising and regulating prostitution? I mean a good reason not to legalise it, based on the real world we live in, not on some unachievable hope that the sex industry might just pack itself up and shut down one day? If you can think of any good reasons, let me know. I'd be interested to hear them. In the meantime, the illegal human trafficking goes on, the infection of girls and their customers goes on, the loss of tax revenue goes on, the National Health Service cleans up the mess and the bad guys just keep right on winning.

But do you know the strangest thing? As we returned from the Bridge on the River Kwai and the coach pulled up next to the ship, I have to admit that my initial hope that the girls in my cabin would have gone home and left me alone was no longer stacking up. I couldn't seem to remember how in the world it made sense when I came up with such a lunatic idea, and yet I remembered quite clearly that the matter seemed perfectly reasonable to me at the time.

I don't want to go back on the Baboulene word on this matter, but a small part of me was disturbing my resolve. I had to keep fighting off a secret hope that maybe just a couple of the girls were still there. Their soft skin fragrant with oriental aroma; their hair tickling my face as they bent over me; their hands cool with oils as they prepared for the long night ahead. OK, maybe just three girls then. Just as a final goodbye to all that nonsense. That would be an appropriate farewell. But after Bangkok that would be it. No more. Never again...

However, back aboard the ship, events had overtaken us. Everyone was running around like crazy trying to find us. The ship had been sold. We had previously been told to prepare for a sugar run between Queensland in Australia and Penang in Malaysia, but that was all off. The ship was to drop down to Singapore and await its lucky new owners. No further cargo movements would take place. A skeleton crew would remain aboard for the handover. We cadets were to fly home immediately, in time to make it on to a college course at the Tyneside Marine College on the coast near Newcastle in the north-east of England.

Our plane was leaving the next day. A day of packing, filling in forms, paying-off the ship and trying to get around everyone to say goodbye, followed by a frantic drive across Bangkok sitting in the middle of a huge pile of bags in a white Toyota minibus. I entered a jumbo jet that was gleaming in the blinding sunshine at the old Don Mueang Airport, and emerged from it 14 hours later into a bone-rotting drizzle at London's Heathrow.

Chapter 14

Smilin' and A-Wavin'

When a car is not a car. Cowboys and Indian (food). An unwanted but beautifully lit audience with Root'n Toot'n Cap'n Hoot'n. Exams are coming – the lecturers get nervous.

The arrival back in the UK was something of a whack to the sensibilities. It was January, and for someone who had recently been basking in Far Eastern sunshine, it was not favourable to find oneself in the kind of temperatures capable of rendering a microscope into essential equipment for a big willy competition. Finding myself suddenly back home and with a few days to prepare before college, I decided that I deserved a reward for all my hard work, and set off on a purchasing mission.

So it was that I found myself staring doubtfully at a lowly pile of rusty metal, scuffed rubber and fluffy dice, which the salesman, in a moment of unbridled fervour, referred to as a 'sports car'. He seemed very sure that it was the answer to my dreams, and was anxious to point out the three solid, practical positives it had going for it: the car was unique, it was a head-turner and it was cheap. He forced me to admit that these facts were undeniable, although it seemed to me that it was all of these things for three equally simple reasons: it was old, it was knackered and it didn't have a roof.

The salesman's smile was not dented by my lack of enthusiasm. He looked on me as a father looks on a son who has yet to understand the world, placed a big sheepskin arm over my shoulder and walked me around the car, stroking its flanks with the pride of a racehorse trainer that reminded me of Dick Van Dyke trying to do Cockney.

'You gotta look at things different, my son, if you want success in life, y'know?' He stopped and turned me to face him, holding me by the shoulders and staring deep into my eyes to be sure that his trust was not misplaced. 'You do want success in life, doncha, son?' He relaxed when he saw me nodding and we carried on walking. 'Cor blimey, Mary Poppins, course you do. So look at it like this: you wouldn't be able to afford this beautiful car if it did have a roof, now, would you? And 'old' ain't bad in cars like this one, now is it? 'Old' becomes 'classic' in a beauty of this age, see? People round you ain't seein' an old car wivart a roof, are they? They sees a "classic convertible". See? That's better, innit? This classic convertible's unique featurisations – the ones what set it apart and makes it 'special' – are the very things what brings it into your price range! It's a big win win for you, eh? Win win!' And he punched the air in front of us to punctuate the wins. 'A good old double whammarisation! Win win!'

'Well… when you put it like that it seems reasonable, but you see…'

'Tell you what, son. Have you ever seen them crusty old souls up there smilin' an' a-wavin' from vintage MGs on the London to

Brighton veteran car run? Have ya?' He did the actions – smiling and waving to the gathered crowds on left and right sides with a simply enormous toothy smile on his face. I couldn't deny it. I'd seen them many times. 'There you go then. Note what they are doing wiv themselves: smilin' an' a-wavin', right? Smilin' an' a-wavin'. Look at them kids down there!' He turned a few more circles smilin' and a-wavin' to young admirers all around him. 'Love a duck! See? They're happy and cheerful and them drivers – smilin' and a-wavin' – them drivers, they ain't got no roofs, 'ave they? See? Surely a free spirited lad like you don't want the grief and responsibility of roof ownership, do ya?' He pushed me away and turned scornfully. 'Naaaah! Roofs is for losers!'

I still wasn't certain, and the grimace on his face told me he frustrated that I couldn't understand what he was saying.

'OK, son. You made me do it. I didn't wanna, but you forced me. I'm gonna divulgerise you a big old trade secret here. I'll get murderised if anyone finds out, but you're a good lad and I wanna help ya.' He looked all around to check if anyone was eavesdropping. 'Lissen, son. If, by some him-possible he-ventuality, you don't like this classic convertible sports car MOT Feb FSH two new tyres thirty mpg gd cond throughout, you know what you can do in March?'

I drew a blank. I didn't know what to do in March. I didn't know what he was on about at all. He looked frustrated. He turned me through 180 degrees and whisperised in my other ear. 'Lissen son. People what do waste their money on roofs, you know what they do wiv em in the spring? They take 'em off! All that money blown on a bloomin' roof, and where is it? On the floor in the garage! Ha! Mah mate, you could sell this baby on in March, when no roofs is just exactly how many everyone wants, and you could make a tidy prof. Out of me!'

He suddenly seemed to have sold the car to himself. His arm was removed from around my shoulder and he started backing off towards his hut.

'Now I fink abart it, son, I could sell it for double this price in abart two munf's time. I'm effectively givin' you money, 'ere. I'm not sure I can afford to do this deal. You'd better go, mate. I'm not sure abart this any more…'

Now, some people might have given up and left empty handed at this point, but we Baboulenes are wily negotiators, and after only a small uplift on the windscreen price (but still maintaining a massive potential profit in the Spring, when the price I could get for being the proud owner of exactly no roofs went way up), I persuaded him to part with it. The sucker. As I drove away with the wind in my hair, I couldn't help feeling what an advantage it was to be a winner in life. To outmanoeuvre a car salesman in the intense arena of financial negotiation takes some doing, but I had managed it. It's a wonder a guy like that can stay in business with people like me around. As he waverised me on my way with a big, brave smile on his face, I almost felt mean.

So off I drove towards college. A journey that required me to drive most of the length of the country, and I have to say that despite equipping myself with leather gauntlets and an epically long scarf like they wear on the veteran car run, the smilin' and a-wavin' phase didn't last as long as I might have hoped. During our negotiations, the salesman had regularly referred to the machine as a 'convertible'. I didn't want to split hairs with him, but, strictly speaking, it seemed to require several external factors to come together at exactly the right time in order to encourage it to display any noticeable ability to convert; at least, not in ways that could be considered helpful. For example, during the 150 miles of wintry M1 motorway going north from London, I experienced a cloudburst of rain near Northampton. My 'convertible' was quick to respond, converting swiftly and smoothly from an 'open-topped sports car' into a 'moving aquapark'. I tried to ignore the looks I got as I drove along with only my head visible above the surface, until things changed somewhere near Mansfield, where the temperature dropped and the rain turned into a blizzard. My car was quick to react. It converted smoothly from an 'aquapark' into a 'full load of snow' for me to sit in. Indeed, the entire blizzard seemed to want a lift, so I transported it up as far as Knaresborough, where we found we weren't getting along any more. I stopped by the road, opened both doors and ordered it out. But its spirit stayed with me, and, after four hours of driving, and with all further smilin' or a-wavin' activities formally postponed indefinitely, I tried to turn off the motorway for South Shields and found my arms couldn't manage the project. The reality of this grim, northern cold was beginning to hit home in ways that hadn't cropped up in conversation at the car dealership. It has to be said, I suppose, for the sakes of balance, that the local Geordie species didn't seem to have a problem as they headed out into the freezing night air in their string vests, but for the rest of us (or 'Southern Jessies', as we were formally known) it was face-removingly cold. Eventually I arrived facelessly in South Shields. I was lifted from the car – frozen into the driving position – and placed fully clothed and ever so gently (so I wouldn't shatter) into a warm bath to thaw out.

Once I had recovered from my cryogenics, I found I was at a place called Westoe House, a grand Victorian home attached to the college and converted into student accommodation. I had a bedsit to myself and, apart from the familiar presence of NotNorman and Giewy in the building, I recognised many other friendly faces from my induction course. It was exciting to see them all again. We all had stories to tell of our first trips, and the signs were that I was in for a relatively pleasant time at college. Maybe I could even have a break from the craziness of ship-board life...

Westoe House had strict curfew rules and security guards on the gates. This was because our time at college counted towards our formal sea time (thirty-six months of which were required before one could sail as a third officer). This was highly significant. It happened occasionally that a cadet would finally get his second mate's certificate (also required before one could sail as a third officer), but had still not achieved enough sea time. He then had to go back to sea for another trip as a cadet. After a four-year apprenticeship and having qualified, this was embarrassing, depressing and annoying. The sea time was precious and everybody knew to the day how much time they had got in and how much time they still had to go.

This said, I felt a strangely powerful compulsion to be somewhere other than the confines of Westoe House between the hours of midnight and 7.00 a.m. This was because the rules said I *must* be within the confines of Westoe House between the hours of midnight and 7.00 a.m. otherwise that day didn't count as sea time. I wasn't the only one who felt that rules like this were made to be broken. There was a general feeling abroad that it was just about essential to be outside the confines of Westoe House between the hours of midnight and 7.00 a.m.

I quickly found my feet, signing out as Giewy whenever I left the building. A check of the register would indicate that I had spent my evenings quietly studying alone in my room – apparently, I hadn't left my desk in weeks – whilst Giewy was out being irresponsible. Giewy never noticed this trick, mainly because he was signing out in my name every damn night, the weasel.

The college was a little unusual, in that it was a commercial college. It was paid for by the shipping lines and the Department of Trade and Industry to get us cadets not only through the twenty-two sea-related examinations that defined a second-mate's ticket, but also some academic qualifications to give us something recognisable to take ashore if we ever left the sea. The college also differed from normal colleges in that our lecturers were not proper lecturers. They were mostly ex-sea captains who had been forcibly removed from their beloved ship-board life for medical reasons. After a highly fulfilling life of global travel, in which they were literally and metaphorically at the helm, they suddenly found themselves in a tweed jacket with leather elbow pads, stuck in front of a bunch of cocky youths in a South Shields classroom. Make no mistake – they hated it. Oh, man, how they hated it. They were miserable, cantankerous old bastards who were disgusted at how easy life was for us compared to what they went through. They despised their own existence and wanted ever so badly to make life as hideous for us as they possibly could.

My personal tutor was a good example. Captain Howten – pronounced 'Hoot'n' in Geordie language – was a proud Durham man. He was big and broad, and carried great authority, but minor heart problems had meant no more ships. Now he lumbered miserably around the college like the last of the dinosaurs, lonely and awaiting extinction; the bags under his eyes bent him over and the bags of classwork under his arms slowed him almost to a stop. The most animated he became was when he would wait for us in the doorway of our top-floor classroom and vent his disgust at us as we arrived for his lecture. Holding the door open, he would sneer and swear at us with utter vitriol as we passed cowering in front of him. You couldn't make out many actual words in the diatribe of spit and derision he rained down on us as we crossed the threshold, but the regular use of the word 'shites' got the general gist across.

Once he had given us this personal welcome, he didn't even look at us again for the rest of the period. He faced the windows along one side of the class and droned out the material we were to learn, whilst staring wistfully out across the Tyne to the life he craved beyond that grey North Sea horizon. He had started his career on the old four-masted barques in the 1930s. He'd seen a raw, harsh life on those sailing ships, where men were truly men and life was genuinely tough. He had no time for us. We were mollycoddled and frivolous; we lacked respect and

– ptah! – our ships had engines. We were, in a word, shites. He didn't care if we turned up for his lectures or if we died on the floor. We mucked about quietly whilst he taught navigation and ship structure to the seagulls, which stared back quizzically at him from the window ledge. Maybe that's why seagulls follow ships: they want to try out what they learnt from Captain Howten. We always knew when his lecture was over, because he stopped, sighed heavily, picked up his files and trudged out of the classroom in hunched misery, like a migrating diplodocus, leaving both seagulls and students looking around at each other and wondering if that was it. We knew it was surely only a matter of time before poor old Captain Howten found himself sporting an Open University beard and trying on sandals in Clarks. Thus attired, he would surely go clean off his rocker and wipe out a campus full of cadets with a machine gun before turning the weapon on himself.

The only thing that livened him up was any mention of the government. It was a shite government, comprised exclusively of shites. They made the rules that forced him off the ships and into teaching after a mere stroke or two, so he devoted his life outside the college to anti-government activities. He would come in on a Monday, having been out campaigning for the miners or manning a picket line at the pit head all weekend. With his black eye, arm sling and neck brace, he would tell us not about the intricacies of nautical science, but all about how we should be going with him the following weekend to attend a rally with a speech by Arthur Scargill. He would pass a bucket around and we were invited to donate money towards the cause. We soon found out that passing up the opportunity to give generously had a disastrous impact on our marks for the term… and good marks were imperative if we were to avoid having to re-sit the course or, worse still, being given extra sea time – the ultimate punishment which hung over our every indiscretion.

Captain Howten also took issue with any decision made by the local South Shields Town Council shites. In the first few weeks I was at college, the new one-way system they had introduced for South Shields got right up his nose. He campaigned against it, he protested and agitated, he lobbied the local MP and chained himself to the diggers with the hippies when the work started. (We are talking about a severely bored human being here.) He failed to stop the changes at every junction, but still continued to object even after the work was complete. Every morning and evening, people would gather to watch the spectacle of a grimly determined Captain Howten at the wheel of his Allegro, haranguing all those around him as he followed the same route he had followed for decades, even though this now meant driving the wrong way up a busy one-way street with buses coming towards him at the top end of the town. He had been driving that route since time immemorial and he wasn't about to change now just because some wet shites on the town council said he should. It was quite touching really. In the end, the police shites took his car and license away, and the college – in a desperate attempt to calm him down – gave him a promotion and let him move into a large section of Westoe House so he wouldn't have to drive to work any more. Not only was Captain Howten my tutor, he was now also Dean of the campus on which I lived... and just to top things off nicely, he was my next-door neighbour within the building. My life was rather generously blessed with exposure to Captain Howten.

NotNorman once asked Captain Howten if we could smoke in class. The captain argued with the seagulls for a while about the rights and wrongs, until he realised that the government would certainly forbid it. We were instantly given permission to smoke in his lectures. Indeed, it made a positive difference to his demeanour as he lost no time in firing up a gasper for himself. It had a palpable, calming effect on the man. From then on, during every lesson, someone would ask the question, and Captain Howten would pronounce the words that became a catchphrase for years to come:

'Gentlemen… you may smoke…' (pronounced 'smaaw-uk' by the good captain, in his excellent broad Geordie.)

A week or two later, we decided to have a bit of fun, and we all brought in smokes. Every one of us. We brought in pipes and ciggies and cigars and rough shags and Rizlas and weed – there was even a hookah. Even the non-smokers and the skinny asthmatics from P&O brought in something wet and combustible and got involved. It was a marvellous effort. The question was asked, and the answer came:

'Gentlemen… you may smaaw-uk…'

As Root'n Toot'n Cap'n Hoot'n (as he became known) lit one up as well, and began educating the local bird life on the subject of sacrificial anodes on ship structure and the rules regarding their use as defined by the Department for Trade and Industry shites, we got out our Rothmans and Cubans, our black Bulgarian shags and Columbian golds, our matches and our oxyacetylene torches and began firing up combustible products on an industrial scale. Even the seagulls had roll-ups hanging from the corners of their beaks.

At first, Captain Howten didn't really notice. A certain amount of smoke had become normal and comforting to him. Even as it increased in volume, it was mostly gathering at the ceiling and coming down gradually from there like a moorland fog. He was in a world of his own, so he just continued to remonstrate furiously with a black-backed gull who was struggling to grasp the concept of negative ions, and failed to notice the build-up of smoke. It was probably the hubbub from the class that finally brought it to his attention. The cloud base had reached head height for us in our seats and it was getting hard to see the top half of Captain Howten at all. When he did notice, he thought there was a fire, hit the alarm and began evacuation procedures in the style of Corporal Jones. By the time he realised what had happened, we were long gone. There were no further lectures that morning.

On the first weekend at the college, we went for a big night out. Led by Giewy (yes, I know...) and some of the other older lads who had already completed a college phase and knew their way around, we headed off to Newcastle – piled nine high in a classic convertible – to take on the best of the north-east's vest-clad and crew cuts.

Newcastle is a great place, I'm sure, and the Geordies I got to know personally were amongst the kindest and most generous people I've ever met, but on a Saturday night in Newcastle city centre, going about the place with a South London accent seems to light a fire underneath Geordie sensibilities. The sound grates with them, and their generous nature makes them anxious to help cure you of your affliction. Fortunately, they have a tried and tested treatment, which consists of kicking six bells of crap out of the patient until the accent goes away. And do you know what? It works. I developed an admirable line in being the strong silent type, and got to sit like a lord whilst the others got my drinks in for me rather than have a fight with the locals every time I opened my mouth. Do you remember when I was hoping to find a violent nutter in Gatwick Airport to occupy Ffugg, and found no takers? The reason now became clear. They were all attending an intense nutters conference in Newcastle. There were plenty up here to be getting things done and they were managing the workload admirably. There were nutters around every corner, keen to get down to business. There is a reason why you only see those adventurous travel writer types marching off into crocodile infested waters and uncharted jungles up the Congo. Marching into somewhere like Newcastle city centre is too damn wild, that's why. The place made West Africa seem like a stroll in the park. I became overwhelmed that night with a desire to go to Sunderland. And it's not very often you hear someone say that.

On this first night out, having survived the perils of Newcastle, we ended up at a wonderful spot known as the Kazzboy Club that became a fundamental part of my college life over the next few years. Indeed, some lecturers started whining to the shipping line that in order to teach us anything they had to hold their lectures in the main bar of the Kazzboy or never see us again. From the outside, the Kazzboy was just a faceless, unwelcoming door in a dark, rather seedy part of Shields, down near the river. The street lights didn't work and the wind whipped in off the Tyne. Giewy gave the secret knock ('shave and a haircut' – possibly not the most uncrackable code) and we waited. Nothing happened. It felt like the wrong place to me, but Giewy and his mates seemed positively excited. As we stood in the snow, stamping our feet and wondering if we'd been led here to have our livers removed, it seemed for all the world that there was nobody awake or even alive for miles around. Suddenly, a panel in the door shot back, and a narrow eye checked us over through a peephole. The older lads were known to 'The Management', so the panel shut, and the door opened. Two large-bellied gentlemen in badly fitting jackets and faded tattoos stood grudgingly to the side and watched us with heavy suspicion as we entered (clearly they were graduates of the CHSCSS: The Captain Howten School of Charm and Suit Selection). Even so, being ushered through a secret door at one in the morning was exciting, like walking into the den of an underground society.

Inside, a narrow stairway led us down. At the bottom was another door, which opened out into a huge room. The club was based around a central polished-wood dance floor, but nobody was dancing. In the days when the pubs shut at 11.00 p.m., the dance licence was just an excuse to keep selling beer until 4.00 a.m. At one end of the dance floor was a curry house

– chairs, tables, waiters, red velveteen wallpaper – a totally authentic curry house, set out in the open next to a dance floor. And from your seat behind an admirably cheap rogan josh, you could watch the action at the other end of the club. Because the Kazzboy was the clandestine meeting place for men and women who had a fetish they no doubt kept secret from their nearest and dearest. Here at the Kazzboy – and only here – they could indulge their perversion. These were precious nights when they could let down their hair and, for one all-too-brief night of freedom from their lives of secret longing, they could be happy in their own bodies.

For here, everyone at the far end of the dance floor was…

… a cowboy.

We stood open-mouthed at the scene. Every last one of them was a Butch or a Sundance; a Buffalo Bill or a Jessie James. There were stetsons and six-shooters, sheriffs and Cheyenne; there was a-whoopin' an' a hollerin' and a Yessirreee! The Wild West might have left Wyoming at the turn of the twentieth century, but it was alive and well and line-dancing the night away right here on Tyneside. Yyyyeee-haaaa!

We turned instinctively away from the loonies dressed as cowboys and towards the protection and relative sanity of the curry house, never for a moment taking our eyes off the action at the OK Corral end of the club. They had all the props they needed – a Wild West bar complete with nervous barman, a metallic-sounding piano, poker tables, wooden signs, a lasso and saddle – there was even half a wagon! There was a stage at the furthest end of the bar, and as we got ourselves comfortable, a quick-on-the-draw competition was already under way. One totally authentic cowboy (with an unfortunate Geordie twang to his best Wyatt Earp) took on another in a shoot-out to the death. They had big Smith and Wessons, sweaty stubble and mean expressions. There was the posturing and the big talk and when they drew their guns and the shots rang out – man alive! – the gunfire was nothing less than terrifying. As well as all this Western authenticity, there was also an enormous amount of good old Northern banter going along with it too. It was amazing, and it was very funny. We hadn't been there ten minutes when one Geordie sheriff swaggered up in his chaps, pulled a gun on a cattle rustler who was laying low in the curry house and growled:

'Stick yer hands up, yer bum!'

The cattle rustler wasn't quite sure how to obey that particular instruction without putting us right off our sag aloo.

It soon became clear that the shoot-out was an ongoing and organised competition. Each new stand-off was heralded by the music (that whistly, high noon theme, taken from *A Fistful of Dollars*, I think), the swagger and the threats, the tension, the bad acting, the sweaty brows, the twitching trigger fingers, then... BANG! BANG!

This was followed by an argument (in whining, high-pitched Geordie voices) about whether the Cisco Kid or Black Jake got his shot off first. Everyone turned with bated breath to await Sheriff 'Whip' Withenshawe's decision. The Whip sweated in unshaven close-up as the pressure mounted. He spat out his chewing tobacco, paused, then with Clint-like authority and Lee Marvin's deep toned drawl, he pushed back his hat and came down on the side of, 'the Kiiiiiiiiiid'.

His adjudication was followed immediately by an even higher-pitched tantrum from Black Jake about whether the Cisco Kid, having shot first, missed or not. Things were going from bad to worse for Black Jake who was now not only dead, but was losing the argument about how he got that way in the first place. Then it got personal. Black Jake claimed that, although the Sheriff called himself 'The Whip', he was really the Cisco Kiiiiiiiiid's Uncle Trevor from Wallsend, and the adjudication was therefore unsafe. Judge Dread would be back next week, and Black Jake asserted that true justice would be back with him. The sheriff, having his honour brought into question, rose to his feet with barely-controlled fury, pushed his hat forwards again and, with fingers trembling over his widow-maker, challenged the yellow-bellied son-of-a-rattlesnake to a shoot-out.

'Eeeee, arl fill yus full of lead, hinnie!'

Whip Withenshawe seemed genuinely furious, and later we found out why. It wasn't simply that his honour as a law enforcer had been called into question, but Black Jake had gone too far when he broke the club's sacred code amongst cowboys and referred to him as 'Trevor' in public. People's real first names just didn't help the Wild West atmosphere, so they were strictly banned in favour of an individual's chosen pseudonym, and no other form of address was allowed. Black Jake had broken the code by calling The Whip 'Trevor', and The Whip wasn't going to let him get away with it. He challenged Black Jake to a dual, and when Black Jake turned him down (pointing out that he was dead already and was effectively conducting this argument from beyond the grave), Whip Withenshawe got so mad he stood up and, to gasps of horror from the townsfolk, exposed Black Jake to the whole community for the Jeremy he really was. Trevor went even further, announcing to the world that not only was Black Jake's real name Jeremy, but that some people called him 'JJ'. Black Jake was incensed. For years he had kept his shameful Jeremyness a secret, so despite his recent demise, he rose to his feet as menacingly as only a freshly-outed Jeremy can. The music started and the tension built again towards another shoot out. Black Jake was angry over the favouritism afforded the Kiiiiid. Whip Withenshawe was angry over being uncovered as a closet Trevor. You could hear the anger in their voices as they bore down on one another. They stood face to face, the midday sun beat down, the crowd held its breath, the barman ducked behind his bar and it was down to two Wild West legends, Trevor and Jeremy, to sort this thing out once and for all.

BANG! BANG!

The sheriff froze and his knees wobbled. The gun fell from his hand and he clutched his belly. He staggered about with his mouth open and eyes pleading, bumping into furniture and choking on a packet of theatrical blood. This guy was no Black Jake. He wasn't going to argue about whether he'd been hit or not. He was breathing his last and he was going to milk it for everything he could. It was more like watching the Dying Swan sequence from Swan Lake than High Noon at the OK Corral as he spun on one leg and staggered in circles for ten minutes clutching his heart. They even had tables and sugar-glasses and swing doors (that didn't go anywhere) and other props that a stricken sheriff could blunder into and turn over and burst through and smash up on his way to a death that never seemed to arrive. It was wonderful stuff – like watching an Italian striker going down for a penalty. When the sheriff eventually fell to the floor, cowboy friends and relatives rushed to his aid; his wife cradled his head to listen to his last, croaked message of love, then, with one final death wobble on the floor, he died. There was great applause from all around the club, but this was too much for his 'depurdy', Baby Face Braithwaite. He rose from the sheriff's side in smouldering rage to challenge Dead Black Jake to a shoot-out – and the whole thing went merrily rolling round again. It was hugely entertaining. I particularly enjoyed the occasional fist fight that involved everybody. It was triggered by a surly looking bunch of Apaches bursting through the swing doors every hour or two. They had apparently sneaked over the border from their reservation in Accrington Stanley.

It occurred to us that this was no place to have an actual fight or to really die. You'd be staggering about trying desperately to get someone to call for an ambulance, and all these cowboys and cowgirls would just applaud your antics until you stopped breathing. There would be no getting through to the real human beings under the hats – the Mabels and the Lionels, the Ackroyds and Blenkinsops. They'd be too busy line dancing around you to be of any genuine medical assistance.

We never joined in with any of this, of course, despite our fascination and the fun they seemed to be having, but you had to admire these people for doing what they wanted to do without embarrassment. I was even grudgingly envious. They were having such a good time. They clearly got enough out of it to make the journey across town dressed like that worthwhile. I mean, can you imagine that journey? I was threatened with a beating in Newcastle earlier that night simply for being from Somewhere South, and yet these guys from Wyoming got off scot free. Maybe it was because they were packing heat.

Once we were finished at the Kazzboy, it was 3.30 a.m. We were full of curry, exhausted from laughter and ready for bed. We made a note to come back early on the first Saturday of the following month when the place was due to be ambushed by a coach load of Mexican bandits from Chipping Sodbury. I couldn't wait.

'What do we do now?' asked NotNorman. 'We can't get back into our rooms. Where are we going to sleep?'

'Don't worry,' said Giewy, winking at us like a wassock, 'We'll show you the way back in.'

Giewy and his peers from the previous intake had it all worked out. We followed them back and soon we were staring up at the steep sides of Westoe House. Actually, we didn't just stare up at it, we noticed an open window high up on one side and spent a happy half-hour throwing snowballs into someone's room. It was fun – and we must have dumped at least a hundred snowballs each in there. A good, honest endeavour someone could discover and appreciate later in the day, particularly as they would have absolutely no idea how or why there came to be so much water all over their floor. Excellent. We also lifted up Captain Watson's car, turned it round with our bare hands and replaced it tightly against the wall, with the nose in close to the garage door at the end. It was hard work, but we reap what we sow in life, so it would be worth it. Apart from the fun of seeing the man scratching his head and wondering how on earth his car turned itself round, it would be almost impossible for him to get it out from that spot, even if there was nothing parked behind. A very satisfactory night's work.

'OK, lads,' said Giew. 'Here's how we get back in…'

The older lads led the way along to the far end of Westoe House. The lights from the security gate could be seen, but we were in the shadows some way along and couldn't be seen by the guards (actually, we could be seen because of the somewhat brash flashing lights on the Christmas tree we were carrying, but more on that in a minute).

With two hands, Giewy indicated a drainpipe as if it was a top prize in a game show.

'OK. You do the Romeo thing and climb up here.'

The drainpipe was alongside a trellis on which a climbing rose was sleeping away the winter. 'See up there? Third floor? That window has been deliberately left open. Jump in, run across the room and you're in the main corridor. Up you go – and say 'Hi' to Tommo as you cross his room. He's used to it – buy him a beer tomorrow and he'll be fine.'

Perfect. My precious bed was becoming a priority, and here was a way to be reunited with my loved one. NotNorman started his climb. I was next.

'Here, Windy,' said Giewy, handing me a Christmas tree. 'Don't forget this.'

We had passed a pub on the way home that still had a Christmas tree up at the front, complete with merrily flashing, multicoloured lights and a fairy on the top sporting an ominously forced smile, as if she was hiding a deep rooted discomfort from her seating position on the top of the tree there, but wanted to keep smiling for her public. We decided to rescue the pub from the bad luck that results from leaving a tree up after twelfth night, and took it along with us. We all felt a driving need to give the tree a new home in the toilet bowl of the staff toilets back in Westoe House. However, there was a bit of an issue with this particular item of stolen goods. It had a battery in the base so that the lights flashed in somewhat vivid and attention-grabbing ways during the long walk home through Shields, and continued to do so despite all attempts to turn them off. It was as if the tree knew it was being stolen and was crying out for help. Fortunately, no police cars drew up to investigate the light show.

The lights were bright and cheerful, particularly against the background of a crisp winter's night, and I did feel that carrying the thing up the side of a wall might leave me somewhat exposed. All the same, we'd be quite safe once it was through the window, so I took the tree, with its lights, decorations, fairy and all, and began my climb. I think it was my inebriated state which made it seem so important to lug the tree into the house, but as the yellows, greens and reds flashed gently round my head, I did feel a sense of mission. It would look just perfect, flashing away in that toilet bowl. Once in place, we would twist the fairy's head through 180 degrees. With her forced smile, she would look uncannily like the girl from *The Exorcist*, and that could only serve as a positive contribution to healthy staff bowel movements. Anything to help. We were hoping this would be the third event in the tipping of Captain Watson over the edge. First, his car had turned itself around and cornered itself up against the garage doors whilst he wasn't looking, then his room had filled itself with water, and now there were Christmas trees with possessed fairies emerging from a toilet that could normally be relied upon to resist festive blooming. We were hoping to witness Captain Watson stumbling from the building sucking his thumb later in the day.

The climb was vertical, but it was surprisingly easy to work my way upwards. The combination of drainpipe and trellis made it a cinch, despite the encumbrance of a Scots pine, the accompanying light show, NotNorman's arse above me, a line of sailors below and a fairy screaming silently for help through a clenched smile just behind my head. As I waited for NotNorman to get in through the window above me, I looked back down. I was a good 30 feet up – high enough to decide quickly not to look down again. What I did notice in my glance downwards was that, behind the orderly queue of drunks head-to-toe on the trellis beneath me, Giewy and his mates were waving us on from the ground. With hindsight, it did briefly occur to me that only us new boys were actually attempting the north face of Westoe House, and that the encouragement of the older lads from down there at base camp had a certain 'happy-to-help' vibe to it that I didn't quite like. They were smiling like fairies, if you see what I mean. But it was too late now, and my suspicions were not raised enough before NotNorman began to move again. He climbed in the window, dropped to the floor, and I made my way up. As I put my hand on the frame, and tried to manoeuvre body and fir in through the window, I was conscious that NotNorman had made it across the room. He opened the door at the far side, and some light splashed into the room. I heard NotNorman speak gently in the stillness of the room.

'You awake, Tommo? Don't wake up... it's just us. Cheers, mate.'

I was struggling a bit, so I called in a loud whisper.

'Oi, NotNorman! Come and take this tree, will ya? I can't get in the window!'

I saw Notters approach, his large frame looking strangely unfamiliar in the stroboscopic switch from red to yellow and green as the coloured lights flashed calmly across the town. I felt the tree being taken from me. It moved across towards the door.

The main light then banged on in the room, and staring at me from the switch was… Captain Howten, wearing Rupert-the-Bear pyjamas, holding a flashing Christmas tree and looking at me with a face like thunder. The fairy next to him looked at me too, in tightly clenched innocence, as if she was the stoolie. I was so shocked that I nearly just let go. Captain Howten was always a volcano about ready to blow, and I was terrified of him at the best of times. Now, as he came at me with outstretched fingers flexing ominously, with his enraged face and a morbid fairy bearing down on me, both changing from red, to green and then yellow every two seconds, it was like a visitation in a nightmare. I tried to get back down, but the guys coming up behind me were not aware of the last minute changes in personnel above, and were still trying to come up.

'Get back! Get back!' I shouted. 'It's Root'n Toot'n Cap'n Hoot'n! He's coming!'

I was then treated to the absolutely unique sound of eight young sailors panicking on a trellis. There was also absconding laughter from the street level below. I then felt large hands grab my jacket and I sailed in through the window of the third floor of Westoe House.

'Sit doon there and divvn't move!' fumed the captain, throwing me against the wall. He then ran to the window and looked out to try and identify others.

'You… you… you… you… shites!' he shouted hugely across the town. 'I'll get you all for this… every shiteing one of you!'

He turned back towards me, his eyes blazing. He took two paces, then stopped, thought a moment, turned back to the window and hung out into the street again.

'And divvent call me Tommo!' he screamed, banging his head on the window frame with the exertion. We'd clearly touched a nerve with that one.

Down below, the security guards had heard the rumpus. They arrived at the scene of the crime, where they collected up cadets as they dropped into the flower beds around the bottom of the trellis like fruit falling from the trees. Meanwhile, up at the now unmanned security gate, Giewy and his mates sauntered unchallenged into the accommodation and headed off for a well-earned sleep. They did indeed know how to get in after hours. The trouble was, we were sacrificial to the cause. From the whole group of us new boys, only NotNorman got inside, and even he was later identified, because I had brilliantly named him through Tommo's window.

The following week we were carpeted by Captain Howten. NotNorman and I were given an additional six months sea time to add to our required total. Not only was this disastrous in itself, what made it worse was that now even Giewy was doing me up with practical jokes. And I thought college would give me a rest from all that.

Electricity was the first lecture of the day, three days a week. The early start, combined with the horrific difficulty of the subject matter, resulted in students usually being outnumbered four-to-one by gulls. As the term progressed, it became evident that we were in trouble with Electricity. We had to pass the exam, but we didn't know one end of a volt from the other. If you needed a fuse to be changed in this neighbourhood, you were better off calling in a seabird. This wasn't exclusively our fault. Captain Howten also knew nothing about electricity. Indeed, after he had held the door open and showered us in spit for ten minutes for being shites, he then stood at the window and piled further spit and derision on the subject of electricity in general for its part in ruining the world, then went on to teach us other things. During electricity lectures, we had learnt from Captain Howten how to blackball scabs at a picket line, how to intimidate a constituency MP during his surgery hour in town and how to tell a Guillemot from an Arctic Tern through a classroom window. But by the time the exam rolled around, we wouldn't have known a watt from an amp if they were put through our nipples (although such material could be learnt through practical sessions at the Kazzboy Club on Wednesday nights). It was not a happy circumstance because we had to pass every single one of the twenty-two exams set over the four years in order to qualify as navigating officers. Failure meant a re-sit and more college time. I couldn't see any way we could pass this one however many times we sat the class. It was depressing, to be honest, because electricity was so totally irrelevant to our lives at sea, and so damn difficult to understand, but there it was. We weren't the only ones feeling depressed about it. One day, Captain Howten actually turned from the window and looked at us. That's how bad it was. He appeared even more miserable than usual, and sighed a mastadon sigh as he made his pronouncement.

'Howay, lads. I have to go clear ova the uther side of the camp-oos to see the dean of the main college. I mean, reet waaay ova the uther side, there, and so whilst I'm gannin, you have to promise me that you worn't look in this envelorpe heeya.'

We all stopped talking and looked at him. What was he on about?

'Y'see, this envelorpe heeya has the electricity examin-ear-shun peea-pus insade it, like, and I'd hate for it to get into the wrong hands, ya knaar? You boys make sure it's kept good and safe, noo, cos I'm haway for at least fifteen minutes, so it really is important that I can rely on youse shites, reet…?'

He put the envelope on his desk, patted it forlornly then shuffled out of the room without a backward glance.

We looked at one another in disbelief, then sprung into action like a crack troop of SAS soldiers. This was a lifeline. We posted lookouts at each end of the corridor, another two on the door, and then worked in pairs transcribing the questions onto rough paper. The job was done in minutes and the envelope returned to its formal position as if untouched by human hands. Agreement was reached that we would deliberately get a few wrong each to keep it all real. We did a good job. Indeed, it was evident from Captain Howten's face when he came back that he was worried that we hadn't actually looked at the papers after all, such was our convincingly angelic demeanour.

We realised what was happening. This was a commercial college, funded by the Merchant Navy. Howten was paid on results, and didn't want to lose his job. We recognised that he wouldn't be so helpful on the important subjects, where our lack of knowledge might result in shipwrecks and loss of life, but he'd help us with the pointless stuff like electricity. It was just as well, really, as I was also having a bit of a sweat with meteorology, maths and ship stability to name but three other irrelevancies, so every little bit of help was welcome.

One hour before the official end of the electricity examin-ear-shun on the following Friday morning, NotNorman and I walked free from the hall out into the winter sunshine and breathed deeply on the cold, sweet air. We suddenly felt a lot more optimistic about our prospects of success. We could see a whole new method for passing exams opening up before us, and a backup career as qualified electricians becoming available should the need arise. In fact, so sunny were we in our disposition that we gave ourselves the rest of the day off, and indeed, the weekend off, and decided to take a trip to the playground of NotNorman's youth – the Lake District of Cumbria.

Little did we know how long it would be before we would see the college again…

Chapter 15

BambiGate

Roofless People. Survival in the face of bad jokes. NotNorman's money-making scheme – Windy is squeamish. A surprise present for a salesman. Fun in the car park.

As the snowfall steadily brought the north-east of England to a standstill, and the radio advised people not to travel unless it was absolutely necessary, NotNorman and I put on our smilin' and a-wavin' gear and our best stiff upper lips and headed out of South Shields in an open-topped sports car for the comfortless exposure of the Pennines, bound for a drinking weekend in the north-west. NotNorman was very keen to show off his family and friends, and the area in which he grew up: the Lake District of Cumbria. He was proud of where he lived and obviously had a wonderful childhood. I was excited to visit the Lakes, and to meet his NotMum, his lack of brother, his non-ex sisters and his failure to be a good father.

So off we went, in my NotConvertible, and how we were turning the heads! To see a couple of handsome lads, young and carefree in their classic two-seater, crossing the Pennines with the roof down, the wind in their hair and snow up to their necks, was clearly something a bit special to these sheltered people. However, even though the public looked at us as we motored by, we didn't do much smilin' and a-wavin'. NotNoman made it clear after only a few miles that he wanted me to stop. All the same, it was great to be so alternative, young and attractive.

We discovered another interesting thing about driving a convertible. Not only does it bring additional excitement to the travellers, but any maps you have in the car become caught up in the thrill of it all, too. At first, as you drive slowly through the town, the maps are happy to lie neatly on the passenger's lap in traditional map fashion. But once you get a bit of speed up, they like to leap up when you least expect it and wrap themselves around the driver's head in order to get a better view. They put up a surprising amount of resistance to getting them off, too. It takes two of you to get matters back under control, and whilst you are thus distracted, the car makes a break for it across the fields towards Yokenthwaite. By the time we were up on the Pennines, relationships between the sailors and our cartography had gone downhill. As fully professional navigators, we were expert in the use and manipulation of maps, and we felt hurt by this one's behaviour. We felt we deserved more from our working partner; without us, it would have no meaningful role in life, but there was no appealing to its conscience. During our map's third attempt to envelope my cranium, at 60 mph on a main road, the ensuing tussle saw a complete breakdown in relations. The map ended up leaving the vehicle by the rear and attaching itself to the windscreen of the lorry speeding along behind us. And do you know what? The cheeky sod of a lorry driver stole off with it. We slowed down to get it back, but he was off. He smashed through a farm gate and the last we saw he was bouncing through a herd of wild-eyed stampeding cows. He was driving like a maniac – and all for one measly map. We even heard the guy shouting with delight at his booty. You just can't trust anyone these days.

They say that the wonderful thing about banging your head against a wall is when you stop. When we finally made it, after several hours, to Bowness and stopped the car, the dark pain and misery of the journey was replaced, as if by magic, by a snow-spangled village overlooking Lake Windermere. The ice particles that had been whipping our faces turned into dancing snowflakes. The biting wind that had been gnawing our very bones became a warm glow as we surveyed the Christmas-card scene before us. I adored Bowness the moment I laid eyes on it, not just for saving me from hypothermia, but for being everything you would want it to be. Its welcoming vista heralded the beginning of a magical weekend. The Lake District is so beautiful at any time, but I loved it in the winter. The tourists are gone, the locals are relaxed, the scenery unparalleled and deep, fluffy snow tops it all like icing on a cake – it was breathtaking.

The weekend went perfectly. Big dinners, beery nights, wintry walks and roaring fires in country pubs with NotNorman, his NotFamily and no-friends were enjoyed by, em, nobody. (OK, OK, I'll stop now...) Before we knew it, it was Sunday evening, and it was time to go. However, as luck would have it, we couldn't. The car was snowed in so deeply we couldn't even find it on the driveway let alone drive back over the Pennines. The radio told us that the whole area was completely cut off, and the television news had those wonderful pictures they trot out every year of a blizzard through which a series of headlights glides gracefully sideways off the road without a hint of a smile or a wave from the driver. There was nothing for it but for us to take shelter, dig in and implement our perfectly-honed survival techniques... in the pub.

NotNorman knew the landlord of the King's Ransom very well. He was a fat, bald jovial man who stood with his hands on his hips and turned his head on one side when he was listening to you. He was known locally as GoLarge, because his pub did not skimp on the portions of excellent, traditional English fare. GoLarge had a small head – although it seemed to vary in size depending upon how hard he had to think – and a remarkable laugh that rendered him helpless. It consisted of one huge, long 'Haaaaaaaaaaaarrrrrrrr!', followed by a long line of 'heh, heh, heh, heh's that continued until he was skinny and blue and his head was the size of a raisin. When you heard the expression 'dying of laughter', you felt it was actually possible for GoLarge, as his ability to breathe back in again was disabled by his laughter. GoLarge was also famous for making crap jokes. Endless, endless double entendres and Beano material which somehow became funny, firstly because they were all sponsored by the RAC (Real Ale Consumption – that was one of his), and secondly, because he just never stopped. Here are a couple of things you have to say every day if you are GoLarge. He would shout up the stairs to his wife:

'Oi! Maggie! Can you help me get this crate of beer upstairs, love?'

'Why don't you just leave it down there?'

'Cos I already drunk it! Haaaaaaaaa-aaarrrrrrrr, heh, heh, heh, heh!'

If you are GoLarge, here's what you have to say whenever you hear the sirens of an ambulance go past.

'Well, he's not going to sell many ice creams at that speed, now is he? Haaaaaaaaaaaaarrrrrrrr, heh, heh, heh, heh!'

A delivery driver stuck his head round the door to hand something over for GoLarge's wife. He called across to GoLarge.

'Excuse me, does Maggie Holland live here?'

His response was instinctive. 'Aye, she does. Just dump her on the doorstep there and we'll put her to bed later! Haaaaaaaarrrrrrr, heh, heh, heh, heh, heh!'

If it was a particularly good – or even original – joke, he would turn to us with open-mouthed delight, in the style of Kermit the Frog, to see how it had gone over with his public before collapsing with laughter himself and beginning the process of haaarrring himself into a skinny tiddler before re-inflating on the intake cycle back to the size of a bouncy castle. It was so infectious, and he was a wonderful host despite the jokes and, to be honest, we had been pretty much living at The Ransom for the whole weekend with or without snowy excuses. It was a cosy, picturesque pub, with great food, frothing ales and an irresistible habit of failing to recognise any sort of closing time. Our pattern was to turn up late morning, get pleasantly sozzled with a light-hearted and friendly bunch of locals, and stay that way for, well, permanently. Nobody got off-yer-face drunk, and yet nobody ever got round to sobering up either. It was a seductive lifestyle, and one that made for a very relaxing, stress-free passage of the hours... days... weeks... years.

We rang the college each morning from NotNorman's hallway and explained how things hadn't improved. We would wring our hands and say how hopeless it all was, and they would hope we were holding up OK and say how hopeless it all was, and we'd all agree how hopeless it was and we would promise to try our hardest to get back tomorrow. The phone would go down and we would smile broadly at each other, get our walking boots on and tramp across the snowy fields through the chill air to the King's Ransom, where we would stomp our feet in the doorway, hail a hearty good morning to our fellow refugees and get down to the business of survival.

Now, pubs need deliveries to stay meaningful, and deliveries need clear roads. By Wednesday, the beer was holding up fine, having a good long shelf life, but the pub menu was wearing a little thin. NotNorman and GoLarge had indulged a confidential conversation that had set Notters thinking. As we left that night, I asked him what was wrong, and NotNorman explained to me on the soberingly chilly stomp home across the moonlit fields that the following day at the pub might easily cost us nothing.

I didn't know what he meant until the next morning. As we prepared to leave the house, I couldn't help but notice NotNorman going to a good deal of trouble to conceal a certain object under his long coat and down the side of his boot.

'Right! All set!' said NotNorman as the object became invisible. 'Can you see it at all?'

I stared back in disbelief as he continued his fashion show, cat-walking back and forth to ensure it could not be seen from any angle. In the end he was satisfied, and set off into the street. I was horrified. His coat was large and effective. It hid the object, but it didn't hide the fact from me: NotNorman was carrying a high powered rifle.

'Look, if it's got that bad?' I stammered, running to catch up. 'I'll pay for the beers, OK? There's no reason…'

'Rabbits,' said Notters. 'It's for the rabbits. GoLarge'll give us two quid a pop. Fiver for a duck!'

'Oh, I see,' I said, quietly. 'You're going to… to…'

'Now I think about it,' said Notters, licking his lips, 'I rather fancy duck for lunch, don't you?'

He stood still for a moment, considering the à la carte options and therefore the route we would take to pick up menu items along the way. Having grown up in the Lakes, NotNorman was comfortable with the huntin', shootin' and fishin' lifestyle, and all those sorts of earthy, northern things that I didn't get involved with in South London. I was profoundly uncomfortable with the murder of innocent wildlife. Meat should be obtained naturally, in the civilised manner by which we've obtained it for decades: wrapped in cellophane in a supermarket. Going out and killing it ourselves was just plain immoral. Or something.

'NotNorman, I think we should be getting back to college. We've been out a long time, and in all honesty, the roads are clearer now. We could drive…'

'We'll go for duck,' he said finally. 'Worth more money, and they don't understand ice, so you can pick 'em off dead easy in this weather.'

As we stomped off across the fields I could tell from the way he sniffed the air, slitted his eyes and slapped down the small talk that he was serious. I was going to witness ducks being shot because they couldn't understand ice. And confused rabbits running, terrified, in circles before… it didn't bear thinking about. Knowing NotNorman, I didn't trust that these would be swift and clinical deaths. The whole thing might make us a fiver, but it was not a prospect I relished. I was trying to think of a convincing way of calling him off, but I was already too late. As we hit the brow of a hill, NotNorman froze and put his arm across my chest to still me. I followed his steely gaze, looking for the poor bunny-wunnys kissing their crying children goodbye, and the exhausted quack-quacks trying fruitlessly to run away on an iced-up pond. There weren't any rabbits, and there weren't any ducks, but that wasn't good news. There, in the field ahead of us… were three deer.

I saw the pound signs in NotNorman's eyes roll round and stop at 'Jackpot'.

'No, Notters! No!' I hissed in an urgent whisper. 'You can't shoot one of those! It's… it's…' Well it was scary, but I couldn't say that.

'Yes, it's illegal, I know,' said NotNorman, never taking his eyes off the quarry. 'But the place is locked down by the snow – nobody'll catch us. And GoLarge'll give us forty or fifty notes for venison.'

NotNorman looked all round the horizon, assimilating logistical information like an army general.

'I need to get nearer, and down wind of them,' he said. 'Stay here and keep down.' And he set off to my right.

I stood frozen to the spot as NotNorman dropped out of sight of the deer and began to move around the contour line below the brow of the hill. The deer were nosing snow out of the way and grazing on the grass below. They suspected nothing. I was tempted to startle them, but I couldn't bring myself to do it, and I couldn't bring myself to turn away either. I lost NotNorman below the brow at the far end of the trees. He settled invisibly into the grass and I couldn't pick him out. I was sure he must be visible to me – and let's be honest here, NotNorman's was not the type of physique to melt easily into the background – but he simply disappeared. I was wondering where exactly he was and what he was planning next, when, suddenly, there was an enormous: BLAM! Birds scattered into the sky and the deer all ran, jerking this way and that, off into the woods. For a few seconds the report from the gunshot echoed back to us from the surrounding mountains. I felt disorientated, then looked back across the field. The deer were gone. All except one, which stood stunned for a second or two, then slumped slowly to on to its side in the snow.

NotNorman ran out towards it, waving for me to come across. I didn't move. NotNorman knelt down by the deer. He drew his knife and got busy as I dawdled over.

'Get on with it, Windy! People will hear the gunshot. We gotta go!'

He did some things to it which I managed to miss by delaying my arrival. Blood is always an urgent psychological trigger, but it looks even worse in the snow. There was a small but growing patch of dark red beneath the body of the deer, spreading from snowflake to snowflake, like strawberry juice leaking into a sugar bowl. There were also drops of blood splattered further away, and they glistened, suspended in the deep white snow like scarlet tears. NotNorman was pumped with success, and was regaling me with testosterone-laden excitement in his words. I could tell his heart was beating fast and he was buzzing from the experience of taking a life as he worked on the body. But I couldn't listen to him. I looked at the fallen deer and felt awful. He told me to cover over the evidence as he lifted her on to his shoulders and set off towards the pub.

I kicked and scooped snow over the blood, pleased to make it disappear, then ran to catch up. I had a lump in my throat as I watched the deer's head lollop on NotNorman's back as he walked. It was a female. She was big. Deer always look small and dainty, but up close they are much larger in body than their skinny legs suggest. And they are beautiful. Her tongue flopped from her open mouth, but her smooth fur and dappled lines were heart-breakingly perfect. NotNorman saw victory and success. I saw Death. Stark and uncompromising.

We arrived at the pub and stood in the car park. NotNorman put the deer down and stretched his back from the effort. It hadn't snowed heavily for a day or two, and the roads had been cleared to some extent. We were told that it was possible to get out through Kendal to the M6 now, and although we had no intention of passing this information to the college, there were a few cars in the pub car park. That meant there were strangers around and NotNorman needed to be careful.

'Right, I'll get GoLarge to open up at the back. You carry it over to the rear door, there. We can get it straight into the kitchen from there with nobody seeing.'

NotNorman headed for the front door. I looked at the deer. I couldn't touch her, let alone pick her up or move her. Forty quid. One beautiful life for forty quid. Life. £40. It somehow didn't add up. Not at all. Could I seriously be eating this later on? Could I, in all conscience, continue to eat and enjoy any meat if I couldn't accept the animal death that inevitably went along with it? Oh, the problems of a conscience. Life is so much easier without one.

NotNorman reappeared, this time through the back door. He saw the lack of deer at the entrance and stomped angrily across towards me.

'What are you playing at? We need to get it out of sight. Take a turn, lazy tosser.'

'I… I can't…' I said, meekly.

'Why? You gonna give me some sort of bad back routine, or something?'

I nodded towards the valley.

'Someone's coming.'

NotNorman looked off down the hill and, sure enough, a jeep was wending its way up the road towards us.

'Oh, crap! It's Stone!' said NotNorman.

'Stone?'

'Sergeant Stone! Police! The feds!' He hauled the deer back up on to his shoulders. 'We gotta find a hiding place!'

'Right!' I said, leaping down behind a bench.

'Not you, you idiot! The deer!'

I stood back up a little sheepishly and peered through the clear, cold air. Sure enough, it was a police jeep coming up towards us. NotNorman began to cast around for a suitable hiding place. None was obvious. The police car was getting nearer. NotNorman was getting desperate. He began to run towards the copse at the end of the car park. I assumed he was going to chuck it into the grass at the far end and just hope for the best, but as he jogged heavily along, he stopped and tried to open the boot of a car in the car park. No luck. He tried another. No luck. Then another.

The boot opened.

He threw the deer inside, slammed the boot and leaned on it with casual innocence a full quarter-second before the police car swung into the car park and stopped in front of the main door of the pub.

A large policeman emerged from the driver's seat and puffed his cheeks. He was as rotund and unfit as any of the locals who frequented the pub. He looked like a local farmer in a policeman's fancy-dress outfit. The hardest work I had seen undertaken since my arrival in the Lake District was being done by the button trying to hold Sergeant Stone's jacket together at the front. It would definitely go off pop at some point and probably maim someone.

'Morning,' he said to me in deep, suspicious tones. Everyone knew everyone round here and I was conscious that he was wondering who I was, but then all of the locals had done that since day one. Then he spotted NotNorman and his face brightened.

'Ah haaaaa! NotNorman! You back from the sea for a while, mate?'

NotNorman strolled over with overly dramatic ease. 'Ha, ha, ha! Yes, yes. Just came back for the weekend and we got snowed in here! This is my mate, Windy.'

The policeman looked on us like a proud uncle and rubbed his hands together. 'Excellent, excellent! Well, I guess I wouldn't be doing my community duty if I didn't buy you both a pint, right?' His broad Cumbria accent was warm and friendly. 'Do you think GoLarge is still sober? Come on, let's go shake him up!'

He ushered us through the door as we looked at each other. Fortunately, Notters had left his gun and his knife in GoLarge's kitchen. So far, we'd got away with it.

Inside, the fire was roaring already. GoLarge was rollicking along with a couple of locals who were getting stuck into their first few pints of breakfast. They were all pleased to see us, and seemed perfectly happy to see Sergeant Stone. It didn't scan with me. Local policemen don't share a casual out-of-hours pint with you first thing in the morning in London, but as the ales crashed down on the bar, it became clear that Sergeant Stone was going to mix directly with his public with the kind of single-mindedness one didn't associate with an officer of the law who was on duty and in charge of a police jeep. It was a refreshing approach to policing and one I could only commend. Sergeant Stone was also a man who had a point to make on just about every subject that came up, and was prepared to go to great lengths to ensure that everyone understood it. So we sat drinking with him all day long and into the evening.

It was getting dark when we left the King's Ransom. I guess it is possible that it was early evening, but it might have been midnight for all I knew. We only left because Sergeant Stone did, and he only left because his day's work was finished, including a couple of hours' overtime. We stepped outside with him and we all hugged warmly and reassured each other that we were each other's best mate. The good sergeant got in his car and kangaroo-hopped back down the hill, his cheerful baritone reverberating around the mountains happily as he went.

GoLarge appeared beside us, and as soon as Stone was far enough away, the faces were serious and we turned to go and retrieve our livestock. Well, deadstock. The cold air was sobering, but it still took me a few moments to focus the sixteen cars in the car park down to the four that were actually there. There was a van – that wasn't it. A Mini Cooper that hadn't moved for twenty years. Nope. A Nissan 4 x 4. Nope. And an Austin Maxi. And that was the lot. The Ford Morgue with the rather special optional extra we were looking for… had gone.

'Oh, noooo! No, no, noooo!' howled NotNorman as he vainly tried the boot catch of the Austin Maxi. 'Forty quid!'

I knew it was no good. The car into which he had deposited the deer definitely wasn't there. NotNorman turned despairingly to GoLarge and me, hoping against hope that one of us had an answer that would put him back in touch with his forty notes. GoLarge put his hands on his enormous hips and nodded sagely.

'I bet it was that bloke who was working in the corner through lunch,' he said.

That made sense. There was a man in a dark blue suit who had been drowning in paperwork around a plate of ham-and-eggs and a lager shandy throughout the morning. He had receding hair, a look of pain and heartache and the general aura of a failing salesman. The car was a salesmanish thing too. That was him. GoLarge continued to nod. Then a broad smile began to creep across his face. His eyes twinkled. His eyebrows raised so high that they appeared to float in the air above his head. NotNorman looked at him quizzically.

'What? What's so funny?'

'Imagine – it might be weeks before he finds it…'

Smiles crept across our faces too as various scenarios began to pan out for what life held for our salesman and his new pet as he drove around the country. His life was sad enough already without random mammals decomposing in his boot.

'He'll have a right go at his kids when he finds it,' GoLarge put on a soppy Mancunian accent for the man. 'All right you lot. Which one of you put a dead goat in the Corolla?'

We sniggered. Then snorted. GoLarge's accent, along with the word 'goat' just got to my drunken sensibilities massively, and we descended into uncontrolled mirth.

Then NotNorman got an idea. 'No, no, no! His wife will sniff the air next time she's in the car with him,' he sniggered. 'My goodness, Edwin? Was that you? What on earth have you been eating?'

My head spun. The idea of a rotting deer being mistaken for a fart would have had Corkage running directly for his mosquito outfit. I was laughing like I'd never laughed before. Bent double one moment, roaring at the night sky the next and then crying on GoLarge's shoulder as he did his Edwin voice again.

'Eeee! Did you tread in summit, love?'

I don't know if you've ever been drunk before. Ordinary things become hilarious. Genuinely hilarious things go off the scale and send you into orbit. For some reason, at the worst extreme, serious things have you in stitches and you become highly irritating to people being serious. I was at the 'off into orbit' stage. Even the word 'Corolla' was suddenly the funniest thing I'd ever heard. NotNorman and I rolled about as GoLarge reinflated for his next 'Haaaaaaarrrrr!' Good grief, I was helpless. Each time one of us became capable of speech, another scenario was proposed.

'Here, here, listen! He'll get pulled over on the motorway, right? By a cop car.'

'Yeah, right. And four deer'll get out, in traffic cop uniforms.'

'Is this yours, sir?'

'What? I never put that there! I never! It's a plant!'

'Bloody funny plant if you ask me, sir. Baaaaaaa! Baaaaaaaa! Would you blow in this bag please, sir?!'

And we were all sent directly to the floor once more, helpless as kittens and rolling around with booze-fuelled laughter at the image of a traffic-cop-deer-herd pulling poor Edwin over. And I kept seeing goats on police motorbikes, too. Beat-cop bongos. Gazelle CID. It became quite uncontrollable. I don't think I have ever laughed so much in my entire life as I did that night in that chilly Lakeland car park. The wonders of alcohol, eh? Don't you just love it?

Unfortunately for me – and for all of us in terms of this story – the truth is that I don't know what happened to that deer.

Edwin must have found the beast sometime, and it must have been a surprise to say the least. Even today, the thought of a deer in the boot of the car of a hapless salesman, who has no idea how it got there, brings a smile to my lips. BambiGate, they'd have called it on the news.

Now I think about it, poor old Edwin might set about removing this smile from my face if he ever reads this and finally gets to the bottom of the corpse in his boot and the Great Unsolved Mystery of his life, divorce, prison sentence, career failure and that beating he received from four cops with hooves and furry faces.

Back at college, one chilly morning at the end of February, NotNorman and I received letters telling us what we were in for. We were to stay at college for one more week, during which time we would complete a radar course. We would then have three weeks' leave before joining the MV *Global Panorama* in Vancouver, Canada for a trip down the west coast of the United States, the Pacific coast of Central America then various countries in South America, starting with Columbia and Peru. Wow! The letters also included signing-on papers for the *Global Panorama*. We would normally expect to sign these at the London office on the day we left the UK to join the ship, but because we were indentured to the company, we would be signed on by officials at college. We didn't understand the significance of this until we asked around, but soon two clear advantages emerged. Firstly, people like NotNorman, who lived in the north, didn't have to travel via London. Secondly, we could organise our own travel, on company expenses, and join the ship directly by whichever route suited us best.

We had heard of people using their one free joining and leaving flight to or from ships to have exotic holidays – there was no stipulation that you had to fly directly home from a ship or directly to a ship from home – and now we understood how it worked. Notters and I thought the thing through over several pints, a Wild West shoot-out, a saloon bar brawl and a tikka masala (with poppadoms shaped like cowboy hats), and decided on our course of action. After college, we would go home for a fortnight, then fly ourselves to Calgary on expenses a week before we had to join the ship. I had a friend working the ski season in a resort called Lake Louise close to the border between Alberta and British Columbia. NotNorman was not the skiing type. He'd never been before and wasn't sure he really wanted to try. I explained to him that there was more to the mountains than skiing. Although I was really rather good at skiing and would certainly be out bonding with fellow experts, he would have a wonderful time even if he stuck to his Hush Puppies the whole week. Eventually I persuaded him. We would holiday in Lake Louise before making our way down to join up in Vancouver. Perfect.

This said, something was still bugging me. Something wasn't right. During the following radar course, and the fortnight with my long-lost family back in South London, I met up with some of my old school friends. They were deeply troubled by 'A' levels or were already hating the jobs they had taken on having left school at sixteen like me. I listened to myself telling them of my world travel and the fun and games I had had around the world. I had got lucky and I was definitely enjoying it. So what could possibly be the problem…?

Chapter 16

Skiigotistical Personalities

The irritating ruggedness of ski instructors. Windy gets a privileged position. And a headache. Downhill all the way! Notes on combining window shopping and skiing. Windy loses his balance.

Two weeks later, NotNorman and I could be found en route to joining our next ship in New Westminster, close to Vancouver on the west coast of Canada. We had one more week of leave, so we stopped off in another of the world's more wondrous regions to do some skiing in the Rocky Mountains of Canada.

Actually, that is not strictly accurate, because at the time our story begins, we were actually getting drunk in a bar in the

Rocky Mountains of Canada. We were high up in a place called Lake Louise, on the border of Alberta and British Columbia, selected because of the presence of my Australian mate Carlo, who was working the ski season with his beloved partner and greatest love – his ego. Ski instructors are like that. All dashing and handsome and pleased with themselves, just because they wear puffy red jackets and look good on skis. It's sickening the way the girls fall for it. Carlo was blokeish and shallow. When he wasn't helping girls with their positions in the mountains during the winter months, he was skippering yachts through the Caribbean all summer. He was one of those people who envious types point at and say, 'Poor lad. No roots. No qualifications. Underneath that loud exterior, he must be desperately sad. He must crave a proper home and career…' Well, no, actually. He was one of the most contented human beings I've ever met. Shallow and loud? Yes. Drunk and promiscuous? Totally. Lots and lots of short-term relationships? What do you think? But hour-by-hour doing absolutely what his heart desired? Oh, yes. Did he give a fig what the rest of the world thought about it? Naahh.

On the Saturday we arrived, Carlo and his mates were preparing themselves for a day off on the Sunday. When you are a skiigotist, you spend your evenings claiming to those around you that you can do something more ridiculous and stupid on skis than the other skiigotists, and then on your days off, you all go out on the steepest mountains you can find and try to prove it. As we met with Carlo and his thrusting mates in the bar, they were getting very excited by the manner in which they had decided to impress themselves. Apparently, if you are stupid enough, you can get yourself dropped off by helicopter in some remote area of the Rockies near the moon, and then cheat death all day trying to ski home again. NotNorman and I wished them luck, and promised to raise a glass to them over a long lunch the next day.

SKIIGOTISTICAL PERSONALITIES

I guess they had been planning an early night, what with helicopters and mountains and 170-degree slopes to deal with the next day, but our arrival did warrant a couple of beers and, being a special occasion, we did also award each of those beers a celebratory Schnapps chaser. And as the alcohol inflated the egos, it inevitably became an evening of storytelling, mostly concerning heroics on the ski slopes. One by one, the baton passed from thrusting young rooster to thrusting young rooster, and each would top the other with stories from the slopes that would curl your hair; stories that took the highest of mountains and the most arctic of conditions, and mixed them with Klammer-esque speeds, Shackleton-like survival and James Bond's suavity.

One of these thrill-seekers – a French-Canadian called Jean-Luc – with piercing blue eyes and four cubic metres of swept-back, blond hair, told us how there was once this guy (there was always 'this guy' in every story. I don't know who 'this guy' was, but he sure went through the mill) in his ski class who keeled over with a cardiac near the top of Mount Whakapapa in New Zealand. There was no time to lose. Our quick-thinking hero cobbled together a kind of stretcher from a clever arrangement of ski poles. He laid the patient out and suspended the guy on it, then Jean-Luc hung the stretcher round his own neck. This meant that whilst skiing his patient back down, off-piste all the way from Whakapapa to Taupo, and leading the ski school the whole way down, Jean-Luc never once had to stop the mouth-to-mouth resuscitation effort. Yip. That's what he told us. He skied down, watched where he was going, performed heart massage and mouth-to-mouth the whole way down, and gave pointers to the beginners who followed him faithfully down the hill, into the hospital, up to the theatre and – whop! – onto the operating table. He said the only tricky bit was trying to get the whole ski class through the revolving door at the hospital entrance with skis on. There was a bit of a pile up there, by all accounts, but all in a day's work for the hero Jean-Luc. I was only disappointed that he didn't go on to perform the heart surgery, using his ski poles like giant knitting needles in the guy's chest cavity. Great story all the same, and we all laughed and had another beer, and then another Schnapps. And then this other bloke told us how he won his silver medal at the Tokyo Olympics, and another told us how fast he had to go to escape a yeti on the dark side of Mont Blanc, and everyone nodded and said they'd had problems with that damn yeti too, and we all laughed and had another beer, and then another Schnapps and then another story.

Each story heralded a new round of drinks, and each round of drinks made the next story even more outrageous than the one before, and after a while, four clear truths became evident. Firstly, I loved these guys. They were hilarious. They were fun. They were the best mates I'd ever had. I was having a brilliant time and I wanted to stay forever. Secondly, I wanted to be a ski instructor. I wanted to have girls swooning all over my puffy, sponsored, bright-red ski jacket. Thirdly – and this is a little bit embarrassing – it gradually penetrated through the fug of my drunken brain that it was me who was telling all the stories. And fourthly (this was quite a revelation), it became clear to me as I listened to yet another wild ski adventure emerging from the mouth of Yours Truly, that I was much, much better at skiing than I ever previously realised. It was only just dawning on me that I was really very good at skiing indeed.

My stories got so bad – the memory of this bit makes me shudder to this day – that in the end, I was telling them how I had this great technique for skiing uphill. It's all in the leg muscles, you see. I reasoned that surely it must be possible, with powerful thighs and good technique, to ski upwards, don't you think? It all made perfect sense to me as I described the expressions on people's faces as they came down the mountain and met me going up, and soon enough I had these ski instructors believing that I could do it (they were all drunk too, don't forget). I had them adopting a sort of pooing position in the bar, and pushing outwards with their thighs, and pulling back inwards again, and I was telling them they were doing well, and that they'd get it in the end if they persevered.

By 2.00 a.m., I was a ski hero. They felt honoured and privileged to be in my presence, and thanked Carlo for introducing me to them as they looked up to me with an almost religious awe. I was about to tell them the story of the day I went skiing down the indigo strip of a particularly steep rainbow, when Carlo made an announcement.

'OK, blokes,' he called in his ocker Aussie drawl. 'Just wanted to raise a glass to me pommie mates here. Welcome to Windy and NotNorman!' A cheer went up, and a further half glass went down the necks of all present. Then came the bomb. 'I know Windy is dying to get out there on the slopes tomorrow and show us his stuff, so in honour of the advances he's obviously made since I last saw him ski like a friggin' starfish into a shop front in the Dolomites, we've organised a seat for him on the helicopter tomorrow!'

A huge cheer reverberated around the bar and the lads clapped me on the shoulder and raised their glasses once more. As the greatest skier any of them had ever met, I would be guest of honour on the next day's adventure. I smiled and accepted the accolades and thanked my public... until I realised what had been said. My face dropped and it was my turn to adopt the pooing position.

'Oh! Ha, ha, ha! No, no, no, really, lads. It's all very kind, but really I can't.'

The lads implored me to come. Jean-Luc fell to his knees. 'Please, Windy. I 'ave reached a plateau and it is only a man like you 'oo could teach me some new zings. Please!'

I was firm. 'No, no. Really. Jet lag. It's very kind of you and all that, but ouch! Ooo, my back! It's giving me jip. Just last week, the doc said…'

'Really, Windy. It's our privilege. There's a spare seat and we've paid for it and everything.'

I was firm. 'Please, lads, don't do this. I need to rest tomorrow, and then there's the insurance to think of, and… and… and you know that old malaria thing of mine is coming back, and I really have –'

'Too late now,' grinned a Blizzard-sponsored ski jacket with a frankly embarrassing blow-dry and a voice like Clint Eastwood, 'it's all booked up!'

Oh, shit.

As the cheer went up I laughed along, but the first opportunity I had, I took Carlo to one side and harangued him with a certain degree of sober urgency.

'Carlo, you taught me everything I know. I *haven't* advanced since we went through that shop front together. You have to get me out of this!'

He waved me away in broadly drunk Aussie tones. 'You'll be fine, mate. It'll be fun!'

'No, Carlo. I won't be fine. I'll die. I'm even scared of helicopters, let alone the skiing bit.'

Carlo shook his head at me and tried to focus. Since I had taken him to one side, this had already turned into the longest serious conversation of his entire life, and he was beginning to get bored with it. 'Windy, listen, mate. I'll get you down, OK? Trust me, it'll be a riot. Now will ya stop putting a downer on the party? Let's get another drink.'

As I trudged miserably back to a hero's welcome at the bar, I consoled myself with the knowledge that once we all went to bed there was no way they would be able to get me out there in the morning. I would lock myself in my hotel room, and there wasn't any number of grizzly bears in the mountains that could ever chisel me out. As soon as I was out of their sight that would be the last they would see of me until long after the danger had passed. Indeed, I began to think that maybe NotNorman and I should change our plans. Lake Louise was dull. There's only so much snow a man can take before he craves solid ground again, and that time had arrived for me. I shared my feelings with NotNorman, suggesting we look at a city break in Vancouver for the rest of the week, but for someone who had never been skiing in his life, he had suddenly become hugely attracted to the local environment. He said how good the mountain air would be for me, and how he'd regret it if he didn't help me to make the most of the opportunities on offer. For someone who wasn't going to ski, he seemed to have taken to the place in quite a big way. He was beaming all over his face.

I knew what I had to do. As soon as the door on the hotel room was locked behind me, I would be safe from any ridiculous heli-skiing trips. They wouldn't get me out of that hotel room for all the puffy red jackets in the world.

Don't you treasure those memories you have of nights that ended up with just you and a select group of friends – friends you will never forget – with whom you shared a perfect sunrise?

We didn't go to bed.

With a bit of breakfast to fill in for the lack of sleep, and a brace of coffees as concessions towards sobriety, I never got a moment on my own, and no chance arose for me to slope off and hide. Before I knew it, the time came for the dead-man-walking bit and, in another of those moments of reflection on life, I found myself wondering what in the name of God I was doing in a queue of expert skiers climbing into a helicopter in the Rocky Mountains of Canada. I was also nurturing the kind of headache that would show up on a photograph, and simultaneously trying to puzzle out what had possessed me to place such a headache next to a helicopter engine, and why NotNorman was allowed to wave goodbye from a safe distance before heading off to bed whilst I had to go through with this. Things just weren't adding up to a holiday. As the helicopter thwacked off into the mountains with me on board, and the testosterone began to fill the air, I seemed unable to join in the merry banter and pumped excitement of these thrill-seekers.

I suppose that you, dear reader, could rightfully expect at this point, from material masquerading as travel writing, a prosaic description of a breathtaking sunrise over the Rocky Mountains, viewed from a helicopter. My prose should surely be inspired and flowing, but to be honest with you, my heart wasn't in it. I'm sorry to disappoint, but I was somewhat distracted by a greater sense of foreboding than at any time I could remember. I was reflecting on my genuine skiing experience to date, and becoming increasingly concerned that things were unlikely to work out well.

I had been on a school ski trip to the Tyrol when I was fourteen. They stood us up on perfectly flat nursery slopes, and we fell down and laughed. They stood us back up again, and we squealed like girls and fell down again, and laughed. Then we got our skis tangled, and couldn't get back up. And we tried, and failed and knocked each other over again, and laughed, and bent the poles, and rolled around, and we tested the patience of the instructors to its very limits. It was all great fun, and very safe, but we didn't advance very much as skiers in that week. Then a couple of years later I went on another trip, this time to the Italian Dolomites, and this time with Carlo. He had not yet qualified as an instructor, and had a somewhat revolutionary – and possibly illegal – approach to teaching people how to ski. He took me directly to the top of the mountain, put a ski on each foot, and whilst I stood gingerly trying to get my balance, like a newborn giraffe, he pushed me off the top. I still fell down immediately, just as I had done on the nursery slopes, but this time I had the satisfaction of descending 300 yards in the process of falling over. It was more productive falling over, and as I rolled down the mountainside, screaming and flailing arms, legs, skis and poles in all directions, Carlo skied down backwards beside me, continuing to deliver his lesson. When I eventually came to a halt, Carlo swished up beside me, stood me back up and, just as I was telling him how unacceptable his methods were, he pushed me off again. The next fall took a total of around three seconds to complete, during which time I hit around 45 mph and descended 350 yards. He stood me up again, gave me a shove, and I did 375 yards. Before long, I realised that remaining upright was preferable to a week in intensive care, but my failure to fall over in good time near the bottom led to my rather famously crossing a road and starfishing into a plate glass window on the front of an Italian delicatessen. Carlo liked that one. He liked it so much that he felt it necessary to stop our lesson, take his skis off, and go inside to ask the shoppers – who were picking themselves up off the floor and retrieving their shopping from the four corners of the shop – what I had looked like from the other side of the glass.

So, the truth is, I suppose I might have just kind of perhaps mildly exaggerated a few of the stories about my skiing experience the night before, and was not looking forward to the thrills and spills of heli-skiing. At best, I was going to hold these speed freaks back and be embarrassed at having to bring up the rear in a nervous snow plough. At worst, and rather more realistically, I would break every bone in my body.

After a good long time in a confined space next to a helicopter engine, the infernal machine landed, and I struggled out, carrying my hangover in both hands. The chopper had blown up tons of snow all around, so we couldn't see a thing as we unloaded our skis and backpacks. It was like being in a blizzard that roared at you. Eventually, the noise got worse, the chopper lifted again, and slewed off. It was a few minutes before the snow cleared and the sound dropped to nothing, then...

... Wow.

Just wow; there are no words to describe the panorama. The silence, the solitude and the scale of vivid wilderness. I know I was preoccupied with other things, but this was unbelievable. It left me with my mouth open, and yet utterly speechless. Everyone was humbled into silence. For a couple of minutes we just stood there, isolated from the rest of the world and 3,000 metres up in the sky, feeling the chill in the bright morning sun, listening to the intense silence, and turning circles to take in the view. A precious and extraordinary calm... before the storm. Gradually the excitement crept back in and the boys started getting ready to roll.

I also began to return to reality. We had landed on what seemed to be a tabletop the size of a tennis court. I was quite near one side, so I edged over to take a look at what my skiing prowess would be up against. Well, jeeeez, we couldn't go off that side! It was sheer! A cliff edge! I worked my way round to the next side, looking for a more gentle entry point, but this – man alive! – this was even worse! It was stomach-churningly ludicrous. I kept going, but with a creeping sense of impending doom. The third side was worse still. I couldn't even see the sides of the vertical drop without lying on my stomach and peeping my head over. I was lying on an overhang! There was no skiing off there no matter how good you were – at the very least you needed a hang-glider to go off that side. I went across to the last remaining edge, full of trepidation. I prayed that there would be a recognisable slope, at least shallow enough for me to cling onto with hands and feet as I slid down. As I leaned over, the high clouds far below and the circling vultures beneath them confirmed my worst fear: this whole thing was too much for me. We were on a mountain that from a distance must look like a giant letter 'T' in space, with a lethal drop on all sides. I was not going to be able to do this. Not at all. And no, I am not exaggerating. It was seriously, seriously too steep to ski off from any side. It was nuts.

The boys were getting themselves nicely pumped up, a-whoopin' and a-hollerin' with the excitement of what was ahead of them as they put on their skis and tightened their boots. I was shaking as I drew Carlo off to one side. Despite all my impressive words the night before, there was no way I could ski down.

'Em, Carlo, this... em... this little trot back to the village...'

'Yeah, isn't it wicked? Mate, this is living!'

'Em, no, Carlo, this is *not* living. This is dying. I can't ski down here. It's... it's... it's suicide.'

He laughed with unhappiness in his voice. 'Oh, please don't crap out on me, Windy. Just follow us. You'll be fine.' He clapped my shoulders and nodded at me encouragingly. 'I'll see you're right, OK?'

'No, really, Carlo. I... I can't do it. It's way too steep and I'll...'

'Windy, Windy. Stay with me here, OK? We go off that end there. Sure, it's quick to start with, but you just gotta hit those first few moguls right, then it begins to level out.'

I pointed over the edge. 'N-N-No, it doesn't! That edge there? It never levels out! Never at all! This is... base-jumping, not skiing! Are you seriously trying to tell me that we have to...?'

My voice was breaking up. It was pure, unadulterated fear. Jean-Luc came over, his brow furrowed with concern. 'Is there a problemme 'ere? Why aren't you gearing up?'

'Bloody Windy's lost his bottle. Doesn't want to ski.'

'Sacre bleu, man! What about all zat sterff last night about skiing down ice walls and beating ze Finland downhill champion at Breckenridge and...'

'Yes, yes, well, look. That was all rubbish, OK? I was drunk. I made it all up. I was lying. Satisfied now? I can't do this. There. I said it.'

I folded my arms. It was embarrassing to have to admit the truth, but I could not ski off here without killing myself so I had to speak up. All the guys were gathered round me now. A dozen testosterone-pumped men, and as the truth became clear they didn't look very happy. There was a degree of teeth-gnashing and fist-clenching and I was called some unprintable names.

Carlo took a breath. 'Well, answer me this then, you genius.' He held my cheeks in his gloved hands and looked deep into my eyes. 'How do you propose to get down, then, eh? There's no bus home from up here.'

He slapped my cheeks and did that 'Duuuh' thing that kids like so much these days. And as the others all laughed cruelly at me, I became suddenly and awfully aware of the predicament I was in. There was no alternative to going off the side of the cliff.

The boys continued to prepare, looking at me sideways and cursing under their breath as I went to the edge again. Then I went all around the edge again. I had to do this; I simply had to. But it was utterly preposterous. As far as I could make out, even on the most forgiving side, the first couple of hundred feet were simply free fall. I was much too scared and no clever words could get me out of this one.

I began taking my gear off again. 'I can't do it, OK?' I blurted, my voice cracking with emotion. 'You can't force me! It's too steep. I just can't!'

Carlo listened to the heated suggestions of the others (most of which were impolite) whilst I knelt in front of him and pawed at his trousers, begging him to save me. Finally, Carlo made the decision.

'We have to stay together, and we can't leave him here. I'll have to get the chopper back. Nothing else for it.'

The chopper! Oh, praise the Lord! We had options! He could get the chopper back!

A couple of the lads looked like they wanted to hurt me. They swore and threw their gloves on the floor and generally stomped about. One of them, the Clint-style American, came over and poked me in the chest. He spat as he spoke.

'That chopper is 300 bucks for ten minutes, and YOU are sure as hell going to pay for it, boy.'

'Ha, ha! No problem! You can have a helicopter each. The helicopters are on me, lads! I'll buy you helicopters all round as soon as we get back! OK?'

I meant it too. Anything to get me off this needle in the sky.

I heard the pilot through his engine noise shouting back down the radio. 'What? I'm 50 miles away! Who is it, eh? What? That British jerk-off? I knew it. Jeeeeez, I'm gonna have him!'

Good grief. Now he hated me, too. I was beginning to feel that flinging myself off the precipice might be preferable to death by ski pole. As we packed up our stuff and awaited the chopper's return, the guys filled the time by taking it in turns to express their hatred of me. Normally in the past, when I've upset people, I've been able to run away (I'm a very fast runner), or hide behind large friends, or what have you. Their hatred rarely lasts long, as distance or other objects are placed between me and the aggressors. In this case, however, there was nowhere to go. I was stuck in the middle of the lion's den with nothing to do but feel feeble and more than a bit scared that one of these blokes was going to hurt me. I don't remember ever feeling so uncomfortable in my entire life.

Eventually, the helicopter came back. We loaded it up in silence and to my enormous relief, took off safely from that needle in space. As the chopper took off, there was no talk on board – the engine noise made sure of that – and I ensured there was no eye contact by staring at the bulkhead next to my face and planning my exit from Lake Louise the moment we landed. I was even contemplating not bothering to pack; I would just put on a false beard and slope out of town the instant the door opened.

The helicopter touched down, the snow flurried up, and we unpacked all the gear again. We ducked down as the rotors sped up, and the chopper lifted off once more. I took a deep breath and prepared to make good my escape. No nice goodbyes. No shaking hands. I just wanted to get away. Now. But, as the snow cleared, I found I still could not escape. A different and freshly horrible scenario emerged into view.

This wasn't the helipad in Lake Louise. There were no hotels, happy skiers, ice sculptures, cheery lights, laughter and safety. This was… this was… terrible.

'Carlo! Carlo! What… what… what are we doing here? I thought we were going home and you've taken us to the top of another mountain!' I dropped to my knees, pawing at him again, like a dog about to be shot. 'I told you I can't do it, this is too much for me, and you said we'd go home and now here we are at the summit of another mountain!'

'Yeeeah! Isn't it great? Maaan, we're gonna have a good ski today. This is the life, right?'

I was almost in tears. 'No, Carlo, no. Please have mercy, I can't do this stuff, and, look, I'll give you money. Anything you like. How much do you want – all of you – to just call the helicopter back and –' I looked around, and the other lads were all looking at me. But not with hatred and loathing. They looked kind of weird. They were smiling.

The snow had cleared and I looked around. Yes, we were at the top of another mountain, and yes, we were very high up and off piste. But the slope was manageable, even for me.

'You didn't think we were gonna go off that other one, did ya?' said Carlo. 'Are you crazy, or what? Get your gear on, Windy. We've got some skiing to do!'

And with that they all – to a man – burst out laughing. They were utterly out of control and falling about like a herd of GoLarges.

It had all been a joke. I mean, it was a *joke*. The entire thing had been a setup, just for me. I teetered around for a while, trying to get my head around it, as the guys rolled around in the snow laughing, giving themselves high fives and then coming over, hugging me and telling me what the look on my face had been like and how they'd never forget it.

I learnt something about myself that day. I learnt that drink is an evil motivator of egocentric storytelling. I vowed that I would never, ever make up rubbish again. I would never get drunk again; and I would never, ever tell stories ever again unless they were the rock-solid truth.

Now move on to the next chapter and say nothing…

Chapter 17

A Close Shave
for Bernard

Notes on French culinary practices. Queen Anna of Bobble causes a fight: Bernard and YouBear, head to head.

Following a most amazing day of heli-skiing – it was fantastic, you really should try it one day – I got back in the evening to find that I was one of the gang and I was surrounded by friends. True friends. We were close, us guys. We were a band of brothers, united by extreme sports and honest bravery. You could say we were Like That. As a celebration of our unity, we decided to go for a meal together. We picked up some hangers-on from outside, like NotNorman and some other girls, and we set off to hit the town. On the way we pushed each other into the snow, as close mates do, we threw lots of snowballs, and some of us even did hilarious impersonations for the girls of what one of us looked like at the top of a pinnacle in space and scared to poodom.

Before long, we could be found seated around a table for twelve in a French restaurant downtown. We were welcomed into a homely, darkly wooden but well-lit space by synchronised waiters with black shirts and white aprons buzzing around serving dishes cooked with flair and served with pride. Informal, but high quality. My favourite.

As we looked through the menu and discussed the possibilities, we all agreed that we didn't want any live animals to eat. This is the nub of the problem with the French. It seems that the higher the quality of the food, the more alive it has to be when served. You order a meal called something exotic and tasty sounding like, 'Racklette meon bajerres Normandie flambette jus de climpie clompie' or something. You think it sounds intriguing, and you get excited when they replace your standard cutlery with specialist equipment that requires a mains connection. Then two waiters emerge with a flourish, lift the lid on a giant silver platter – *et voila!* Two live adult badgers, which the chef has delicately annoyed by burning their feet on an oven and drizzling balsamic vinegar in their eyes. The waiters bow and leave you with nothing but a cheerful 'bon appétit' and a pepper-pot the size of a baseball bat with which to subdue the beasts. Now, I know all that tripe about how animals must be killed for us to eat meat, and I have no problem with that. Indeed, I used to go on shooting trips hunting deer in the Lake District in my younger days, so I'm quite used to all that but, I mean, really. I do feel that the minimum cooking time should at least be long enough to ensure the wretched beast doesn't cry plaintively for its mummy when introduced to the fork.

Anna knew about this. She was Canadian, so she had grown up alert to the tricks the French might pull on you in the form of 'wrestle the entrée' opportunities. She wasn't going to fall for any of it. She was a pretty girl, with a heartbreakingly cute face and long blonde hair cascading from beneath a bobble hat which carried a curious sex appeal. I don't know how exciting men generally find bobble hats, and maybe it was simply because Anna was inside it, but I did find myself imagining her in *flagrante delicto* whilst wearing her bobble hat. I couldn't help myself. It was a curious fantasy, as they go, because as the story of BobblyAnna and me unfolded in my mind into something seriously sexy, and her bobbly hat bobbled in ways of which I never thought them capable, she would wait until the peak of my excitement, then grab the bobble hat with both hands at the sides, pull it down over her face and laugh through it with a noise like a flushing storm drain, which somewhat spoiled the sensuality of the moment. You try it. Imagine her now, getting sexy in her bobble hat, and I bet it goes all wonky on you, too. Weird.

Anyway, I wasn't going to find out if Anna was amenable to a bobble, if you see what I mean, because she was undergoing intensive private skiing lessons from Carlo. I don't know how much she had learnt, as her ski lessons seemed to take place exclusively in her hotel room. From the noise that emanated from her room, I would have thought she was suffering horribly from his methods, but at least they were putting the hours in. Indeed, Carlo had told me privately that they were in fact wearing skis and boots at all times, and her technique was becoming 'unparalleled', which he clearly thought was a rather clever in-joke for ski instructors. I tried my hardest not to imagine what was going on in there, but my progress through the day was endlessly encumbered by visions of bobble hats bobbling teasingly around Canada. All the mountains had bobble hats on. I wondered if I could one day persuade a girl to cut leg holes in a bobble hat and wear it as knickers. And I found myself stroking bobble hats in shops, my guilt causing me to take a sudden interest in socks when anyone came by.

Putting bobble hats to one side, the point was this: Anna the Bobble fancied fish, but she also knew that she had to be careful with her order in case it had to be fervently slaughtered at our table by a mad French butcher called Hubert (pronounced 'You-Bear' by our French hosts). BobblyAnna had prepared in advance. As we entered the restaurant, she peered into the huge tank outside the kitchen to see if there was anything alive in there. There was an unruly mob of crabs loitering around at the bottom and that was it. The tank was otherwise empty and her fish would have to come from the good old freezer. You can't get deader than that, so she felt perfectly safe priming up the taste buds for trout; up on the board as a special for the day. She smiled at the waiter, folded the menu, and placed her order. As soon as she did so, there was a corporate intake of breath from the entire restaurant and a sudden silence descended. Something was wrong. We heard the name 'Bernard' whispered behind people's hands (pronounced 'Bear-nAAarrr' by the French contingent) and then the name was shouted angrily at the waiter across the room. The waiter shouted something incomprehensible back. He was angry. He pointed at Anna and threw his arms up in the air as if there was nothing he could do about it, then amidst a great deal of general heckling, he disappeared back into the kitchen.

Two minutes later YouBear crashed out through the double doors looking like he'd just finished his audition for *The Texas Chainsaw Massacre*. In a blood-spattered white apron, and with a kiddies' fishing net gripped murderously in his hand, he headed for the fish tank amidst a chorus of boos.

Anna was horrified to discover her mistake. A closer look into the aquarium revealed Bernard the Trout. He was minding his own business up in the top corner of the tank; almost invisible amongst the bubbles created by a flow of water, and completely invisible if one didn't lean down to see if there was anything near the surface.

We quickly gathered from the translation of Jean-Luc that Bernard had escaped capture the first couple of times that YouBear had rolled his sleeves up to chivvy him into a pan. YouBear was fond of a few glasses of wine, so Bernard had been able to dodge his efforts at capture. YouBear had become flustered at the jeering crowd; he'd lost confidence and had been forced to give up, scurrying off back to his kitchen to cleaver out his anger on confused but uneaten badgers. Bernard had become expert at dodging the net. He had survived for weeks now, and had become something of a favourite amongst the locals, who deliberately didn't order him; they took him to their hearts instead of their stomachs. They felt his surviving multiple death sentences should earn him a reprieve and they lived off soups and other blameless foodstuffs in order to ensure the safety of their pet. This greatly annoyed the proprietor of the restaurant – the grim old bat, Magdalene (pronounced locally as: 'Grim Old Bat') – firstly, because whenever she looked at Bernard, she saw dollars which were now being denied to her; and secondly, because she didn't take kindly to the levity with which the locals had named the fish after her son, who breathed through his mouth and whose eyes were on the sides of his head, thereby, I felt, justifying the soubriquet.

So here was YouBear. He was angry, focussed and determined that this time he would not be outsmarted by a trout called Bernard. He huffed and sneered as his customers booed him roundly, and completely ignored the one customer who was pulling at his arm, her bobble hat bobbling provocatively as she tried desperately to change her order.

In the background, and with quiet authority, Bernard girded his loins (or he would have done if he had any). He dropped slowly to the shadowy far corner of his tank like a submarine taking up its position. The fish solemnly knocked out his pipe, placed it in its rack and removed his cravat. The time had come to go into battle.

YouBear, too, was psyching himself up. He paced in front of the tank, took six dramatically deep breaths, bounced on his toes, then made his way back again as he mentally ran through his game plan. Once focussed, he moved across to a rack and lovingly handled the line of fishing nets. He selected one, then the next and ran the handles smoothly through his hands as he assessed them for weight distribution and quality. He settled on a TroutMaster 2.4 (with TightMesh™ technology), made a couple of practise sweeps, then, satisfied, he turned to face the tank and slid aside the cover. As he dropped his net in top-left, the crowd started to chant: 'Ber-naaar, Ber-naaar, Ber-naaar!' and the crabby things on the tank floor raised their arms up at the net in a Mexican wave, their pincers clacking like castanets – at least they were enjoying themselves.

At first, YouBear tried to coax Bernard into the net nice and gently. He knew that patience was the secret. He'd lost his rag on previous occasions and was determined to keep his cool. Barely perceptible movements of the net towards Bernard were supposed to make the whole affair fuss free, but Bernard was never going to fall for that. He yawned sarcastically and rolled with the net, like a high jumper sliding over the pole. YouBear closed his eyes, counted to ten, swapped hands and started a controlled sweep towards the other end. His right hand was far more clumsy than the left, and Bernard had no trouble with the even numbered passes.

To add to YouBear's frustrations, he kept catching the net on the cheering crabs, who took it in turns to take a ride out of the tank and experience the thrill of YouBear shaking them clear of the net, glaring at them and blowing their hair back with some warmly delivered French swear words, then throwing them angrily back into the water to be welcomed home by their laughing friends. Whichever way the net went in the water, the crabs all raised their arms and eyes, and followed it faithfully back and forth as if there was a prize for whichever one of them could catch it next. The crabs were having a whale of a time.

The water in the tank was becoming stirred up, raising debris and introducing bubbles. All to the benefit of Bernard, so YouBear introduced his other arm. He was trying to corner Bernard between hand and net to leave him with nowhere to run, but Bernard always seemed to find the gap and flash off down the other end. A couple of times things got a bit tight. YouBear nearly got him out and Bernard had to leave the water to find the gap, but each time – and to great applause – he found his way back into the tank despite desperate lunges at his tail by the Fish Butcher of Lake Louise. Poor Bernard couldn't go on forever, though. Eventually, YouBear trapped Bernard in the top corner. Bernard made his move. He jumped from the water and the world went into slow motion. YouBear dropped the net and grabbed for him in mid-air. Bernard was slippery, and twice he escaped YouBear's grip. But – disaster. He fell outside the tank and down onto the floor. The faces of the crowd turned to slow motion horror. Then suddenly back to full speed as YouBear went headlong after him on the floor. Bernard was off across the room, running on his tail, pumping his fins like a champion, adding a point and a wink to the camera for good measure. He headed off under the tables and chairs with YouBear diving after him like a goalkeeper.

As YouBear crashed angrily around under the tables, customers all around the restaurant passed Bernard around, behind their backs and from lap to lap. They gave him a quick breather in a cabbage soup or head-down into a glass of chardonnay to keep his chin up whilst the fish Gestapo of Magdalene and YouBear searched from table to table for the fugitive.

In the end they had to give up. Bernard was brought out from under someone's hat and carried shoulder high, clasping his fins above his head in victory, back to his tank. He was placed back in the water, bloodied but unbowed, to a clackety welcome from the crab castanet ensemble and a cheer around the restaurant which nearly took the roof off.

None cheered louder than Anna, of course, who in a touching moment of silence in the restaurant, apologised to Bernard. He kissed and forgave her, waving away her apologies with gallant French flair. Anna asked if she could see him again, but Bernie said he didn't think inter-species relationships were quite the done thing in Lake Louise – unless she would keep her bobble hat on for him – but I won't tell you what happened next, as, having exaggerated this story out of all proportion (when I solemnly promised I wouldn't do that anymore in the previous chapter) I don't want to go on to spoil the movie version for you.

Suffice to say, if you ever go to Anna's house, I guarantee it will be nothing more exciting than a nut roast for dinner.

Chapter 18

The Topping
of Pantsby

*Thoughts on job satisfaction. Dinner in the mess. A topping time
with the new captain. Ffugg gets the blame. Heeeere we go again!*

I was sad to leave Lake Louise. It was mesmeric. I had found
yet another place where I could happily spend a lifetime. But
time inevitably started to clump NotNorman and me round
the head and push us out through the door to go and join our
next ship in Vancouver.

We took a coach down from Lake Louise to Calgary, followed
by an incredible train journey from Calgary to Vancouver.
When we planned our trip from the UK, we had seen Calgary

and Vancouver as relatively close together (two professional travellers that we were). It was in fact more than six hundred miles. The train fare cost almost as much as the airfare to Calgary from the UK. Yeeesh. Thank goodness we could claim back the aeroplane ride. Mind you, we almost went up and down as far as the plane as well; the train ride from Calgary to Vancouver involved a drop of around a mile.

We got into Vancouver and worked our way back across town to New Westminster, overlooking the Fraser River at the easternmost end of Greater Vancouver. It seems to me that all the cities of the world that have a certain magic to them are set in natural harbours. Sydney, obviously, and Wellington in New Zealand spring to mind. Vancouver is just as dramatic. Indeed, the shipping routes in and out of Vancouver from the Pacific are staggering. A mountainous fjordland. How come nobody seems to have noticed? Why aren't we all flooding here for our holidays? It's an amazing part of the world. Surely Vancouver is destined to play a major role in the evolution of the Pacific Rim. Buy property on the stunning coastline north of Vancouver. I predict you will make money.

We arrived at the port in New Westminster and were greeted by a sight that was becoming all too familiar. *Global Panorama* was another elderly lady, and I felt my usual sense of excitement, but combined with a strange underlying unease. It was a strong realisation that my shipboard life wasn't a holiday. It wasn't just an adventure that would end sometime and we could all go home. This was now my life. A life of constant travel as one ship replaced the next. Did I even *have* a home? No, I didn't. This ship was my home – until the next ship. Would I ever get used to that feeling? Would I ever feel totally comfortable with that? It didn't seem possible that my family home was only going to be a place I visited occasionally. It was an unpleasantly empty feeling.

NotNorman did not seem to be encumbered by such thoughts.

'Don't you ever think there will be a time when you live and work in the Lake District again?' I asked him.

NotNorman shrugged. 'Naaah. How could anything match this? You wouldn't want a job shoreside, would you?'

'No,' I said. 'Of course not. Not at the moment, anyway. I just love the feeling of being on a permanent holiday. But don't you think that, you know, something is missing? Don't you feel that in the long term…'

NotNorman pointed at me as if I'd hit the nail on the head. 'Permanent holiday,' he said. 'That's exactly it! This is the best life ever!' He picked up the letter we had received from the London office and shoved it under my nose. 'Look where we're going: Seattle, San Francisco, LA, Costa Rica, Nicaragua, Panama, Columbia, Peru – how could any other job match that?'

He was right, of course. For the moment, it was a holiday. It was an adventure. Why care about the long term? Just enjoy it while it lasts. He was right. It must be something else that was bugging me, and it had been there for a while. I snapped out of my analysis. I must be shallower – more Carlo – about things. Deep thinking was for saddos.

'A life on the ocean waaave!' I sang. 'La, la, la, la, la, laaa, la, laaaaaa!' Thumping good tune, that. I really must learn some more lyrics.

We put on our uniform whites and I checked myself in the mirror. I couldn't fool myself, even if I fuzzed my eyes up, so I sighed, took off the bobble hat and headed for the officers' mess. It was lunchtime on the first day, and we hadn't got filthy dirty yet, so we took the opportunity to look smart and eat in comfort. I felt more confident than ever that I would be able to take charge of my life on this ship. I would be able to contribute and impress, and to be my own master to a much greater extent. One of the reasons I was feeling so positive and buoyant was that we had a new captain.

The new old man went by the name of Captain Pantsby. A skinny, weedy, stick insect of a chap – the type of chap who has to run about in the shower to get wet. He had an embarrassing comb-over and wide, surprised eyes made all the wider by large, round spectacles that gave the impression, when you were in conversation with him, that there was a monster creeping up behind you that he couldn't bring himself to tell you about.

So far, my relationship with Captain Pantsby was going very, very well. I had met him when I'd formally signed on. We'd shaken hands, and I had successfully negotiated around fifteen seconds of small talk. I was relieved to see a new captain because this gave me a chance to start again with a clean slate. I could show my true self; the self who studied, worked hard, knew what he was doing and didn't get into the captain's bad books. I didn't intend to do any of these things, of course, but it was critical to give the right impression to the man at the top. This was now my third ship, and I knew how to project a positive image. The key to success was this: at all times when you are exposed to high ranking officers, you put on this ridiculous act as though you are the most serious-minded, best-dressed and cleanest intellectual the world has ever seen, for whom quality is paramount, nonsense will not be tolerated, and failure is not an option. You have to look like you *care*. Then, as soon as they are out of the way, the beer comes back out, the feet go up on the table again, the vulgarity kicks back in and the laughter rings out around the brothel once more. It's such a con, and yet it is absolutely the only game in town. Everybody does it. I had got into a good deal of trouble through giving the wrong impression to Captain Benchmerson and Captain Howten. On this ship, things would be different. I would be Officer Material every time Pantsby came within a nautical mile. I would never let my guard down.

We entered the officers' mess to find Captain Pantsby already present, sitting like a praying mantis at the head of his table, rotating his head to chat with the chief engineer and lying in wait for flies to land on the table.

'Afternoon, Captain. Good afternoon, Chief,' I said, acknowledging them with my shoulders back and deeply professional sincerity before heading to my seat at the junior navigators' table. Do you see what I mean? Despite all that talk about fun and permanent holidays, here I was, on my first day, with my uniform whites blinding the captain in the officers' mess, and my very best shrewd operator cloak on.

Then two things happened at once. As we sat down and assumed attack positions for the incoming fodder, NotNorman hit me with a bombshell.

'You do realise what's bugging you, don't you?' he said, buttering a roll like he was plastering a wall. I shrugged in the negative. No, I didn't know what was bugging me, unless he meant these stupid packets of butter – why do they make them so impregnable, and how come NotNorman had tons of the stuff going all over the place? 'It's bloody obvious from where I'm sitting,' continued Notters. 'You're in love, mate.'

I stopped in my tracks. My grip loosened and my knife dropped on to the plate with a clatter. Oh, my God. I gulped, and realised that my heart was in the back of my throat. I suspect it had been trying to get my attention for a while.

NotNorman pointed his knife at me and spoke from behind a front-of-house display of partially-masticated bread and butter. 'Greece, matey. It's been since Greece.'

I felt a surge of... of something I'd never felt before. I knew that I had found WonderGirl spectacular, but it hadn't occurred to me for a minute that these feelings could be... could be... I gulped again, felt myself shaking and... and...

And it was at that very moment, there and then as I was trying to get my head and heart around it all, that Captain Pantsby gave me a copper-bottomed, cherry-topped beauty of an opportunity to prove my professional worth to him.

'Cadet? Could you pass me the cream, please?' he asked, his head turning like a satellite dish to face me.

I did my best to shake WonderGirl from the front of my brain. WonderGirl – of course – no – forget WonderGirl. This was it. The perfect chance to be the disciplined professional Captain Pantsby would want to see in one of his apprentices. I zeroed in on the aerosol can of long-life cream, sizing up the task at hand. It was there on our table. It was a good size and shape for gripping. It was in an almost perfect position to be passed. I was in prime physical condition myself – well up to the job. I would pass the cream to the captain and, goddammit, he would know that the cream had been passed by a competent future officer. I was NOT going to mess this one up.

'Yes, Captain WonderGirl. No problem, Captain,' I said smartly. I jumped up, and began pacing back and forth across the end of the table, sizing up the situation. I closed my eyes, took some deep breaths and concentrated my mind with the focus of a samurai on the perfect trouble-free execution of the can-passing mission. It looked like this: I had to pick up the can and carry it on a level plane an estimated eight feet, maybe nine, across to the captain. I planned for ten, just to be safe. I would use my hand for the actual gripping of the object – no, make that two hands – and both of my legs for the haulage operation, transporting the target in a direct line across the open ground between the tables. Good thinking. He'd appreciate that. I tried to think around the problem (the way they advise you to do in the management manuals). A strategic approach was the way to win the day, and I had a solid plan in place. Watertight, was the word. Infallible. I saw no need at this point for backup. Of course, I would have to be tactically aware in order to handle unforeseen events as they arose during the journey, but I was as prepared as I could be. WonderGirl appeared in my conscience. She smiled supportively. I could do it for her! We could do it together! I took one more deep breath… and went for it.

It is worth remembering at this point that the concept of long-life cream in an aerosol container was new to the world in the late 1970s. It was magic stuff for ships, as most of the duration of a lengthy sea passage was without decent dairy products, so these new spray cans were brilliant. I hadn't even used one at this point, but they had been the talk of the Merchant Navy in recent weeks, and I could see from the drool down the Pantsby chin that they were certainly popular in his neck of the woods.

I picked up the aerosol can of cream with both hands, never once taking my eyes off it as I marched it – with both legs – across to the captain. The job went very well. I put the cream down on his table, well in from the edge. It sat solidly in place, and I turned to run victoriously from the officers' mess, punching the air and with the front of my shirt pulled over my head. But...

... as I arrived at the captain's table, he held his plate of apple crumble up in front of me, implicitly requesting me to deliver actual cream rather than just the can. I had only laid firm plans up as far as the Can Handover Phase of Operation Creamery, so this was a complication. My mind flew into action. I thought round it, I thought through it, I played scenarios out in my head and I didn't see a problem. In fact, I could see benefits. I was already performing well and I realised that, in the drive to gain status in the captain's eyes, this was a golden opportunity. As he proffered his plate up towards me, his giant, magnified eyes shone with child-like expectation through his porthole spectacles. I was his mother and he was back there, the infant Pantsby, anxious for cream on his pudding, and in the symbolic world of the insecure child he was not about to get cream from a cadet; he was about to receive succour from his mother. It was as much as he could do to stop himself from calling me Mummy.

I removed the lid, and held the can horizontally above his plate. His mouth drooped open with expectation. His breathing stopped. His eyes loved. His tongue begged and glistened. I squeezed the button with officer-like decisiveness, and we both waited for the sweetness of the thick cream to augment his pudding to perfection, to make him feel safe and cared for, and for the good captain to associate that parental warmth with me. It was agreed. We would connect and bond in a special relationship that would set me up for the whole trip.

Whatever route we take through life, we just cannot tell around which corner fate lurks, smacking a baseball bat purposefully into his hand. Today was my day to walk around that corner. As I said, this was my first time. I had never met one of these confounded spray cans of cream. I didn't know the can should not be held horizontally. Why should I know? I assumed it would come out like cream does from a jug. And in my defence, the captain cannot have known any better than me, judging from the way he begged me to give it to him.

As soon as the button was pressed with the afore-mentioned crisp authority the can rasped rudely at the captain, and, in three seconds of milky-white deluge and strident farty noises, his head disappeared in a thick bulging cloud of foaming cream, coming to a nice point just short of the bowl of apple crumble; a bowl he still proffered, angel-like, towards me. A bowl not noticeably contaminated by cream. He sat still. He didn't put his bowl down. He didn't flinch. His head was now four times its normal size and his expression fluffy, white and stubbornly creamy. Everyone stopped eating and looked on in horror – not simply because he now looked for all the world like a dedicated enemy of *Doctor Who*, but more because my actions had looked horribly deliberate. I had just stood there and coiled down a steady jet of cream all over his cranium. I had been paralysed with horror and, for some reason I cannot now explain, I had not removed my crisply authoritative finger from the button. I just carried on topping the old man until I finally – finally – got myself together enough to stop.

For a minute, there was no movement anywhere in the officers' mess. None at all. Not a breath. Indeed, the first movement of any sort came from the South Face of Cream Mountain as it slid off his head, rolled down his shirt and splotted rudely into his crotch. I still couldn't see much of his face, but his giant eyes shone through the creamy foreground like a possum hiding in a cloud. Those eyes spoke to me. They said I was dead.

Now, we Baboulenes are quick in a crisis. Displaying unparalleled presence of mind, I hid the can behind the water jug and had a go at the winning smile. He began to shake, his eyes bulged dangerously and I realised further decisive, officer-like action would be required to rescue the situation. I snatched up the chief engineer's chapatti from his side-plate and began to mop the captain's face with it and, if I remember rightly, I might have said something about how one day we would look back and laugh at it all. I might possibly have even tried a little laugh of my own to help the healing process along.

Captain Pantsby's hands came up and grabbed my wrists, stopping me in mid-chamois. He pushed his chair back, stood up and, without a word, walked with as much dignity as he could from the mess. And the Mess. He left a trail of cream behind him, although he was very effectively catching escapee spludges with his sleeves, shoes and smart black uniform trousers all the way out.

I wasn't done yet. I still had one shot left in the armoury. It wasn't a good one, but it was all that came to mind in the heat of the moment.

'Ffugg! What the hell did you do that to the captain for?' I shouted, hoping vainly that the captain didn't know us all yet, and would naturally assume that Ffugg would be the one to keel haul later in the day. This was a spur-of-the-moment action on my part and, in retrospect, perhaps an ill-judged one. In my mind, I was applying The Rule that seemed so universal on my first ship, that it should be the first tripper – Ffugg – who should accept the blame for the captain's creaminess. But Ffugg didn't seem to understand The Rule. He seemed to behave as if this was his second trip.

He spat his food across the table and leapt out of his chair. 'YOU WOT? RIGHT! ARTSIDE YOU, NAAAARRRR!'

Ffugg came at me, flexing his fingers, gnashing his teeth and brandishing a teaspoon as if he had every intention of using it. As he advanced, he had to walk past NotNorman and, by some mysterious power that I have never since been able to fathom, seemed to trip. He went headlong onto a floor that was lubricated by cream, and slid past me on his belly like a penguin off across the ice flow to go for a swim.

I leapt over him, and hot-footed it after NotNorman out of the mess. As we ran off round the passageway, up the companionway, outside onto the deck and up towards the bridge wing, I could hear NotNorman laughing. His laughter was wobbly from trying to run at the same time.

'What are you laughing at?' I said, sharply. 'This isn't funny, you know.' And I meant it to sting. I wasn't best placed for a comfortable trip.

'"Permanent Holiday",' he laughed. 'That's what you said, wasn't it?'

I felt a smile at the corner of my lips, but immediately curtailed it. This was no time for laughter. I had serious issues to deal with now.

' "Best life there is", right?' his giggles prevented him from climbing any further. Suddenly he roared with laughter, his legs went weak and he fell on the deck.

I tripped over him, collapsed on top of him and we fell together in a heap on the boat deck. I caught his eye and we remembered the other one.

'A life on the ocean waaaaaave!' we sang, and our laughter redoubled. 'La, la, la, la, la, laaaa, la, laaaaaaaaa!'

I lay on my back and we laughed helplessly at the sky over Vancouver. I couldn't believe that I was in trouble with the new captain within two hours of arriving on the ship. NotNorman was laughing fit to burst.

'Did… di-di-did you see what you did to him?' he cried.

NotNorman blew a long, loud raspberry rather like the one the spray can made, and did an impersonation of can-brandishing. 'You just curled it down all over 'is head!'

After a while our laughter abated. We fell into silence. Our minds were on other things.

'NotNorman, how did you know I'm in love?' There was no answer. I leaned up on one elbow to look the man in the eye. 'Well? How did you know?'

He avoided my stare. He looked odd. Sheepish. No, that's not it. Guilty. That was it. And it hit me.

'Nooo, NotNorman! Don't tell me! You – you – you – you are in love with her as well!'

We stared at each other as the implications hit home. We were both in love with the same woman. And we didn't know her name. Or where she lived. But we did know one clue towards finding her. NotNorman nodded at me as he saw me working things out.

'That's right,' he said.

'September the thirteenth,' we said in unison.

I was going to have to get back to Greece to meet WonderGirl at the Paniheeri later in the year. And although I was going to stay friendly towards my best mate, I was going to have to make sure I got there before NotNorman.

Just then a giant baby leapt around the corner brandishing a teaspoon.

'Ah—HAAA!' shouted Ffugg, jumping into the attack like Tinky Winky in a red mist. 'C'MON VEN CHAMP! ON YER FEET! LET'S DO VIS FING NAAAARRR!'

NotNorman and I looked at each other, then we looked at Ffugg and we couldn't help it. We burst out laughing again. I knew it was going to hurt, but I just couldn't stop laughing enough to run away. As Ffugg ghosted sideways across the boat deck like Mohammad Ali, spitting accusations through bared teeth and asking me if I fancied myself, it was quite clear that events to come on this trip were going to be just as uncontrollable as the ones that had gone before.

TO BE CONTINUED

So, from my position in a headlock and having my eyes flipped out with a teaspoon, let me tell you that there will be lots more love and laughter, tears and sadness, joy, chaos and bedlam with me, NotNorman and the others coming soon in the third and final book of my seagoing adventures around the world and, yes, you've guessed it, our next adventure includes a trip back to Greece to find a poor, innocent unwitting Greek girl and show her how attractive we are. The life-changing battle for the hand of WonderGirl...

For news on publication of the third title, as well as live show dates and locations, signed and personally inscribed copies of all my ramblings (which incidentally, make a thoughtful gift), as well as free stuff and a button you can press to tell me how cross you are, go to:

www.baboulene.com

★★★

Acknowledgements

My thanks to both Peter Rutherford and Peter Rutherford
– proper, intrepid travellers who humble and inspire.

Special thanks also to my good friend and inspiration, Captain
Julian Blatchley who, through no fault of his own, was never
called Norman.

OCEAN BOULEVARD

An epic and exhilarating voyage all the way... from a boy to a man

'Interesting, raucous and
very, very funny to the point
that will make your eyes water.' **TalkSport**

David Baboulene

OCEAN BOULEVARD

An epic and exhilarating voyage all the way... from a boy to a man

David Baboulene

ISBN: 978 1 84024 590 5   Paperback   £8.99

David Baboulene runs away to sea in a cloud of romantic dust for the first of his globetrotting adventures. His journey takes him across the world and back, from New Orleans and Houston in America to the Caribbean islands of Barbados and Jamaica, through the Panama Canal to Sydney and Melbourne in Australia, then back across the Pacific – through the Gilbert and Solomon islands, Samoa, Tonga, Fiji and the Azores – to a triumphant homecoming in Liverpool.

But despite the laughs, the real journey in this strangely moving tale takes him all the way... from a boy to a man.

'Top star rating for these tall tales and youthful high jinx. Perfect holiday reading'   MAXIM magazine

'David "Windy" Baboulene is like a Bryson who has really played the field. Ocean Boulevard is truly adventurous, truly hilarious and funny enough to burst your stitches!'   Borders Books

'This truly absorbing and at times astonishing tale will have you laughing out loud... Windy has an engaging, informative and gripping style... a real page-turner'   IN TOUCH magazine

Have you enjoyed this book? If so, why not write a review on your favourite website?

Thanks very much for buying this Summersdale book.

www.summersdale.com